Contents

Editor
Greg Payne

Assistant Editor
Liz Wright

Origination
Sally Robinson

Published by:
Greenlight Publishing
The Publishing House
Hatfield Peverel Chelmsford
Essex CM3 2HF
Tel: 01245-381001

ISBN 1 897738 07 2

© 1995 Greenlight Publishing

The population is exceedingly large, the ground thickly studded with homesteads, and the cattle very numerous. For money they use either bronze or gold coins, or iron ingots of fixed weight. Most of the tribes of the interior do not grow corn but live on milk and meat, and wear skins. All of the Britons dye their bodies with woad which produces a blue colour and this gives them a more terrifying appearance in battle. They wear their hair long and shave the whole of their bodies except the head and upper lip. Wives are shared between groups of ten or twelve men, especially between brothers, and between fathers and sons.

In chariot fighting the Britons begin by driving all over the field hurling javelins and generally the terror inspired by the horses and the noise of the wheels is sufficient to throw their opponents ranks into disorder.... They can run along the chariot pole, stand on the yoke, and get back into the chariot as quick as lightning.

War Commentaries Julius Caesar (100-44 BC)

Preface

Province of Britannia 43 AD

*I*t was early in the morning, bitterly cold, and raining heavily. Aulus, an infantryman of Legio II Augusta, was on watch duty. As he paced the perimeters of his Legion's encampment he grumbled to himself. This climate was not to his liking, and he wondered how long he was going to have to spend in this inhospitable place.

Aulus had arrived with the first invasion fleets six months earlier, and had been involved in considerable fighting with the native Celts. But Aulus was a Roman and knew that nothing could stand in the way of an onslaught by the Legions. Besides, superior gods were on the side of the Romans.

Aulus had signed on for twenty years as a volunteer, swearing his allegiance to the Emperor and pledging his faith in Jupiter, protector of the Legions. He received 225 denarii a year for his services, some of which was saved by the State for his retirement.

The path around the camp was becoming increasingly muddy as Aulus' hob-nailed leather boots cut through the turf. He was armed with a short sword attached to a belt around his waist, and held an iron-tipped spear in his right hand. On his left arm he carried a wooden shield with bronze edging and a central boss. He was wearing an iron cuirass and helmet, and felt secure as he looked back over the row of tents making up the marching camp.

As he pulled his sodden cloak around him to keep out the cold, he didn't notice the silver denarius as it dropped from a split in his money pouch and disappeared into the muddy ground. Later on he would curse his luck, but by then there would be more important things to worry about than the loss of a coin.

Southern Britain 1995 AD

It was a Sunday morning and Alec had been up since first light. He was anxious to try out the new detector he had just bought, and intended to visit his favourite site which was near to an old Roman road.

As he moved slowly along the freshly ploughed field, swinging his detector's search head from side to side, he heard a faint signal in the headphones. The new detector indicated that the target was non-ferrous so he knelt down and using his trowel dug out some soil. Passing the search head over this, he pinpointed the signal. Picking up some loose earth, Alec felt something smooth and round amongst it. His heartbeat accelerated when this came into sight as a blackened disc. carefully cleaning away the soil, Alec found himself looking at a portrait of the emperor Claudius on a silver denarius.

He trembled with excitement ... this was one of the best finds that he had ever made. As he carefully looked at the coin he realised that he was holding a piece of history in his hand, and he wondered who had lost it all those years ago.

* ❋ *

Alec would by no means be alone in such a reaction. By holding a Roman object, untouched by human hand for almost 2,000 years, a personal link is forged with the past. We cannot travel back in time, but by handling artefacts owned by our forebears it is possible to develop a greater understanding of how people must have lived all those years ago.

As a result of the multitude of discoveries that have been made by detecting enthusiasts in this country over the last twenty-five years, it is now possible to built up a fairly comprehensive survey of such objects ... not only from Roman times, but also of the Celtic, Saxon and medieval periods as well.

The sites that have been searched by detectorists - either not known to or abandoned by archaeologists - have yielded a great assortment of coins and artefacts. Most of these, had they not been recovered, would have been destroyed in the ground by ploughing, chemical fertilisers, or building development.

Archaeologists and metal detecting enthusiasts have also worked together on rescue digs where speed has been of the essence.

To the novice detector user, many of his finds will not be instantly recognisable. A fragment of a Roman bronze brooch may look like a piece of Second World War shrapnel, and a corroded iron spearhead resemble a piece of a farmer's plough. Unless you have seen the complete object before, it is easy to get confused.

It doesn't take long for each detectorist to amass a box full of bits and pieces which cannot be identified and have therefore been discarded. Whenever I appraise somebody's collection of finds, this box can often be the most interesting area for study.

Occasionally an object will be found that has no parallel, being of a different style and design from anything previously recorded. It could even prove to be totally unique. Experts may be unable to precisely date it, and will have differing opinions as to its exact purpose.

In some cases your intuition and knowledge of the find spot are the most important clues that will lead to the eventual identification and dating of the object. This is why it is so important to appreciate and understand everything you find.   The more questions you ask yourself, the more information you will acquire. This information will lead you to new sites and could increase your finds rate significantly.

Ignorance and impatience are the most common causes of failure, and the failure rate amongst detectorists to find anything exceptional is quite high.

In the past I have often been asked to assess an individual's finds in order to help him decide which is the best or most interesting site he has been detecting on. To give an example, failure to identify an Anglo-Saxon strapend - found on an otherwise seemingly barren site - could mean that you never bother to return. If you had returned, you might have found the Aethelstan silver penny that was buried near to the strapend's find spot.

This book contains more than 300 illustrations, representing a fairly typical cross-section of finds from the Roman period. All of the antiquities shown (apart from the pottery) have been found through the use of metal detectors, and come from diverse sites around the country. Most of these objects are still in private ownership. Illustrations have also been included of some fragments and incomplete items that you are likely to come across. At the other end of the scale, some photographs show above-average, undamaged, and important items which are very rare.

Precise explanations for every object are not always possible, and in a few cases I have put forward some new theories. At the end of each section, I have included a valuation guide. This gives a range based on condition, within which would be a price that a collector might be prepared to pay for the item concerned.

The condition of any artefact is of prime importance in determining its value. Damaged or corroded pieces are difficult to sell unless they are unusual or rare. Provenance can also be significant, and should be carefully recorded for posterity. A good patina on a piece of high quality and style will add greatly to its value to a collector.

Unlike coins, no two artefacts are exactly alike, which means that giving a precise valuation for every item is difficult. I have been heavily criticised for some of the previous valuations included in the "Roman Artefacts" series of articles published in **Treasure Hunting** magazine, but I have also been surprised at how many dealers used these valuations to appraise their own stock.

The original prices stated in the articles have been substantially updated to reflect the current state of the market. Interest in antiquities is growing all the time; they are still relatively cheap considering their age, and are readily available.

However, I should also mention at this point that all antiquities found in the United Kingdom require an export licence if they are to be taken abroad. (This is irrespective of their monetary value). A licence application form can be obtained from: Department of National Heritage, 2-4 Cockspur Street, London SW1Y 5DH.

Introduction

We are never likely to know exactly what prompted Caesar's first expedition to Britain. In his own writings he does not say whether he aimed at conquest or punitive action. He does, however, state that in most of his Gallic campaigns he found British contingents fighting against him. The invasion of Britain was certainly a wise political move on the part of Caesar for it gave him good reason to retain his commission and avoid recall at the instigation of his opponents.

In late August 55 BC Caesar landed in Kent with only a small force, possibly because he recognised that it was quite late in the year and there would be no time for anything further than a reconnaissance and show of force. After several engagements the British tribes sought peace. Ancient armies were rarely able to mount campaigns in winter and after one month - with the rains setting in - Caesar returned to Gaul taking hostages with him.

In July 54 BC Caesar made his second expedition to Britain. This time he was better equipped having 800 vessels on board of which were five legions and 2,000 horsemen; he landed, unopposed, at Ryde.

Caesar's first major engagement was against the Catuvellauni tribe led by Cassivelaunus. In this he was helped by the Trinobantes and other tribes who had old scores to settle with the Catuvellauni. After storming Verulam, the stronghold of the British king, Caesar accepted the offers of peace made by Cassivelaunus. He left Britain with further hostages and imposed a tax which was to be paid yearly to Rome.

Concern about Britain remained, but it was not until May 43 AD that the Emperor Claudius mounted a full scale invasion. The main force landed at Richborough in Kent and consisted of four Legions: Legio II Augusta (commanded by the future emperor Vespasian), Legio IX Hispana, Legio XIV Gemina, and Legio XX Valeria.

Each Legion was a fully self-contained fighting unit comprising nine cohorts of 480 men each, with a leading cohort of 800 men. With about 19,000 additional auxiliaries, the total force numbered 40,000 men.

The aim on this occasion was to turn the whole of southern Britain into a Roman province, and this was achieved within four years. The general of the army of invasion and first governor of Roman Britain was Aulus Plautius. He made terms with the Atrebates and Iceni tribes, creating client kingdoms. Other tribes, defeated in battle, were disarmed.

In order to consolidate the new province, a system of roads, forts, and fortresses were set up. *Colonia* (settlements) were set up in Colchester (49 AD), Lincoln, Gloucester, and York. Verulam (St Albans) and London became *municipia* (towns). Within a few years over two dozen settlements had been created and many other sites established.

In planning a settlement or town, paved streets were laid out at right angles to one another enclosing rectangular blocks of land. Two main roads intersected at the centre of the town where the forum and basilica were situated. These were government buildings: the forum was an open space for political gatherings, and was enclosed on three sides by columns having the basilica on the fourth side. The basilica was a long aisled hall with a raised platform at each end, used by magistrates for official business.

Ampitheatres for entertainment were elliptical structures, having tiered seating of raised banks which surrounded an arena.

Running water was provided by aqueducts which also served the sewers and lavatories. Public baths were also an important amenity.

Upper class houses were laid out with mosaic floors, painted ceilings and glazed windows. Heating was provided by an underfloor hypocaust system, lighting by means of oil lamps. Furniture comprised of couches, low tables, and cupboards.

Shops flourished, offering a wide range of goods and services. All of this represented an enormous cultural change for Britain's native population.

The new province, however, was not without its problems. When the Iceni client king Prasutagus died in 60 AD, his wife Boudicca succeeded him. The Romans took this opportunity to try to incorporate the Iceni-held lands into the province and this started a rebellion early in 61 AD. Boudicca amassed an army of 100,000 men and sacked Colchester, London and St Albans, burning them to the ground. She was eventually defeated by the governor Suetonius with an army of only 10,000 men. Out of Boudicca's army 80,000 men were killed and the Iceni never recovered.

Under the Emperor Vespasian (69-79 AD) Wales was occupied and the frontier advanced towards Scotland. Eighty new forts were built and hundreds of miles of new roads.

During the reign of Hadrian (117-138 AD) a fortified wall was built as a defence against the Picts of Caledonia. This was started in 122 AD, was over seventy miles long, and took fifteen years to build. The wall was masonry built, fronted by a large ditch, and had small forts at mile intervals along its length. Hadrian's Wall was followed by the Antonine Wall, further north across the Forth-Clyde line, in 142 AD.

At this period the Roman army stationed in Britain consisted of three Legions, with fifty auxiliary regiments - a total of some 53,000 men.

Pic A1.
Obverse of gold aureus of Nero Claudius Drusus, struck by his son Claudius (41-54 AD).

Contemporary coinage consisted of the gold *aureus* (see **Pic A1**), which was equal to 25 silver *denari* (see **Pic A2**). The *denarius* in turn was equal to 4 brass *sesterti*. Smaller denominations consisted of the brass *dupondius* (half a *sestertius*) and the copper *as* (quarter of a *sestertius*). The *quadrans*, or quarter of an *as* was rarely used in Britain.

The copper *as* was widely imitated in Britain and examples can appear quite barbarous. Also, many of the silver *denari* circulating in Britain in the 1st century AD were plated, base metal forgeries. Virtually all of the silver coins found in Britain issued before Claudius (es-

Pic A2.
Silver denarius of Tiberius (14-37 AD. The reverse shows his mother Livia, seated right as Pax (Peace).

pecially Republican issues) bear bankers marks (incised stamps) on the obverse to counter forgery.

The northern Roman frontier held until 154 AD when a Brigantian rebellion occurred; this was followed by a withdrawal in 163 AD from the Antonine Wall.

An invasion at the end of the 2nd century destroyed part of Hadrian's Wall and many forts, but this was restored by Sepitimius Severus who set up headquarters at York in 208 AD.

At this period Britain was divided into two provinces - Britannia Superior and Britannia Inferior - so that a single governor did not control all the military forces.

On the East Coast of Britain pirates coming from Northern Germany were becoming a growing threat and new masonry forts were constructed to help protect against the raids.

Pic A3.
Bronze sestertius of Nero (54-68 AD). On the reverse is Roman seated left, holding Victory.

The 3rd century also saw civil war within the Roman Empire and inflation caused serious damage to its economy. Barbarous radiates (see **Pic A4**) were locally-produced coins, of ever decreasing size and quality, which reflected these problems.

Pic A4.
Bronze barbarous radiates. These are imitations of antoniniani of Tetricus, produced in Britain in the late 3rd century.

Carausius, a prefect of the British fleet who had been successful in combating piracy, rebelled in 287 AD and declared himself Emperor in Britain. He issued better quality coins (see **Pic A5**) minted at London, Clausentum, and Rouen (France) and was a popular leader.

Carausius was murdered by his assistant Allectus (see **Pic A6**) who in turn declared himself emperor. In 296 AD Constantius returned Britain to the Empire, and divided it into three units.

In the early 4th century, the Emperor Diocletian divided the province

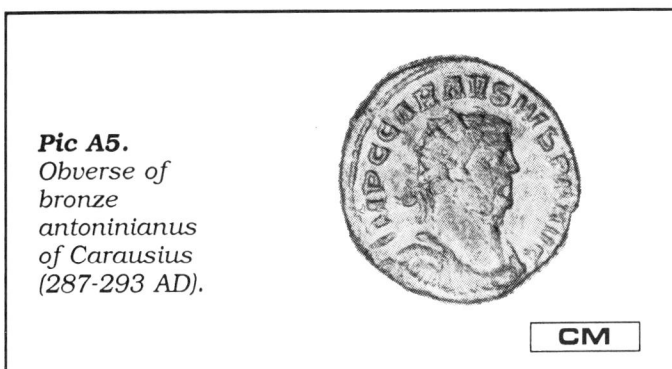

Pic A5.
Obverse of bronze antoninianus of Carausius (287-293 AD).

Pic A6.
Bronze quinarius of Allectus (293-296 AD). On the reverse is a galley. This coin was minted at Clausentum (Colchester).

into four regions (Britannia Prima, Britannia Secunda, Maxima Caesariensis, and Flavia Caesariensis) called the diocese of Britain.

The reign of Constantine (307-337 AD) saw a period of considerable rebuilding and prosperity. This emperor introduced a new coinage consisting of the gold *solidus* (see **Pic A7**), which was equal to 19 silver *milarensia* or 24 silver *siliquae*. This was a time of the building of great villas with their outer courtyards, baths, and mosaics.

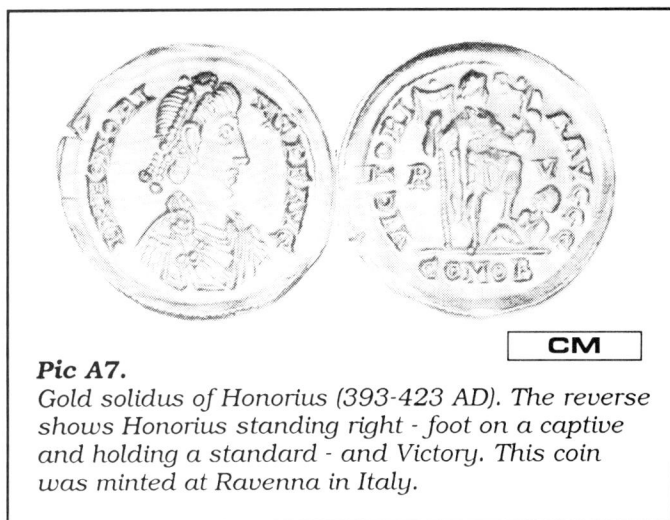

Pic A7.
Gold solidus of Honorius (393-423 AD). The reverse shows Honorius standing right - foot on a captive and holding a standard - and Victory. This coin was minted at Ravenna in Italy.

In 367 AD invaders from Ireland (Scots), the North (Picts), and the Saxons formed an alliance to attack Britain together. The Roman army was defeated on several fronts, but the Emperor Theodosius finally restored order in the following year. He also overhauled and modified the defences of towns and forts. These improvements enabled resistance to continue, even after the Roman army had been taken out of Britain for good in 406-7 AD by Constantine III. A plea to Honorius for help in 410 AD was answered with the reply that the Britons were "to defend themselves".

9

Notes For Collectors

For anyone taking a serious interest in collecting antiquities, there are certain criteria that should be taken into account when acquiring new pieces.

When you examine an artefact that is being offered for sale, the first question that you must ask yourself is whether the item is genuine (ie from the period that it is stated to be, and not a more recent copy). Next, it is important to look at the surface patina or colour to see if it has been altered or applied; and lastly, you should examine the artefact for any repairs or additions that have been made recently (ie a repaired pin on a Roman brooch).

Once you have satisfied yourself as to the above, you can then make a decision as to whether the asking price is a fair one.

If you are lucky enough to have been personally involved in the excavation of Roman coins and artefacts, as I have, then you will begin to develop an understanding of how objects should look and feel after being buried in the ground for almost 2,000 years.

It is possible, for instance, to be able to recognise the different patinas that develop on bronze and to know the type of environment the object came from; in some cases it is possible to state with some certainty the region or county where the object was found.

In a number of cases I have been offered Roman bronze statues that the vendors claimed were found in Britain; the patinas they showed, however, were typical of bronze objects found in the Middle East. The attempted deception resulted from the fact that an English provenance can add value to a piece.

Stylistically, of course, it is possible to suggest where most Roman artefacts were originally made. However, their distribution and subsequent usage can span several continents.

Forgeries

At present, the production of forgeries covers a wide spectrum of periods and materials. Some are relatively easy to recognise, and may have been intended just as "tourist pieces"; others are so well made that they require microscopic inspection and even chemical analysis to distinguish them from the genuine article.

The more valuable the artefact, the more care and attention that will go into the production of a forgery.

Many detector users were collectors before owning a detector, while others became interested in collecting through their finds. An example of the former is the late Henry Mossop who was one of the pioneers of metal detecting in this country. He was able to augment his collection of Celtic coins from his many finds in Lincolnshire, and he eventually published the results.

At many detector clubs, finds are often swapped between detectorists and although I am sure no club member would seek to knowingly defraud another, you should be aware of some of the forgeries that exist and are being traded.

There are many silver items of jewellery that are being cast, given a fake patina, and then being sold as originals. The most prevalent are: Celtic spiral bracelets and rings with crude snake-head terminals; medieval seal rings and seal matrices; stirrup rings set with glass stones; and even simple strapends.

Generally, the silver used is baser than that which would have been used to make the originals, and has a pitted surface displaying a dull colour. Other signs to look for include lack of detail, and often black highlighting.

Bronze artefacts are not so easy for the forger to reproduce because of the difficulty in creating an authentic-looking patina. Also, in the Roman period the quality of casting was so good that the mould seams were not visible on the finished item.

Cleaning & Preserving

With regards to cleaning artefacts there are now special kits available (advertised in the hobby press), that come with full instructions. However, the old rule still applies of "If in doubt, leave treatment and preservation to a specialist".

In general, bronze with a green patina should not be cleaned. Electrolysis cleaning, using washing soda or citric acid as a solution, is suitable for cleaning oxidised silver.

Barrelling machines and other scouring cleaners are only suitable for modern items. Nothing ancient should ever be cleaned by this method as it removes all vestiges of the patina and softens the details of the design.

Renaissance wax applied to the surface of dry or excavated bronze will protect the patina from chipping and moisture; it also gives the object a slight sheen.

Remember that if you have a collection, it is important to prevent the objects from touching one another. Corrosion, such as verdigris on bronze, can spread quickly. Isolate any item that is affected in this way, and treat it or have it treated.

It is very easy to ruin an artefact or coin by careless cleaning or poor storage. Treat all ancient items with the respect that they deserve. We are, after all, only the temporary custodians of such objects for future generations.

Price Guide

The values given in the price guide sections of this book are for two states of condition. Prices are provided as a benefit to collectors, for insurance purposes, and as a standard by which items can be acquired.

The figures given are based on my own observations and represent the price a collector might expect to pay for any particular item. Market forces constantly fluctuate, so all prices are subject to change both upwards and downwards.

In deciding the condition of an artefact, it is the surface patina that is most critical. Corrosion and damage must also be taken into account. Just because an item is 1,500 to 2,000 years old does not mean that it will have a minimum value irrespective of condition. So much material now exists that standards have risen; it is condition and not rarity which is the essential criteria.

Fine: In this condition an artefact should be virtually complete, although there may be a small piece missing. The surface patina should be stable and even, but there may be slight pitting on the surface or a few minor chips around the edge. Design details are visible but there may be wear on the high points. If there was enamel used in the original design, an average of 20-30% should remain.

A large proportion of artefacts excavated from ploughed fields are below - or only just approaching - Fine condition. This is due to plough damage and corrosion caused by the use of chemical fertilisers.

Very Fine: An item in this condition will be complete, and have a smooth surface usually with an even patina. Design details will be sharp. If enamel has been used in the design there will be an average of 60-70% remaining.

Celtic and Iron Age Finds

During the late Iron Age the population of Britain consisted of many different tribes, all self-governing and possessing no overall political unity. The Gallo-Belgic immigrants, whom we think of as the Celts, had arrived in a succession of waves and settled throughout the south-east of England before eventually occupying other areas of the country.

They brought with them a coinage of gold staters, the design of which was based on earlier Greek coins. When staters were introduced, around 125 BC, they were the first coins to be used in Britain although iron bars and ingots - resembling unfinished swords - were also exchanged and appear to have been a form of currency.

Early in the 1st century BC, coins began to be made in Britain. The first examples, called 'potins' originated from Kentish tribes (probably the Cantii) and were of cast bronze with a high tin content. From 75 BC gold staters were struck, more stylised and abstract in appearance than the imported Gallic coins. Over a period of time the gold staters became debased, first by the addition of silver (to produce the alloy electrum) and then by copper.

Eventually, each tribe was producing its own coins. At first these were uninscribed, but by 45 BC the Atrebates of the south Thames region (under their ruler Commios) were producing the first inscribed coins. By the close of the 1st century BC Celtic coins were quite plentiful and this is a reflection of the growing prosperity of Britain's inhabitants at that time.

Many tribes had constructed hill top fortifications, which consisted of earthworks revetted with timber and surrounded by a ditch for protection.

Following the expeditions of Julius Caesar in 55 and 54 BC, greater trading links were established between Britain and Rome. The interest shown by the Romans resulted from the fact that Britain supported a large population with many rich farms and homesteads, and was able to export both grain and cattle.

Tin and iron ores were mined in this country, while copper was imported. All the Celtic tribes possessed skilled metal workers whose crafts-

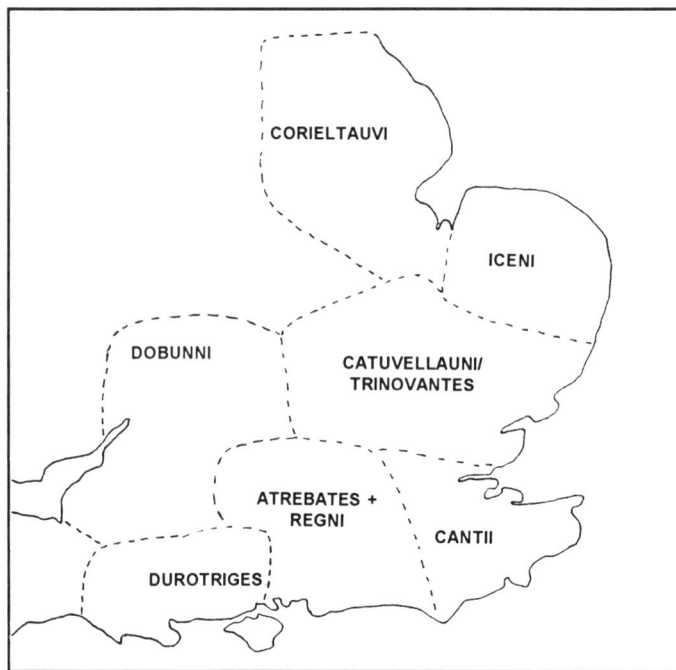

The areas of Britain occupied by the Celtic tribes c 55 BC (based on coin distribution). By the Claudian Invasion of 43AD these boundaries had changed dramatically.

manship was principally turned to making high quality artefacts for the warrior aristocracy. By the 1st century AD the objects being made were showing a strong and individualistic expression in their design. The fine works of art being produced included shields, scabbards, horse trappings, chariot mounts, torcs (sacred neck ornaments) and mirrors.

Until the invasion of Claudius in 43 AD Britain's military structure was based on the form of an heroic society, and the country was a place of refuge from Roman colonialism in Gaul.

The invasion was prompted by the actions of the Catuvellauni (a tribe inhabiting Hertfordshire) who had broken agreements with the Romans. This tribe had also dominated surrounding tribes, and gained the submission of the Atrebates whose leader they removed; this leader, Verica, was a Roman ally.

The native Celts wore their hair long but shaved the rest of their bodies dyeing their skin blue with woad. They worshipped heads, probably as part of their Druid cult beliefs. The Druids themselves were an intellectual class, with "knowledge of the oak" and strong, anti-Roman views.

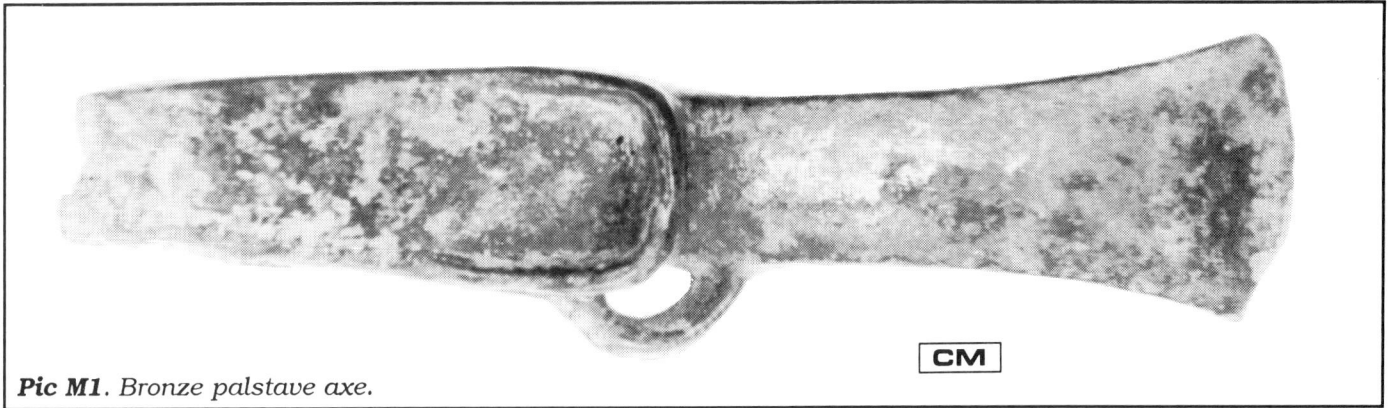

Pic M1. Bronze palstave axe.

The development of weapons from the Bronze Age to the Iron Age was a gradual one. Iron was being used in Britain by the 7th century BC, but was a rare and highly prized metal. Bronze continued in use because it was easily worked and could be smelted down and reused should an object made from it become broken or worn out. Many finds of broken and fragmentary bronze tools and weapons represent founder's hoards. Usually they are pieces of axes, swords etc collected together for resmelting.

Pic M1 represents a palstave dating to around 1200 BC. This was the axe in most predominant use in Britain during the Bronze Age and fragments turn up in Iron Age hoards. It has a stop ridge and side flanges which helped prevent the split wooden haft from slipping. The loop at the side was used to securely bind the haft to the axe.

The next stage of development, which occurred around 1,000 BC was when the axe was cast hollow with a socketed end to receive the haft internally (see **Pic M2**). Again, a loop was provided at the side for binding.

The bronze socketed axe continued to be produced into the Iron Age and was used for trading purposes. Examples have been found with a much higher proportion, than usual, of tin added to the bronze (normally it would have been about 10%) and which do not have a sharp cutting edge.

The palstave and socketed axe represent the earliest metal finds that are likely to be made in Britain. They have become quite common in recent years with an ever increasing amount of hoards and individual pieces coming to light.

Miniature bronze axes (**Pic M3**) of the socketed type appear to derive from later Iron Age sites, usually possessing religious significance. The axes were probably votive and represented an offering to the gods (an alternative theory is that they were carried as good luck charms). Examples with a rounded shaft are Romano-British and later in date.

An unusual and early dress pin is shown in **Pic M4**. This has a solid baluster moulded head with concave sides and three ribs. Below this, the shank of the pin is intentionally S-shaped, resembling the humped shape of a La Tene 1 brooch in profile. The pin almost certainly predates La Tene brooches, although I have been unable to find anything with which to make a comparison.

Early Iron Age brooches from Britain are rare and important finds. The example illustrated in **Pic M5** is an equal sided type, possibly dating as early as the 3rd century BC. It has a hollowed-out and bulbous humped bow. The head and foot parts of the brooch each have rounded lugs forming wings. There are dot and circles moulded onto the face of each disc,

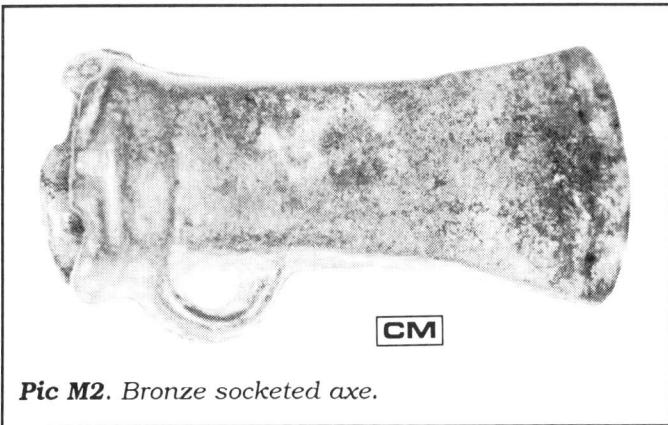

Pic M2. Bronze socketed axe.

Pic M3. Bronze miniature votive axes.

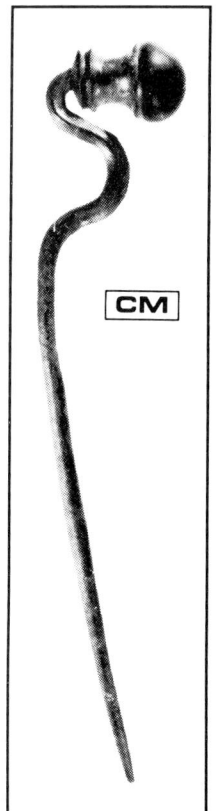

Pic M4. Bronze dress pin.

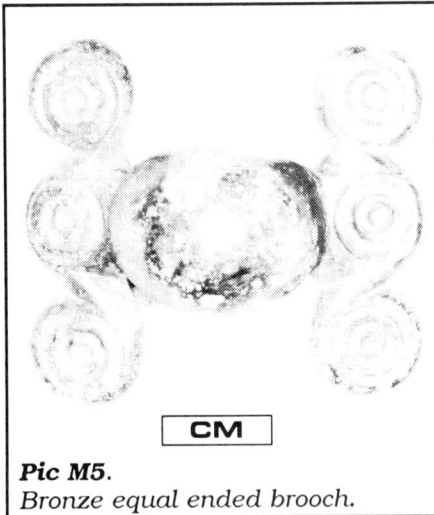

Pic M5.
Bronze equal ended brooch.

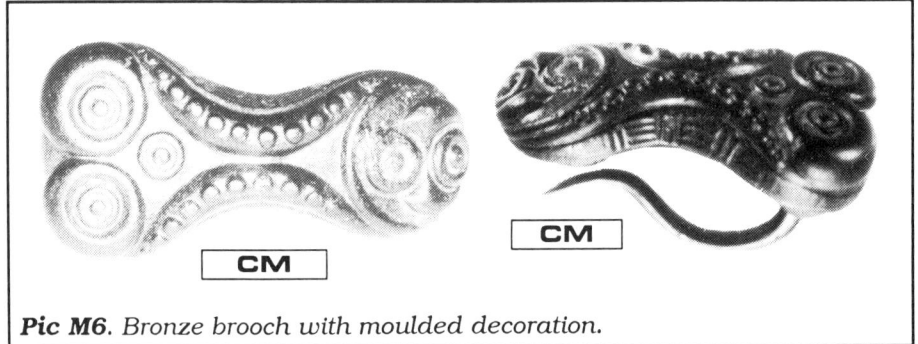

Pic M6. Bronze brooch with moulded decoration.

six in total, and the bronze pin is hinged. The brooch was found in Lincolnshire.

Another early brooch with a hinged pin is shown in **Pic M6**. Curiously, the pin is humped while the bow of the brooch is only slightly curved. The brooch is of solid construction, with a quite elaborate moulded design. On the head and foot are raised rings and dots and there is an additional cable motif between, on the foot. The sides of the brooch are concave, and decorated with basketry hatching. Along each side of the top edge is a line of beading forming two, back to back, outwardly facing crescents.

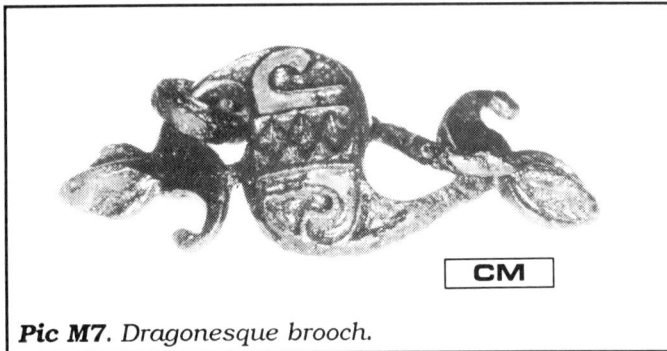

Pic M7. Dragonesque brooch.

The dragonesque is an example of a late Celtic brooch (see **Pic M7**) dating 1st to early 2nd century AD. It was produced in northern England (Brigantia). It is a flat plate brooch with a design based on a broken-back scroll, similar to a capital 'S'. The zoomorphic features develop from this; the head part is a slender trumpet which is capped. The example shown is complete and East Brigantian (York) in style with large petal-shaped ears with raised medial strips (normally these are enamelled). The expanded body of the brooch has traces of blue enamel in a form of spiral, and a central panel of three lozenges.

The bronze pin for the dragonesque is looped around the head of the brooch and runs under the body, with the tail of the brooch acting as a ledge or simple catch plate for the pin to rest on. This example is unusual in that the head is facing left rather than right, making the design a mirror image of the normal style for this type of brooch. This example also differs in that the eyes are not defined. The brooch was found in East Anglia.

During the later Iron Age period iron became more common and was used for basic tools and weapons, bronze remaining in use for decorative articles and fittings. This is clearly evident on Celtic bronze horse trappings which are often enamelled and quite elaborate. Terrets, harness mounts and bridle bits are all examples of horse furniture.

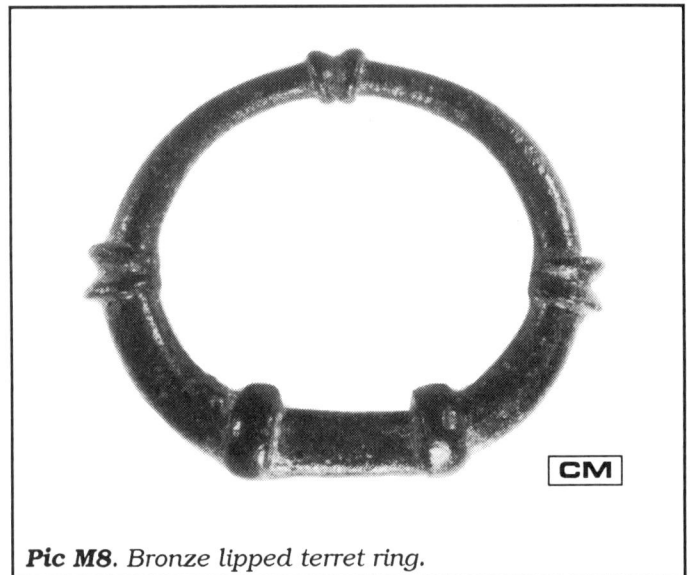

Pic M8. Bronze lipped terret ring.

Pic M8 shows a bronze terret ring which is circular in shape with a flattened base. The form comprises two conjoined trumpets with their mouths acting as collars. These contain a rectangular bar which was for attachment to the chariot yoke. The open ring contained the reins for guiding the horses. The larger-sized terrets might have been mounted on the chariot itself. This example has

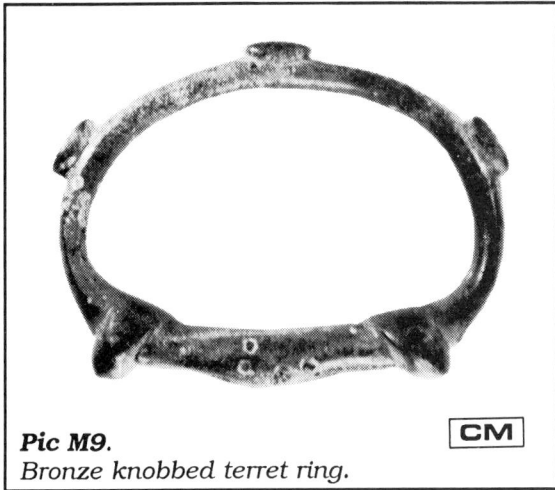
Pic M9.
Bronze knobbed terret ring.

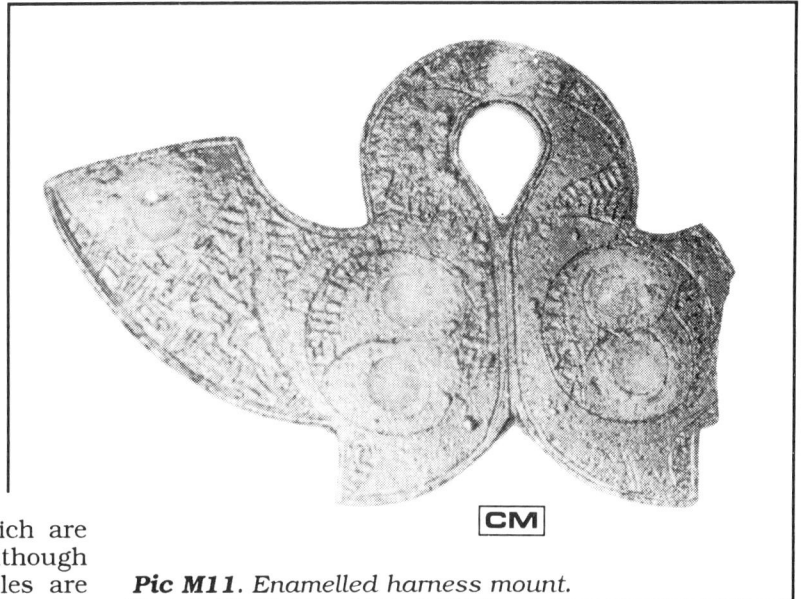
Pic M11. *Enamelled harness mount.*

three lipped mouldings which are symmetrically arranged. Although this terret is plain, examples are known with enamelling within the lips. Dating would be confined to 60-80 AD.

Another terret is shown in **Pic M9**, this time with a moulded knobbed decoration. It is elliptical in shape with a longer base plate (than the previous example), which bulges in the centre. The three knobs are crudely decorated with incised lines of cross-hatching, and the design has worn off the centre knob. This example is later in date than the lipped terret, probably early 2nd century AD.

After the Roman invasion the quality of Celtic workmanship rapidly deteriorated. As the Romans advanced their control in the latter half of the 1st century AD, they absorbed the existing wealth and requisitioned the farmers' harvests. The loss of liberty this entailed, together with the loss of their patrons, diminished the impetus of the native craftsmen and they turned their attention to making utility articles - such as brooches and other ornaments - that could be sold to the Roman legionaries.

Pic M10. *Crescent shaped enamelled terret ring.*

Part of a fine quality terret ring is shown in **Pic M10**. Although this is only a fragment, a crescent-shaped plate can be seen developing around

the ring of the terret. The terret has champleve (sunken cell) enamelling with a curvilinear decoration. A single triangular cell of yellow enamel can be seen on this example.

This style of terret would have been used by the Iceni tribe of East Anglia prior to the Boudicca rebellion, and would date around 40-60 AD.

Celtic art is based on patterns which incorporate a series of motifs or symbols. They include a lotus bud, a cable (similar to a comma), a palmette (palm leaf), a trumpet, a cornucopia (horn of plenty), a triangle with concave sides, and a triskele (three arms). All of the above designs can be seen used separately or mixed together.

Pic M11 shows a harness mount similar in style to a mount from the Polden Hill hoard; this has been dated to the first half of the 1st century AD. Although one lobe has been broken off, the curved geometric form of the mount is quite clear. The six circular cells of red enamel are set within a petal-shaped outline which is called a boss and petal pattern, and is based on the cable motif. Around this there is incised basketry filling. On the underside there is a loop and a strap bar for attachment. This mount comes from Norfolk.

Strap junctions (see **Pics M12** & **M13**) were used for connecting leather straps and were a feature of horse furniture; however, it is believed that some were intended for human use. The example shown in **Pic M12** consists of two bronze rings linked by a central lip. These are flanked by two rectangular grooved panels behind which are hidden two strap bars. This was found in South Yorkshire and is mid-1st century AD in date.

15

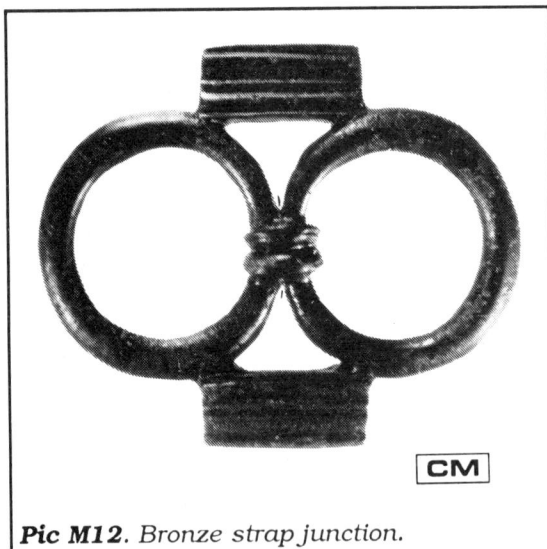

Pic M12. Bronze strap junction.

Pic M13. Enamelled bronze cruciform strap junction.

The example shown in **Pic M13** is much more elaborate and is called a 'petal' or 'cruciform' strap junction. It has a central square panel with a quatrefoil pattern of four petals of blue enamel in the form of an equal-armed cross. This design is Brigantian in origin and can be definitively dated to the 1st century AD. Two of the arms have a petal outline within which are two boss and petal enclosed by a crescent with enamelled cells. The two petal arms are flanked by two rectangular panels which conceal the two strap bars. At the ends of each panel are interlocking triangular cells of blue enamel which would have been alternated with a different colour of enamel (now missing).

The surface patina of this strap junction is quite porous and pitted, the damage having resulted from acids in the ground. It was found in East Anglia.

enamel cells. The two strap bars are concealed beneath.

Pic M15 shows an example with a single strap bar which may be a belt mount or fitting. Oval in shape it has a central rectangular panel with three rows of five enamel cells flanked at each end by a circular boss. It dates 1st century AD.

The strap junction shown in **Pic M16** was probably intended for human use. It again has the two strap bars, but here they are not concealed from view. The bars are circular in section and have the remains of bone discs that at one time were pinned onto the ends. The centre bronze bosses are moulded with rings and dots, and show a cable motif. The bosses are hollow with centrally piercing lugs projecting out.

Pic M14. Bronze strap junction.

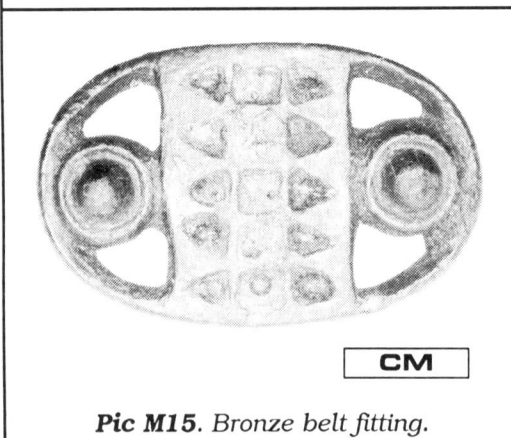

Pic M15. Bronze belt fitting.

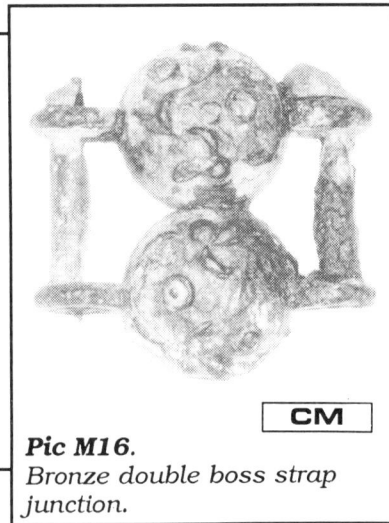

Pic M16. Bronze double boss strap junction.

Pic M14 shows another example of a strap junction. It has paired petal bosses with red and blue enamel centres, flanked by two rectangular panels with alternate red and blue

This strap junction was found in Humberside and again dates to the 1st century AD.

Another example of an item of horse furniture is the enamelled

16

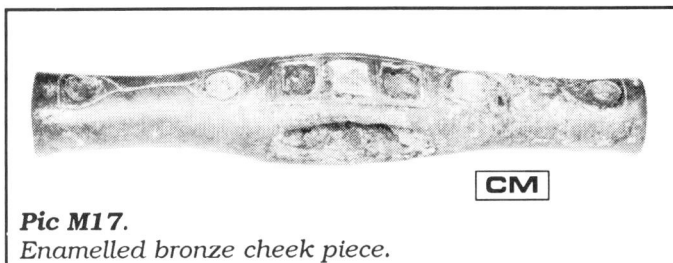

Pic M17.
Enamelled bronze cheek piece.

bronze cheek piece (**Pic M17**) also called a 'toggle' or 'slider'. This is circular in section, rod-like, and is flattened and perforated centrally by a rectangular slot for receiving a strap. On one side are seven enamelled cells, which appear to be alternately yellow and red (the red is much decayed). The outer cells are circular, and enclosed by an incised line of petal form. The three central cells are square, and enclosed within an incised rectangular line. The toggle dates early 1st century AD and was found near Cambridgeshire.

A large proportion of the Celtic artefacts that have been found would have been deliberately buried. Sometimes this burial would have been as part of a hoard, and the owner had the intention of recovering the items at a later date; on other occasions objects would have been placed in the ground as offerings alongside human burials.

The bridle bit of cast bronze shown in **Pic M18** was originally found broken in pieces. The bit had not suffered recent damage, but rather appears to have been ritually broken at the time of burial. (Breaking such objects meant that they could not be used again). The bridle has since been professionally restored by pinning. It was found on a ploughed field in Humberside but there were no associated artefacts in the vicinity.

The bridle is of the two link type. It has two centrally interconnecting mouth bars with a free running cheek ring passing through each terminal. Both bars have a collar moulding and a terminal of bifid or lipped design. The terminals show two circular cells, each containing red enamel which was used to imitate coral. The surface is decorated with dots and incised lines. This horse bit compares in design to the one from the Polden Hill hoard of the early 1st century AD.

Such horse bits are known with more decoration on one end than the other. This suggests that they formed part of a double harness, and the plainer end would have been situated on the inner side where it would not have been seen.

In Britain many ritual chariot

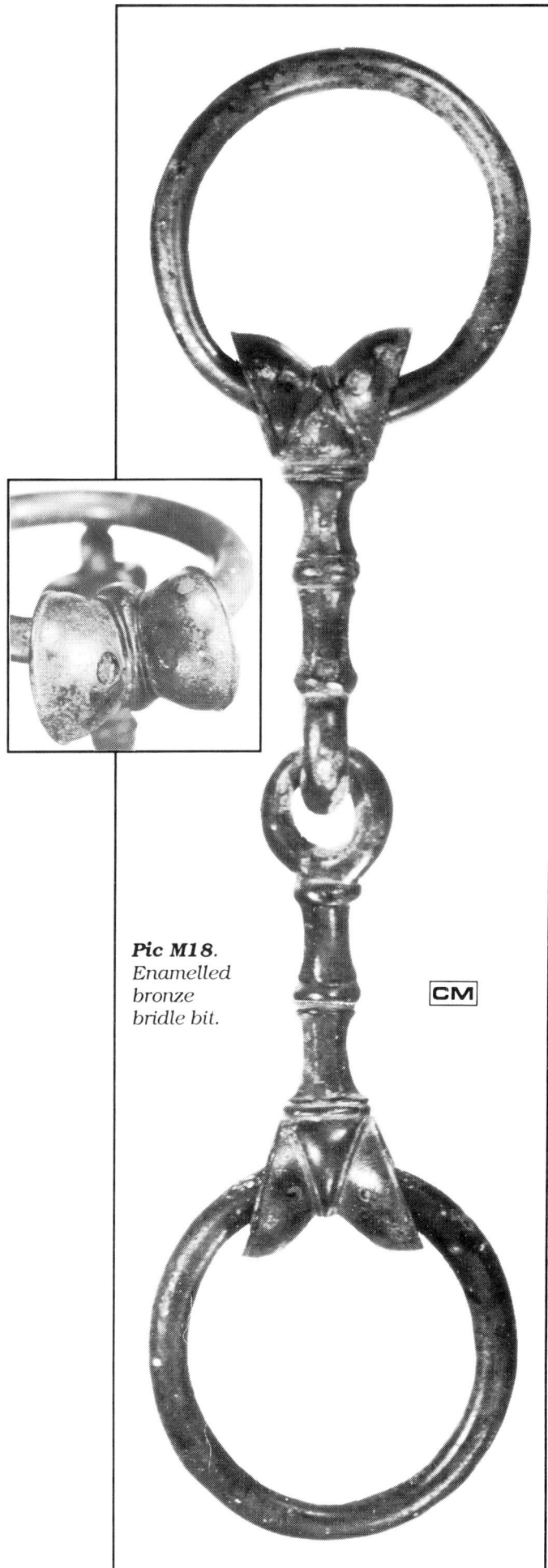

Pic M18.
Enamelled bronze bridle bit.

17

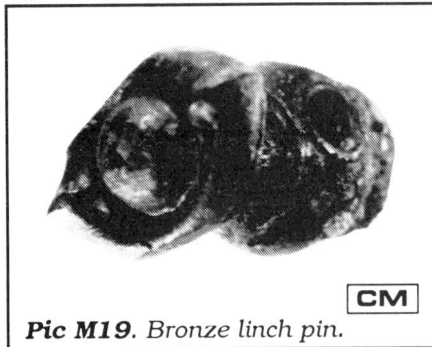
Pic M19. Bronze linch pin.

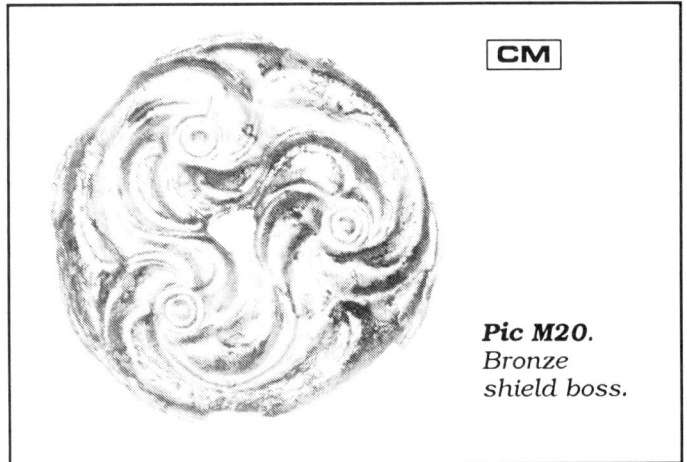
Pic M20. Bronze shield boss.

burials have been excavated, revealing the chariot's continued use in warfare from more ancient times. One important artefact associated with the chariot is the Linchpin (see **Pic M19**). This is a circular sectioned bronze head which would have been attached at its base to an iron shank with a tapered bronze foot at the end. Linchpins were inserted into the ends of the wheel shaft or axle of a chariot to prevent the wheels from working loose. (Some also supported the yoke to the pole of the chariot).

Many of the linchpins known have enamelled heads, but the example in **Pic M19** is of a moulded boss and petal design. The sides are flattened or rubbed by wear. The device possesses a transverse perforation which was for additional fastening or pinning. This example was found in South Yorkshire.

Pic M20 shows a bronze decorated boss which would originally have been fixed to the front of a wooden shield. It was made from thin sheet bronze which was heated and then punched from behind to form a pattern. This style of working is called 'repousse' and was probably introduced into Britain by Belgic tribes.

This shield boss is decorated with spirals emanating from three rings and dots. As a result of the thinness of the metal, the boss can be damaged easily, and the example illustrated has several perforations. Behind the boss is a lead backing plate,

intended to add rigidity and to provide a means of attachment. The advantage of repousse work is that the design is quite easy to produce. The boss dates 1st century and is thought to have been found in Sussex.

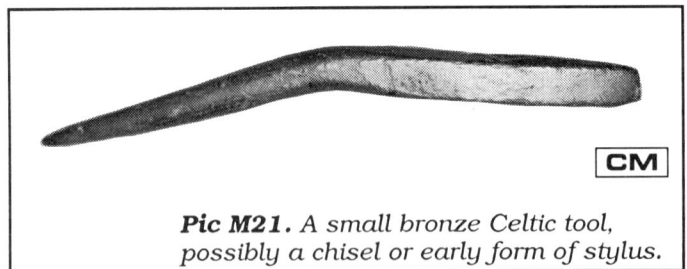
Pic M21. A small bronze Celtic tool, possibly a chisel or early form of stylus.

Pic M21 shows a small, bronze tool of Celtic use. It is solid, circular in section, and has a point at one end with a bevelled edge at the other. This may have been used as a chisel, while the point could have been used for pricking as an awl. Alternatively, it could have been a form of early stylus. It would date 1st century BC.

Although finger rings were rarely worn during the Celtic period, neck ornaments of bronze, iron or gold called 'torcs' were highly regarded. **Pic M22** shows the lower part of a bronze beaded torc. The moulding consists of ten graduated beads terminating in a cylinder at each end

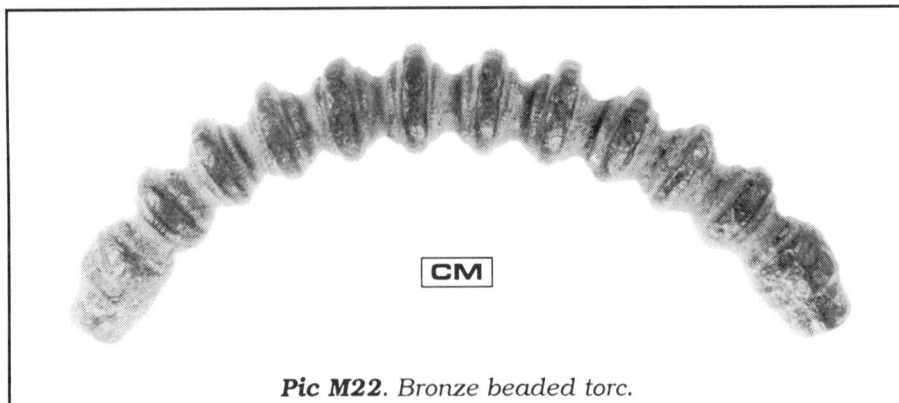
Pic M22. Bronze beaded torc.

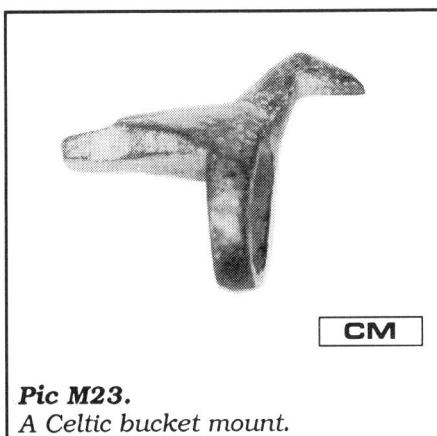

Pic M23.
A Celtic bucket mount.

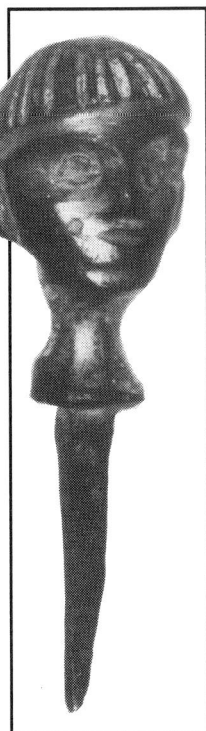

Pic M24.
A bronze pin with a detailed male head.

which is hollowed out. The ends would have been joined to the other two-thirds of the loop, which is now missing; this would have been plain and of circular section. As this type of torc is non-expandable, the two-piece construction would have allowed easy fitting and removal. This example would date 1st century AD.

Torcs have their origins in South Germany during the La Tène period. They were regarded as being endowed with magical powers and were worn in battle. The reason that detector finds of gold torcs hit newspaper headlines is that such torcs would have been worn by tribal leaders and they are extremely rare and valuable.

The Romans also used torcs but in their case it was as a form of military decoration or officer's badge.

An object found in the ground can often be related to others found in the same area by the form or style it displays. Occasionally, a group of artefacts found separately will all belong to the same object.

Although the object shown in **Pic M23** at first glance appears to be a finger ring, it is - in fact - a bucket mount. Fixed through the rim of the bucket, the bird would have been one of a series of animals used as decoration around the top of the bucket. The bucket itself was probably used in sacrifices or religious ceremonies. It would date 1st century BC.

A number of Iron Age pins have iron shafts with bronze or silver heads. The pin shown in **Pic M24**, however, which is possibly Romano-Celtic, is entirely bronze. The pin is quite short and has a detailed male head moulded in the round. The pin has a heavily tinned surface and is thought to date from the 1st century AD.

Celtic artefacts are more difficult to value than Roman examples as a result of their individuality and the fluctuating market conditions obtaining at present.

Price Guide

	Fine	Very Fine
M1: bronze palstave axe	£70	£180
M2: bronze socketed axe	£60	£160
M3: bronze miniature votive axe	£15	£35
M4: bronze dress pin	£75	£180
M5: bronze equal ended brooch	£85	£250
M6: bronze brooch with moulded decoration	£175	£550
M7: dragonesque brooch	£200	£650
M8: bronze lipped terret ring	£70	£160
M9: bronze knobbed terret ring	£60	£130
(If M8 or M9 are enamelled, values are substantially higher).		
M10: crescent-shaped terret ring	£550	£1,750
M11: enamelled harness mount	£750	£2,500
M12: bronze strap junction	£120	£275

	Fine	Very Fine
M13: enamelled bronze cruciform strap junction	£350	£1,200
M14: bronze strap junction	£225	£700
M15: bronze belt fitting	£60	£140
M16: bronze double-boss strap junction	£75	£220
M17: enamelled bronze cheek piece	£165	£450
M18: enamelled bronze bridle bit	£3,500	£12,000
M19: bronze linch pin	£50	£120
M20: bronze shield boss		
M21: small bronze Celtic tool	£8	£20
M22: bronze beaded torc (complete)	£175	£600
M23: Celtic bucket mount	£15	£40
M24: bronze pin with detailed male head	£100	£240

Pic M5

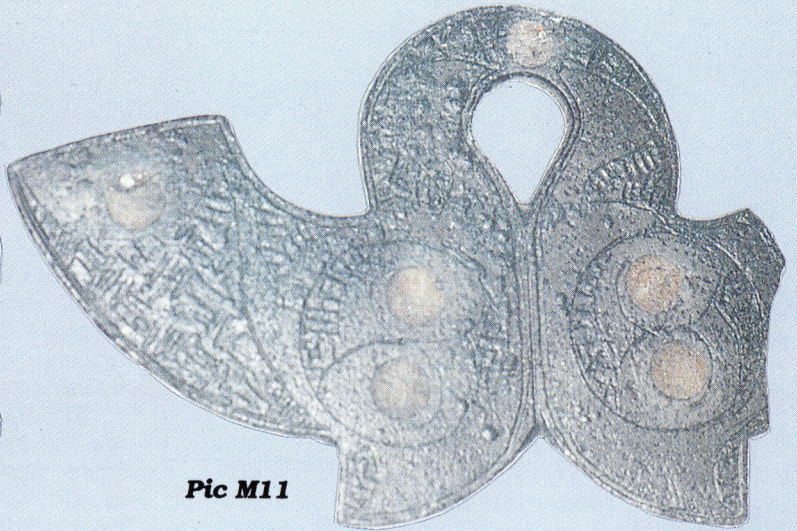

Pic M11

Pic M6

Pic M7

Pic M13

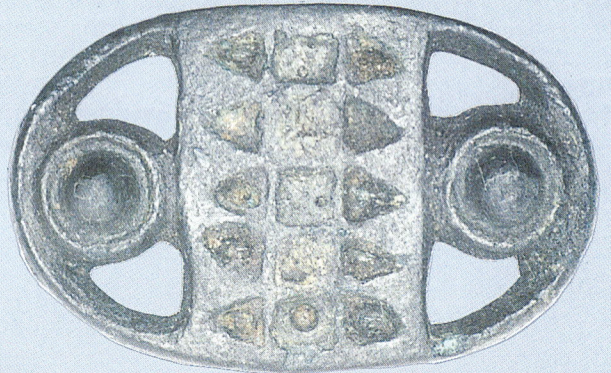

Pic M15

Pic M14

Pic M17

Pic M20

See text for details

Not to Scale

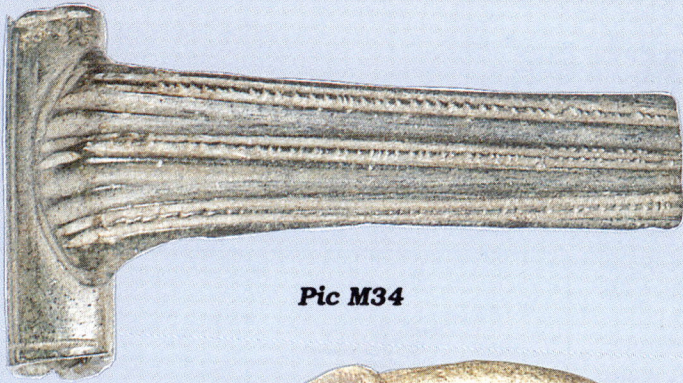

Pic M34

Pic M54

Pic M43

Pic M56

Pic M36

Pic M57

Pic M47

Pic M49

Pic M59

See text for details

Not to Scale

Fibula Brooches

I n trying to date and classify a type of artefact as accurately as possible, it is necessary to compare a large number of the same type of excavated items; preferably, from an assortment of different sites. This is why metal detecting has added considerably to our knowledge of the past.

It has increased the supply of excavated coins and relics, and opened up new areas of research on these finds. It is logical that if people can improve their collections, then it will be reflected in new sources of reference material.

In the case of Roman brooches, this is already true. Four books, all written by the late Richard Hattatt have been published, covering some 1,700 brooches. The examples illustrated and described were mainly from his personal collection, which resulted from purchasing metal detecting finds over a fifteen year period. This clearly shows the archaeological benefits that are potentially available from the hobby of metal detecting.

Of course, it requires considerable funds and research to develop knowledge of this kind, but when it occurs outside of the museum establishment it becomes an important achievement for all concerned in the finding and recording of these antiquities.

Detector users will find that

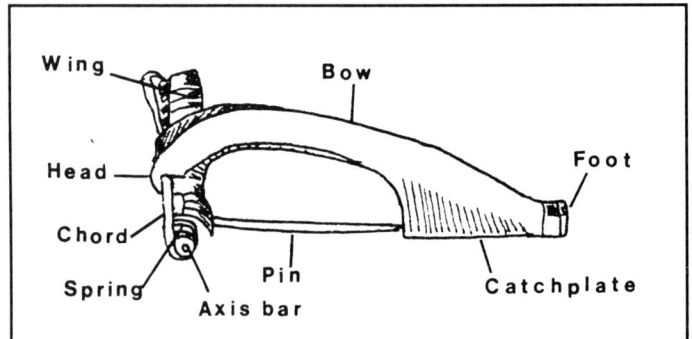

Wing | Bow | Foot | Head | Chord | Spring | Pin | Axis bar | Catchplate

brooches turn up frequently on ancient sites but are generally in a broken and corroded state. Nevertheless, they still present a fascinating series to collect and study. It would, for example, be useful to keep a record of the different types of brooches that you come across. This information can then be compared to the archaeological finds, and allow you to determine the styles most prevalent in your area.

Most of the brooches illustrated in this chapter, were found in East Anglia.

Earliest Examples

Brooches as a functional dress ornament were used in Britain (although not in large numbers) before the Roman Conquest.

An early, but rarely encountered brooch in this country is the equal-ended type referred to as "Upavon". These possibly date from the 4th century BC (see **Pic M25**) although none of the few found in Britain have been accurately dated. Comparisons made to continental finds, however, suggest that they pre-date the La Tene classes.

The example illustrated is formed from cast bronze and has a bulbous, humped bow - hollowed out behind - with an identical head and foot. The pin would have been hinged rather than sprung - a feature common to this type of brooch during the Iron Age period.

An unusual variation of this is shown in **Pic M26**. This example has developed wings which are ribbed with a knob on each end. There is a large dome on the head and foot, which is connected to the bow. Again the pin is hinged. This brooch possible dates to the 3rd century BC.

The bronze brooch shown in **Pic M27** is also curious. It has a flat bow

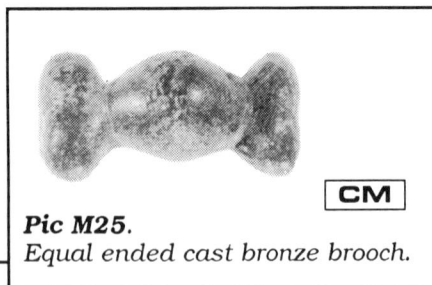

Pic M25.
Equal ended cast bronze brooch.

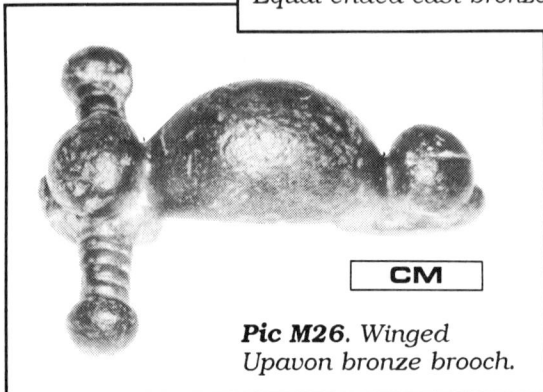

Pic M26. *Winged
Upavon bronze brooch.*

Pic M27.
Bronze brooch with flat bow.

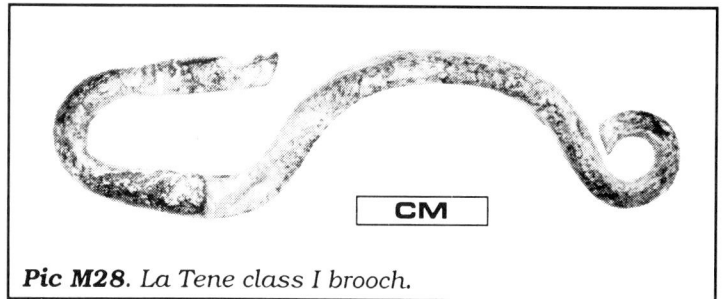

Pic M28. *La Tene class I brooch.*

and extended foot, with moulded decoration in the form of two cups, each containing a bone insert. It appears to have had an iron spring which has now rusted away. This example may be an imported type.

Pic M28 shows an example of a La Tene class I. These were continental brooches made from one piece of metal (normally iron or bronze) with bilateral springs. They had found their way to Britain by the 3rd century BC. This type can be distinguished by its high arched bow and upturned catch plate or tail which is often decorated with a boss (or, more rarely, inset with coral).

The tail becomes extended and is connected to the bow on the La Tene class II, but this form is rarely found in Britain.

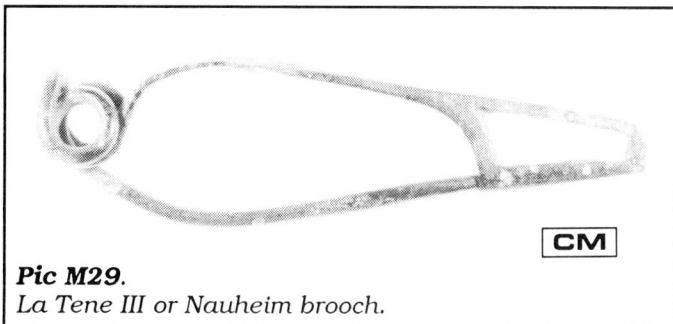

Pic M29.
La Tene III or Nauheim brooch.

In turn, these were superseded by the La Tene III (or Nauheim derivative) in the 1st century BC. This is a much simpler one-piece brooch (see **Pic M29**). Finds of these are more common and serve to confirm the increased wearing of brooches in the period.

The plain and cheap form of this type (which lasted into the mid-1st century AD) indicates a more general distribution amongst the population than the La Tene I.

Another brooch typical of the early 1st century is the "Colchester". This is again formed from one piece of metal but the design now has two metal wings covering the spring (so that it is hidden from view) and there is a hook on the head of the bow holding the spring in place. This type originated in Gaul, but development continued in Britain. Sometimes decoration is applied to the bow,

usually in the form of undulating lines.

The two-piece "Colchester" (see **Pic M30**) dates 50-80 AD and has a separate spring and pin. The brooch head has a lug with two piercings: the top one to hold the chord, the lower one to hold the axis bar of the spring.

This development inspired many derivatives in the late 1st century AD (eg the dolphin, Polden Hill, headstud, and T-shaped).

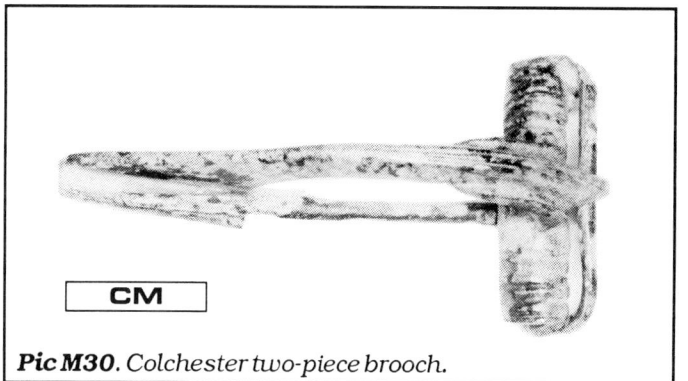

Pic M30. *Colchester two-piece brooch.*

The Polden Hill (see **Pic M31**) is a local variant of the dolphin. The spring or axis bar is secured in the end plate of the enlarged wing of the brooch. On this example the wings are grooved and ribbed, and there is also ribbing along the length of the bow. The catch plate has been made separately and may have replaced the original. This is an attractive and fairly robust example.

In **Pic M33** can be seen another example of the "Polden Hill". This one has much shorter and thicker wings, and has a loop joined to the head.

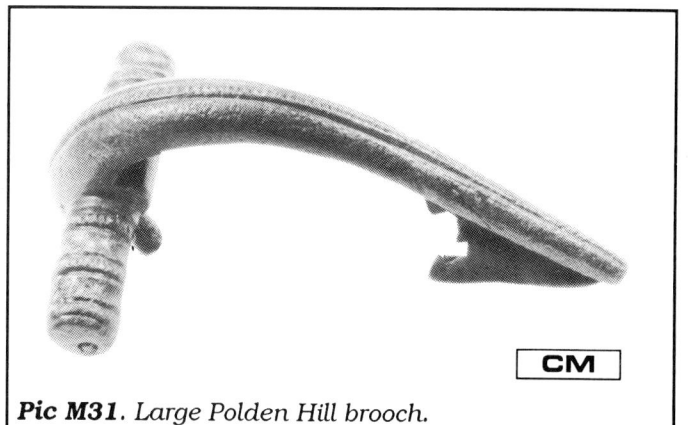

Pic M31. *Large Polden Hill brooch.*

Pic M61

Pic M62

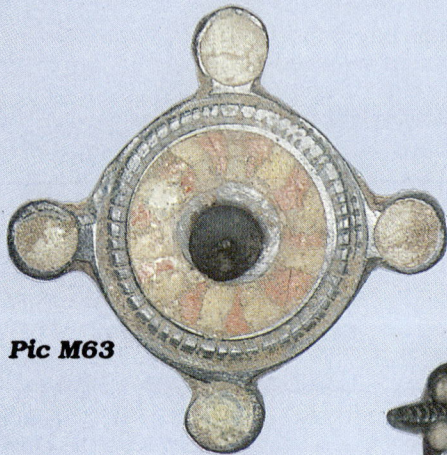

Pic M63

Pic M64

Pic M65

Pic M69

Pic M70

Pic M71

Pic M73

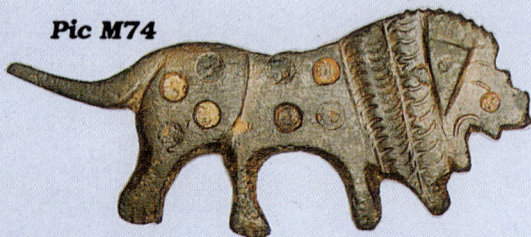

Pic M74

Pic M75

See text for details

Not to Scale

24

Pic M78

Pic M80

Pic M83

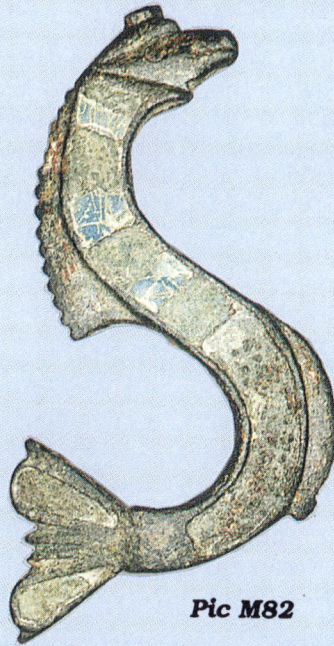

Pic M82

Pic M84

Pic M86

Pic M87

Pic M89

Pic M90a

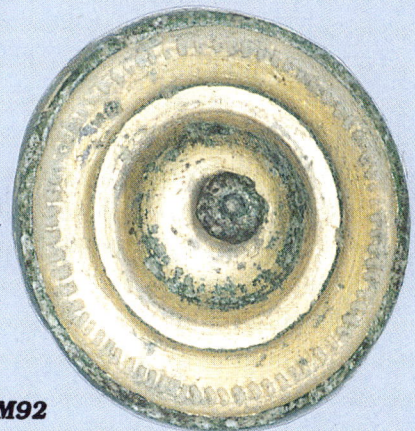

Pic M92

See text for details

Not to Scale

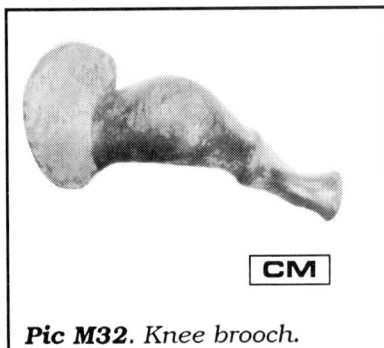
Pic M32. Knee brooch.

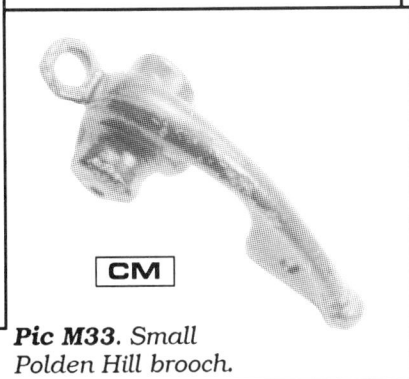
Pic M33. Small Polden Hill brooch.

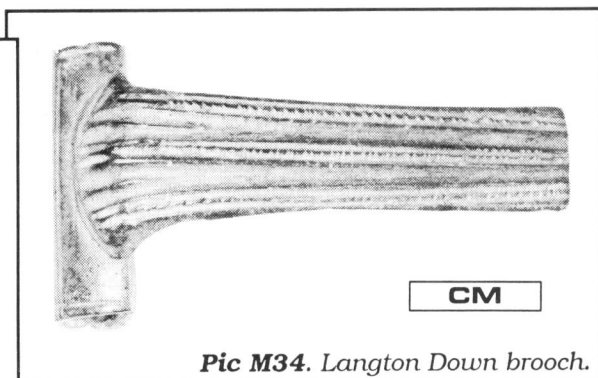
Pic M34. Langton Down brooch.

This was intended for a chain which would have linked one brooch to another (a fashion popular with women during the second half of the 1st century and the first half of the 2nd century AD). It is also important to remember that the chain loop does not occur on continental brooches imported into Britain.

Pic M32 shows another bow brooch called a "knee" brooch; it is a type originating in the Rhineland, where they were quite common. Brought over by the Roman soldiers in the middle of the 2nd century AD, they continued in use until the early 3rd century AD. This example has a semi-circular head plate with a tapering, sharply-turned bow. These brooches are normally quite stumpy, and occasionally examples can be found enamelled, or inlaid with niello (a silver compound). On this example the bronze had been heavily tinned, giving it a silver-like finish.

The Langton Down style (**Pic M34**) was developed in Gaul but saw use in Britain from the time of the invasion until about 75 AD. The spring on these is enclosed within a distinctive tubing of fairly thin construction. The bow is flat, and decorated with grooves and ribs (reeding).

A development from this, is the rosette or thistle brooch (**Pic M35**) which utilises the same style of spring housing. In this design a disc plate

has been added to the bow which is ribbed in the same way as the Langton Down varieties. Additionally, three bolts have been applied on either side of the bow, tipped with red and green enamel. The complexity in the manufacture of these brooches, together with the factor of their fragility, makes them quite desirable.

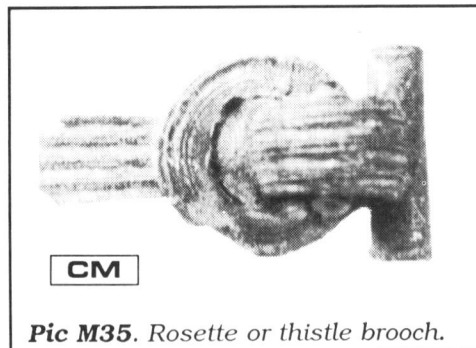
Pic M35. Rosette or thistle brooch.

A more Celticised derivative of the rosette type is the Aesica (see **Pic M36**). The bow has a central rib with a dot and circle pattern on either side of the knobs projecting from its base on each side. The edges of the bow and expanded foot are punch marked. The foot also has knobs at each end and there is a moulded design in the centre. This consists of a crescent above a dot and circle, with trumpets on either side.

An early example of the hinged pin in use on a Roman brooch is the

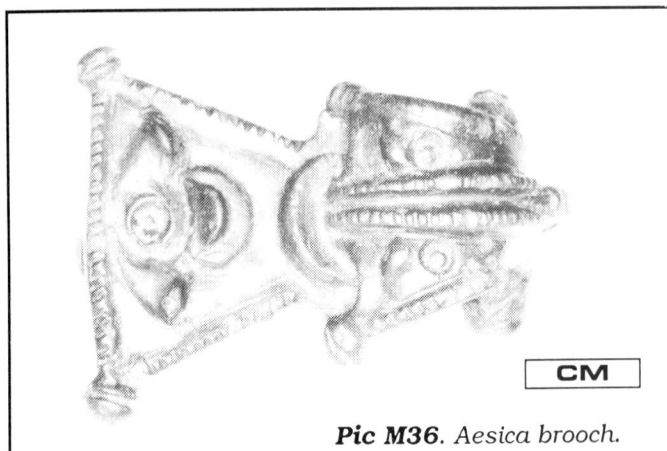
Pic M36. Aesica brooch.

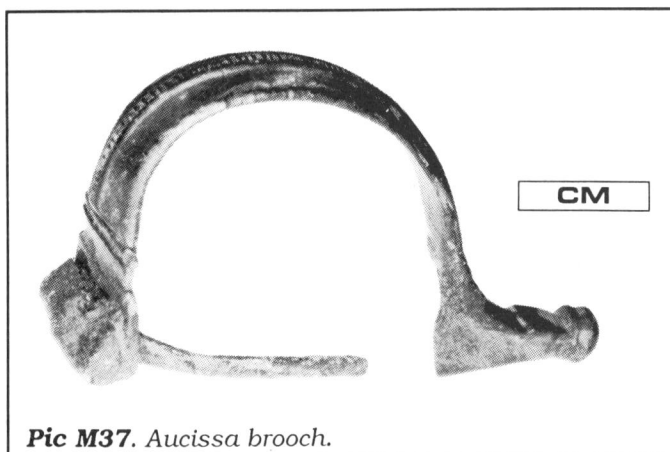
Pic M37. Aucissa brooch.

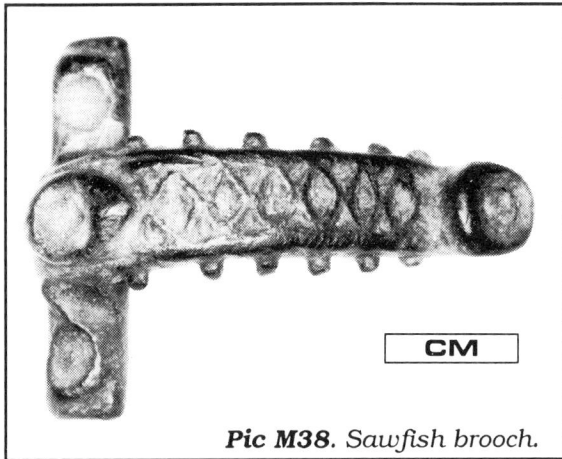

Pic M38. *Sawfish brooch.*

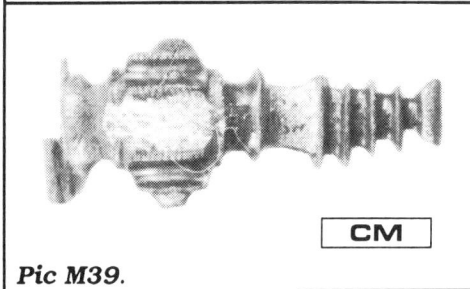

Pic M39.
Hod Hill brooch.

Pic M40. *Tapering bow brooch.*

Aucissa (**Pic M37**) which also came to Britain with the Conquest in 43 AD. It always has a high arched bow, an elongated foot, and pronounced knob. Sometimes the word "Aucissa" appears on the head, which is believed to be the maker's name.

The T-shaped brooch is a development from the dolphin varieties, and dates from the late 1st century through to the 2nd century AD. It has wide, tubular wings and a hinged pin. There is a tremendous variety in the decoration of the bow as can be seen in **Pic M38**. This, termed the "sawfish", has serrated sides and ornamentation on the bow, with recesses for enamel.

Pic M40 shows a simpler form of tapering bow brooch with incised and ribbed decoration.

Pic M41 is a T-shaped brooch with a niello inlay design of two crescents, with a lozenge between, on the head of the bow; this is more wide and flat than the bows of previous examples. In the middle of the bow can also be seen two lateral ribs. This example originates from the Severn area.

Pic M39 is a Hod Hill variety from the middle of the 1st century AD. It has a hinged pin with a fluted and cross-ribbed bow, which has also developed side knobs to the upper part. This is a common type, found in an amazing variety of styles, many of which show tinning.

A possible development from this is the lozenge plate brooch (**Pic M42**). Also heavily tinned, it has a bow with a flat rectangular panel inset, with three circular punch marks. Like the example shown in **Pic M39**, this also has side knobs. The example shown probably dates from the beginning of the 2nd century AD.

Pic M41. *T-shaped brooch with niello.*

The headstud is a native British brooch of the 2nd century AD, and is regarded as being the last of the Colchester derivatives. Its distinguishing feature is an enamelled circular stud on the head of the brooch. The bow is normally richly decorated

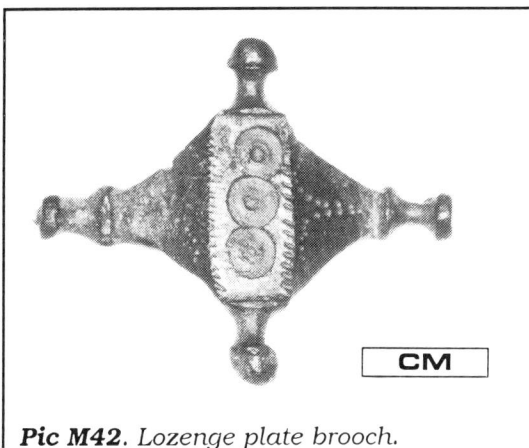

Pic M42. *Lozenge plate brooch.*

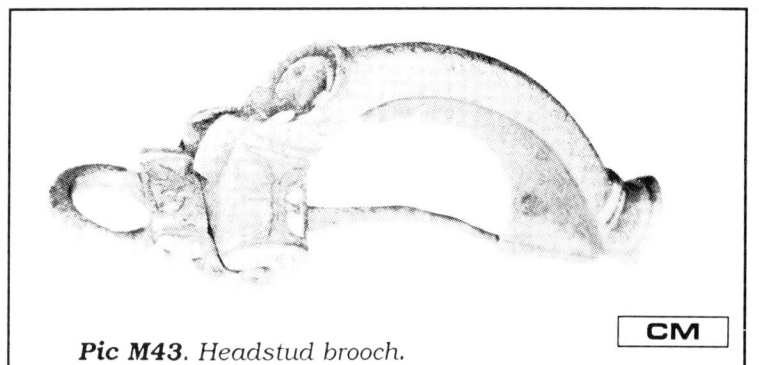

Pic M43. *Headstud brooch.*

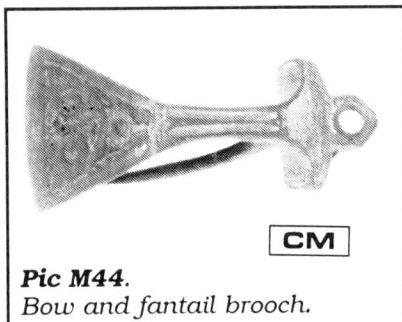

Pic M44.
Bow and fantail brooch.

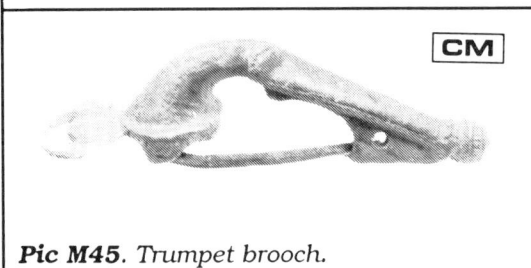

Pic M45. *Trumpet brooch.*

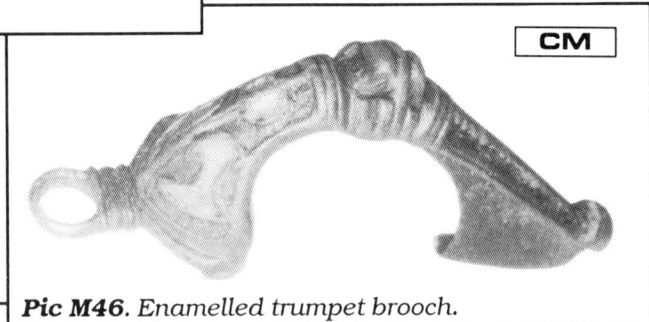

Pic M46. *Enamelled trumpet brooch.*

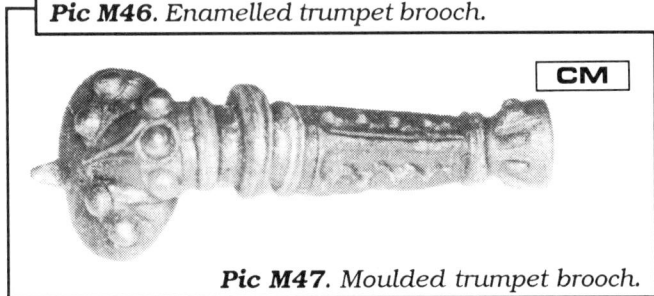

Pic M47. *Moulded trumpet brooch.*

and enamelled. **Pic M43** shows a headstud brooch with blue and white enamel cells on the wings and neck band which supports the head loop. The head stud is of piriform shape and integrally cast. The brooch has a hinged pin with a well-arched flat faced bow of heavy construction, which is typical for this type. This is one of the few brooches where the chain linking it to another brooch through the head loop actually survives.

Pic M44 shows a bow and fantail brooch which dates from the late 1st century and through the 2nd century AD. It has a hinged pin, narrow grooved bow, and a triangular foot which has a Celtic-style scroll pattern inlaid with red enamel. The whole brooch is heavily tinned. Although not a common brooch, I have seen a number of these within collections in southern Britain.

The trumpet brooch (**Pic M45**) is a native British type developed from Danubian and Pannonian imports. It always has a bulbous head and tapering bow, from which the name "trumpet" is derived. This example is virtually undecorated, the only detail being on the foot knob. One interesting feature is the unusual head plate extension with chain loop. This compares with other similar brooches found at Wroxeter in Shropshire. As this one came from the same location, it may indicate the area of manufacture.

A more elaborate version is illustrated in **Pic M46** and this dates to the early 2nd century AD. The head is decorated with green enamelled crescents set in red panels. The bow has a centre globule decorated with acanthus leaves while the leg is lined with triangular red-enamelled cells. The more "Celticised" the design of a trumpet brooch, the more desirable and valuable it becomes.

Pic M47 shows an example of a brooch with a head moulded with two raised dots on either side forming eyes. There are three more raised dots just below the head with three central buttons dividing the bow. The leg has a zig-zag rib running down each side.

The very unusual knee brooch variant in shown in **Pic M48** has a semi-cylindrical head with a rectangular sectioned and hollowed out bow. A probable dating would be late 2nd century AD and it compares in style to an incised example listed by Hattatt (no 483). However, my example is more rigid in shape and deco-

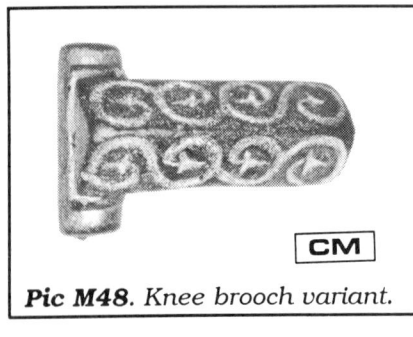

Pic M48. *Knee brooch variant.*

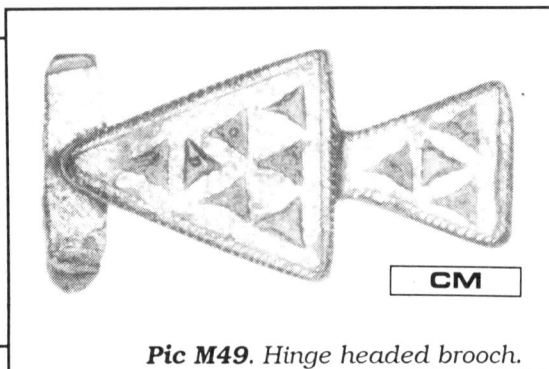

Pic M49. *Hinge headed brooch.*

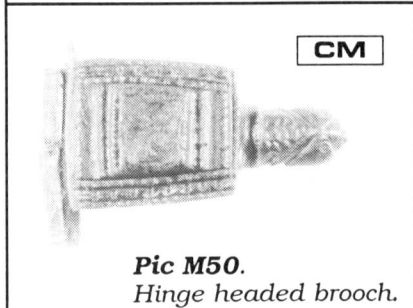

Pic M50.
Hinge headed brooch.

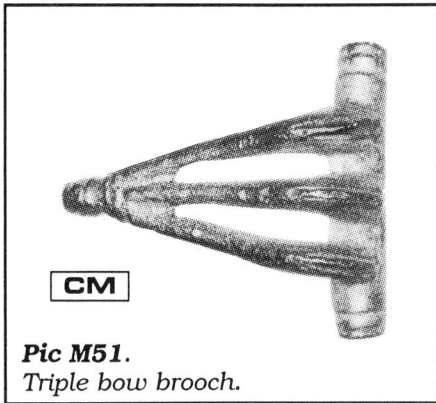

CM

Pic M51.
Triple bow brooch.

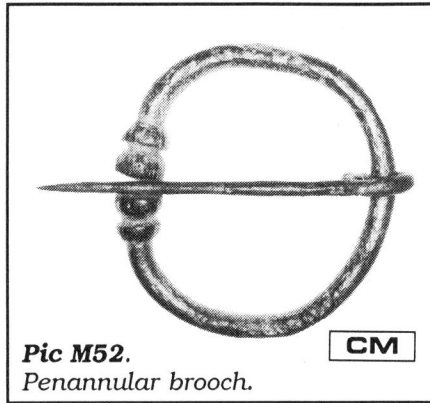

CM

Pic M52.
Penannular brooch.

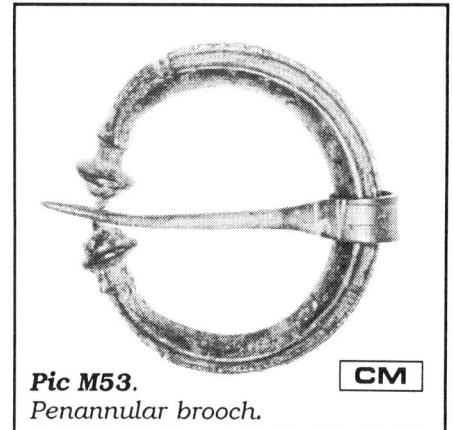

CM

Pic M53.
Penannular brooch.

rated with floral tendrils on each side.

Another unusual brooch is that shown in **Pic M50**, which is a hinge-headed bow brooch dating from the early 2nd century AD. It has a flat, rectangular bow with a zoomorphic foot. Niello inlay has been applied (this type normally has enamelled cells within a lozenge or triangular bow). Many examples have been found in France, and this example is almost certainly continental.

Pic M49 shows a hinge headed brooch with a flat upper bow of triangular shape and a similar shaped but smaller foot. Both contain triangular cells of alternate red and green enamel, and the whole brooch is heavily tinned.

Pic M51 shows a tapering bow brooch of a type I had not seen before until I encountered this example. It

has a bow divided into three sections, imitating the continental P-shaped type. A likely dating is mid-2nd century AD.

Pic M52 shows a penannular brooch. This type originated in the Iron Age period, and continued to be produced right through the Roman and Saxon eras. For this reason these brooches are hard to date closely, although certain clues exist. The terminals are more elaborate on Saxon examples, while the pin becomes elongated. Iron Age types often have a humped pin. This example is Roman, probably dating 3rd-4th century AD.

The other example (see **Pic M53**) is of superior quality with a square sectioned ring showing punched decoration around the edge. The ends are conical but have ridges.

Price Guide

	Fine	Very Fine		Fine	Very Fine
M25: bronze equal ended brooch	£35	£85	M41: T-shaped brooch with niello	£16	£40
M26: bronze winged Upavon	£45	£110	M42: lozenge plate brooch	£18	£45
M27: bronze brooch, flat bow	£65	£175	M43: headstud brooch	£38	£160
M28: La Tene I	£20	£65	M44: bow and fantail brooch	£20	£55
M29: La Tene III or Nauheim	£16	£40	M45: trumpet brooch	£32	£85
M30: Colchester two-piece	£12	£28	M46: enamelled trumpet brooch	£75	£240
M31: large Polden Hill (dolphin variant)	£18	£45	M47: moulded trumpet brooch	£60	£170
M32: knee brooch	£10	£24	M48: knee brooch variant	£40	£90
M33: small Polden Hill brooch	£12	£26	M49: hinge headed brooch	£25	£70
M34: Langton Down brooch	£24	£75	M50: hinge headed enamelled brooch	£45	£120
M35: rosette or thistle brooch	£40	£160	M51: T-shaped triple bow brooch	£30	£70
M36: Aesica brooch	£130	£450	M52: penannular brooch	£25	£60
M37: Aucissa brooch	£20	£65	M53: penannular brooch	£45	£120
M38: sawfish brooch	£16	£40			
M39: Hod Hill brooch	£15	£36			
M40: tapering bow brooch	£12	£26			

Plate, Crossbow & Early Saxon Brooches

Plate brooches were in use in Britain from the time of the Roman Invasion. They achieved their peak of popularity in the 2nd century AD, but continued in use throughout the years of the Roman Occupation and beyond.

The style of plate brooches indicates a degree of affluence possessed by those who could afford to wear them. The small pin used on such brooches, and the limited space between the pin and the back, shows them to have been intended to secure fine - and expensive - fabrics. Also, as another indication of their cost, on some examples the flat upper surface is richly ornamented with coloured enamels, adorned with silverwork, or even set with semiprecious stones.

Enamel is a form of glass to which colouring pigments have been added. It would have been fused to the brooch by heating at a moderately low temperature. The colours normally used were: red, blue, orange, green, and yellow.

Unfortunately, after almost 2,000 years in the ground, a lot of this decoration will have decayed ... sometimes to the extent that it is not possible to appreciate or determine the design. On the few better-preserved examples that have come from the Thames, traces of pewter mouldings are visible that would not have survived had the brooch come from a farmland site.

Plate brooches have the advantage over bow brooches in that when in use the pin and catchplate are concealed from view. As a result of the greater protection provided to the pin it will often survive ... unlike the situation with bow brooches where the pin is more exposed. However, whether the pin is present or not, does not greatly affect the commercial value of such a brooch.

Pic M54 shows a disc brooch of umbonate (domed) type. The dome is enamelled in alternating red and blue triangular cells to form a sunburst pattern. There is a conical boss in the centre. The brooch has a beaded outer border with a notched rim. The surface was originally tinned. This example would date from the 2nd century AD.

The star or sun design may have had significance to followers of the Mithraic Cult, and this would explain the popularity of the design as decoration on brooches of the period.

The imported disc brooch shown in **Pic M55** probably came from Gaul and it is plain apart from a raised hollow centre boss with a small knob on top. Around this is a flat plate with a raised edge. The pin is hinged. This example would date late 1st to early 2nd century AD. The brooch has the appearance of a miniature shield, and a number of brooch designs seem to imitate shield blazons.

A larger variant of this form of disc brooch, has the central boss truncated and flattened at the top, and there are knobs around the perimeter of the brooch. I was able to make a side-by-side comparison of two of these brooches. One was found in Shropshire and had a green patina; the other was from Tunisia and had a dull brown surface. Apart from the colour differences the two brooches were identical and could have come from the same mould. This is an indication of the wide dispersion that

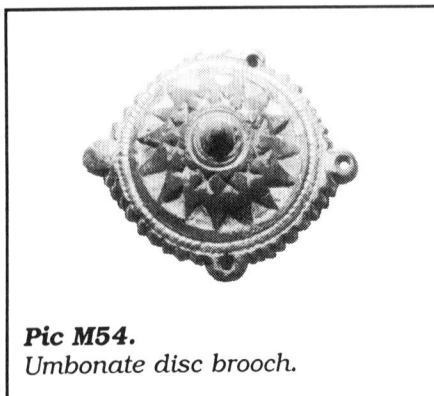

Pic M54.
Umbonate disc brooch.

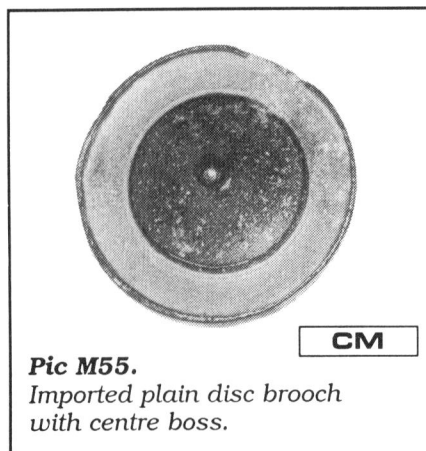

CM

Pic M55.
Imported plain disc brooch with centre boss.

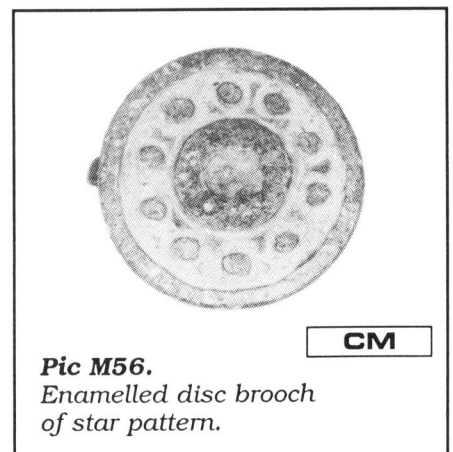

CM

Pic M56.
Enamelled disc brooch of star pattern.

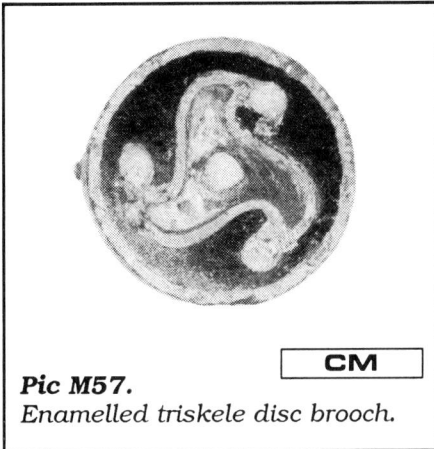

Pic M57.
Enamelled triskele disc brooch.

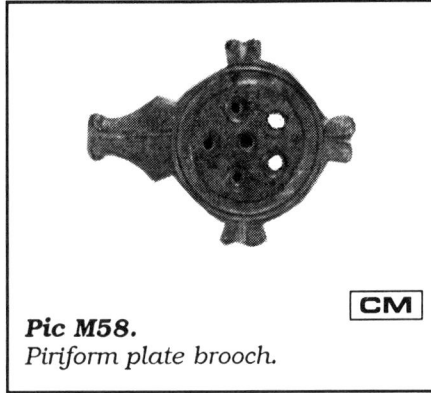

Pic M58.
Piriform plate brooch.

Pic M59.
Lobed plate brooch.

can occur with certain Roman artefacts.

The flat enamelled disc brooch shown in **Pic M56** has a ring of ten dots around a central circle. Traces of enamel remain. This is a native British type dating to the 2nd century AD.

Another disc brooch, shown in **Pic M57**, carries a form of decoration with a strong Celtic influence - that of the triskele, a symbol still being used by the Isle of Man. The design is that of three arms, three being a sacred number to the native Celts.

The brooch has a central disc, from which radiate red enamel arms, each with a terminal disc. The field contains a dark blue or black enamelling, and this brooch is again 2nd century in date.

Pic M58 shows an example of an early plate brooch. It is piriform in shape, having a disc as the upper part with three bilobed knobs; the tapering foot is notched and ends in a similar way. The disc has six perforations which would have held inserts (probably bone). The surface is heavily tinned and the hinged pin on this example is intact. In date, the brooch would come from the mid-1st century AD.

Another plate brooch of the same period is shown in **Pic M59**. It is square-shaped with four circular lobes, each containing a bone disc

rivetted in place. There is a small boss in the centre, which has a dotted punch mark decoration around it. The corners are marked with straight lines representing leaves. This brooch is a Gaulish type.

The lunular plate brooch is another style brought to Britain by the Claudian invaders. At first its design was that of a simple crescent shape, but in the 2nd century in Britain the brooch was produced with Celticised patterns and a highly enamelled surface (see **Pic M60**).

This example is slightly bowed and has triangular cells around the edge and rectangular cells in the centre strip. Traces of yellow enamel are present in the centre, and some red and blue enamel remains on the outside. Pellets included at each side of the centre, would almost seem to have been intended to represent eyes.

A very unusual lunular type brooch is shown in **Pic M61**. This has a perforated central design, while the crescent is ornamented with triangular enamelled cells, red on the outer circle and blue on the inner. The foot is of baluster form with two circular lugs containing a blue enamel centre and an outer ring of red enamel resembling two eyes. The effect is to create a staring face of a strange creature. The brooch would date 2nd century AD.

The plate brooch shown in **Pic M62** is another type with the appear-

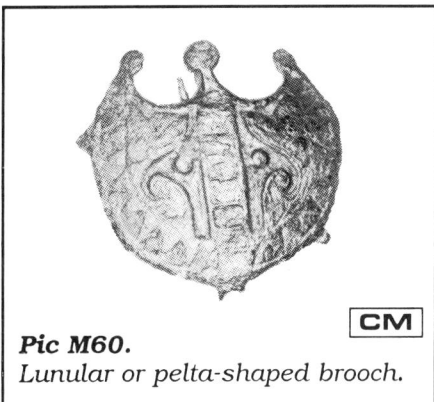

Pic M60.
Lunular or pelta-shaped brooch.

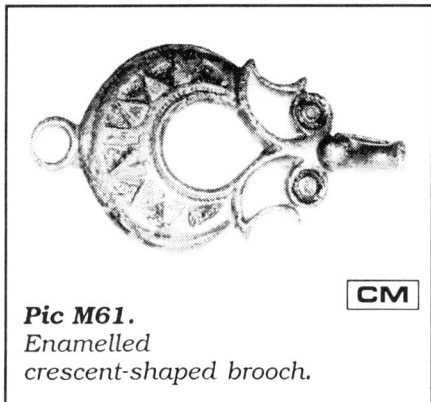

Pic M61.
Enamelled crescent-shaped brooch.

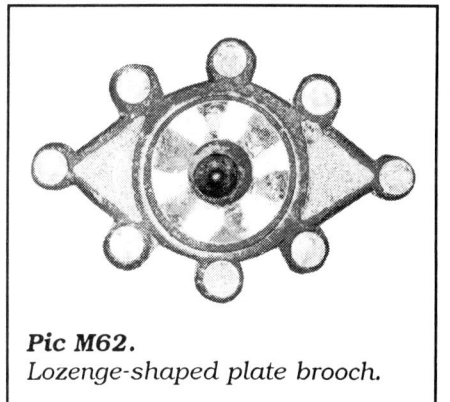

Pic M62.
Lozenge-shaped plate brooch.

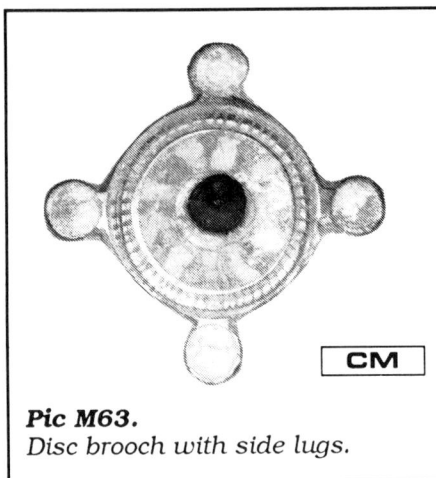

Pic M63.
Disc brooch with side lugs.

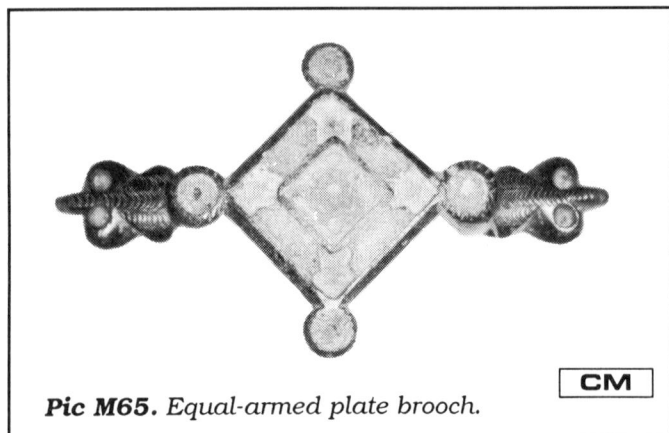

Pic M64. *Equal-armed plate brooch.*

ance of an eye. The central disc has upper and lower triangular sections attached. There are eight circular lobes around the perimeter of the brooch, of alternating orange and blue enamel. The central disc has blue and while individual enamel strips with a conical boss in the middle. The outstanding colours of the enamel, which have survived intact, reveal the beauty of Roman brooches.

A simpler example can be seen in **Pic M63**. This has a similar rivetted central conical boss, from which radiate individual strips of enamel, this time in red and yellow. Four circular lobes are set around the perimeter. These two brooches bear so many similarities that it is possible they came from the same workshop.

Plate brooches developed into a multitude of shapes and styles in the 2nd century. This resulted both from the dictates of fashion, and also from the increasing prosperity of the Roman Empire at the time. **Pic M64** shows a brooch in which the centre disc forms a stepped union between the two smaller tri-lobed lozenge-shaped plates which have the hinge and catch plate mechanism on their underside. The brooch must be of continental origin, and may even have come from the Rhineland. The centre

and outer rings are turquoise in colour while the inner ring has been enamelled in alternate red and blue strips. All of the eight lugs are enamelled orange.

A variation of this is the brooch in **Pic M65** which has a central lozenge with lugs at each corner as the stepped union between two zoomorphic terminals. The central panel is in orange enamel with five blue enamel dots.

Where enamel decay has taken place a loss of the original colour can occur and the green and red traces that survive are not always a reliable indication of the colours used in the original manufacture of a brooch. As a guide, however, blue and red would appear to have been the most common combination of colours used on Romano-British brooches.

Another unusual example of a plate brooch is shown in **Pic M66**. This consists of three discs which are hollowed out to receive circles of bone, two of which remain intact. The brooch has a hinged pin and would date from the 2nd century.

Pic M67 shows a piriform plate brooch with a blue enamel centre. It

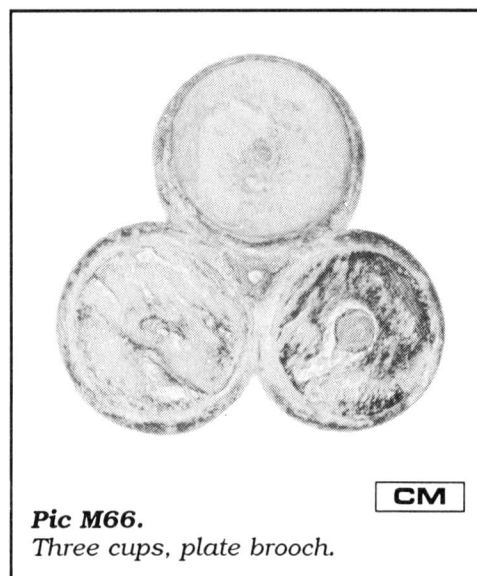

Pic M65. *Equal-armed plate brooch.*

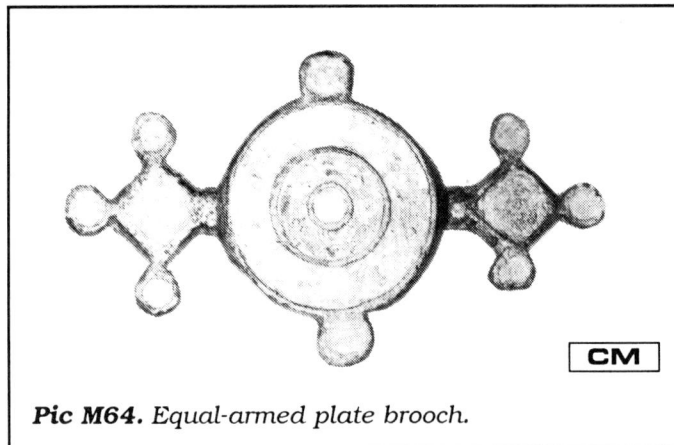

Pic M66.
Three cups, plate brooch.

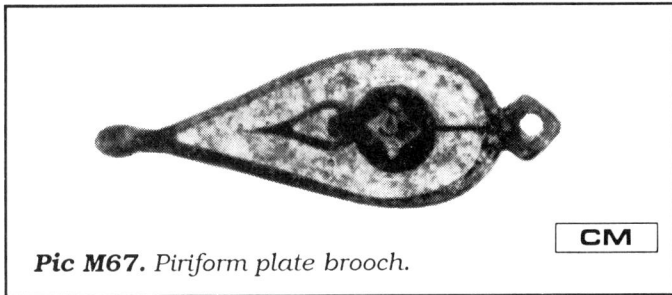

Pic M67. *Piriform plate brooch.*

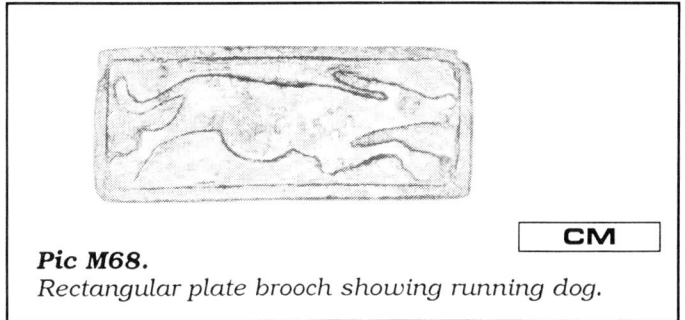

Pic M68.
Rectangular plate brooch showing running dog.

has a chain loop at the top and a small globular foot at the bottom. In the middle there is a plain disc with a four-pointed star inside; below is a piriform ornamentation. The brooch has a hinged pin.

An interesting native brooch from the 2nd century is shown in **Pic M68**. This is of flat rectangular form with a sprung pin. Several different designs are known including fish, sea serpent, hare, and - in this case - a dog. The animal is shown running to the right with an extended mouth and upturned tail.

Curiously, the stomach is shown swollen which could either indicate an abundance of food and good hunting or - more unlikely - that the dog is pregnant. No traces of enamel survive and, although the perimeter usually has an applied silver border, no trace of the metal remains on this example.

is shown shorter on the hare brooches; the hare also has a smaller, downward-sloping tail. The hare was a very popular animal to be shown on Romano-British brooches. This example has bronze dots along its body within the single enamel cell. The eye is again enamelled.

Stylised animal forms such as the above are termed "zoomorphic" and are the most collectable design of all Roman brooches. Most of these brooches are flat, but three-dimensional examples are known.

The horse and rider plate brooch shown in **Pic M71** is a well-known zoomorphic. Commonly found in Norfolk, Suffolk, and Cambridgeshire, these brooches date mainly from the 2nd or 3rd centuries. The

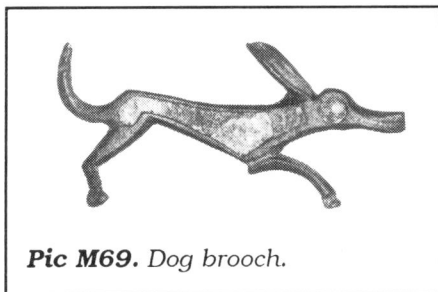

Pic M69. *Dog brooch.*

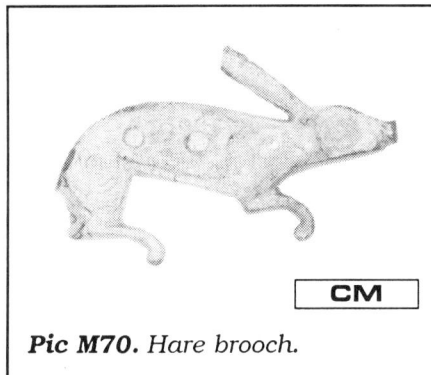

Pic M70. *Hare brooch.*

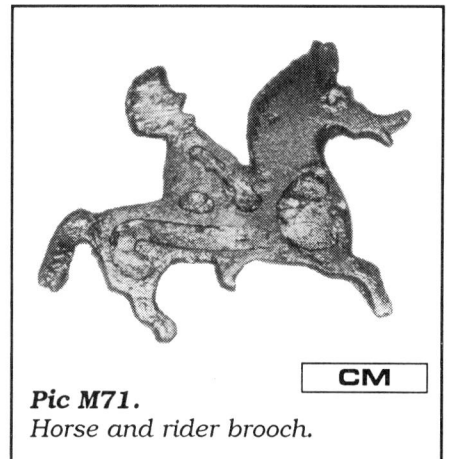

Pic M71.
Horse and rider brooch.

Pic M69 represents an excellent example of a running dog, again with extended mouth and upturned tail. The body has been provided with a long single cell for enamel, and some of the blue colouring remains. The eye is also enamelled. This brooch shows Celtic influence in its form.

In ancient Britain the dog was regarded as a symbol of the Celtic healing divinity Nodons, and had cult associations with both healing and death.

The hare (see **Pic M70**) is also represented on brooches and can be confused in appearance with the dog. Both tend to be shown running and are portrayed with long ears. The main difference is in the snout, which

galloping horse has a well-defined head, with a mane represented by notches. The rider has his head held back and has a pointed nose and notched hair. There are four cells of blue and red enamel. Examples vary in size and detail. Sometimes the rider is shown holding a baton or sword, and sometimes the horse's and rider's heads can be moulded in the round.

The horseman was of high status in Romano-Celtic life, and associated with warrior gods who were depicted on horseback. Many of the horse and rider brooches have been found on temple sites (rather than domestic ones), by archaeologists, indicating a cult significance. Epona,

Pic M72. Horse brooch.

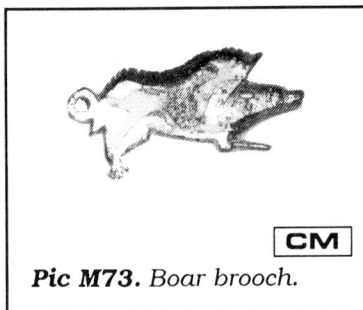

Pic M73. Boar brooch.

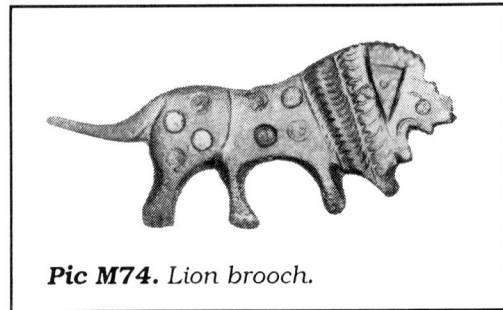

Pic M74. Lion brooch.

the horse goddess, was worshipped in Britain. She was linked with healing springs, and was depicted astride a horse (sometimes with a dog and raven beside her).

The horse shown in **Pic M72** (also one of the illustrations on the front cover of this book) is scarcer as a brooch than the horse and rider. The horse was admired for its beauty and speed, and in Celtic religion was linked with deities of the sun and warfare. The example illustrated has finely detailed moulding. There are five rectangular enamel cells at the front of its body, with a long green cell along its back. A red strip runs along its belly. Remains of silver inlay are visible around the enamel cells. This brooch has developed a glossy hard green patina that is much admired by collectors.

The boar brooch shown in **Pic M73** has a heavily silvered surface with a single green enamel cell in the outline of a stag. The boar represented war and hunting, and is shown with its spiny crest erect, indicating the animal to be attacking. The fearless nature of the boar was greatly admired by the Romans.

Pic M74 is a representation of a lion walking to the right. There are eight enamelled circular cells on its body, within which traces of blue and orange are visible. It has a mane represented by two ridges with incised wavy lines. This example is unusual as all four paws are shown

The stag shown in **Pic M75** represents a rare example of a zoomorphic brooch. The animal has lost its legs which would have been originally attached to a ground line linking them together. There are five circular cells of turquoise enamel set within a single red enamel cell. The decoration includes incised marks around the head.

Pic M76 shows an even rarer brooch which is a representation of Eros astride a panther. The panther's head is moulded in the round, and the animal is shown wearing a torc or collar around its neck. There are circular cells for enamel on its body. The rider is rivetted in place through the body of the panther. He has incised marks on his body but the details of his head have worn away. This brooch is possibly of Gaulish origin, and would date 2nd-3rd century AD.

The zoomorphic plate brooch shown in **Pic M77** represents a perched bird, possibly an eagle, crow or raven. The arched neck suggests a pecking bird, and I believe this to indicate a raven.

Ravens were shown with the Celtic sky god, and also with Epona. The example illustrated has three cells for enamel along its body.

Pic M78 is a three-dimensional, hollow-bodied zoomorphic brooch. It is a representation of a sitting hen or cockerel with an enamelled body of orange, and blue cells forming the closed wings of the bird. The tail is upright and curved. The bird has a

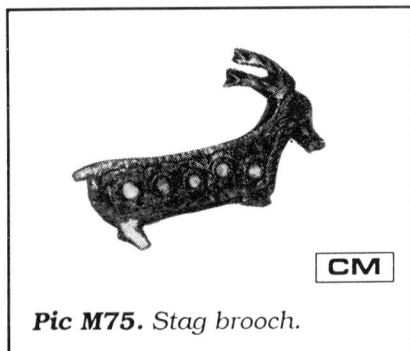

Pic M75. Stag brooch.

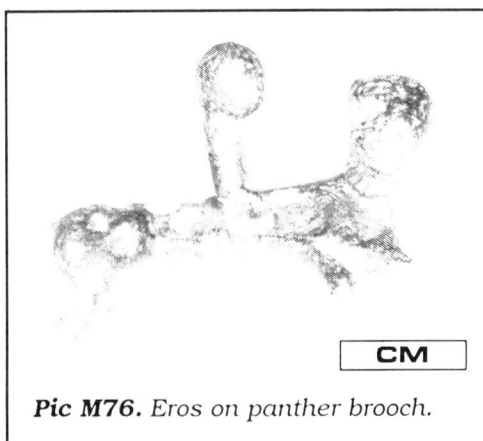

Pic M76. Eros on panther brooch.

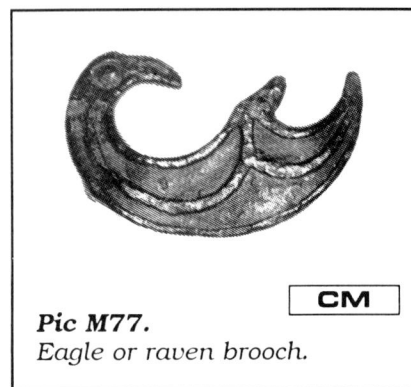

Pic M77.
Eagle or raven brooch.

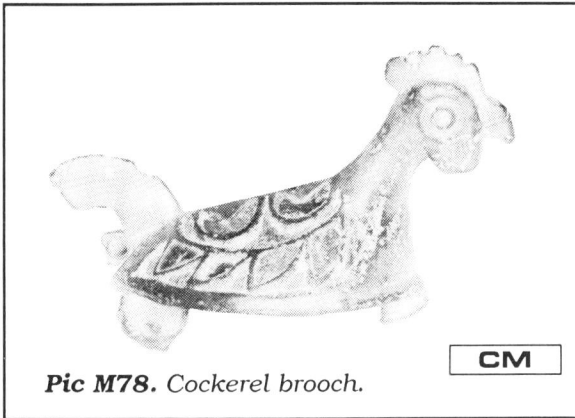
Pic M78. Cockerel brooch.

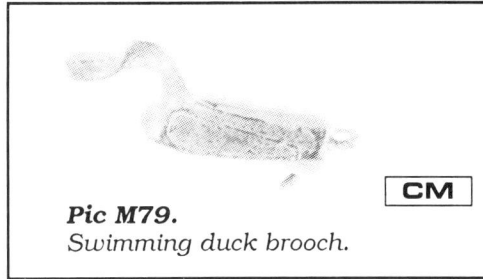
Pic M79.
Swimming duck brooch.

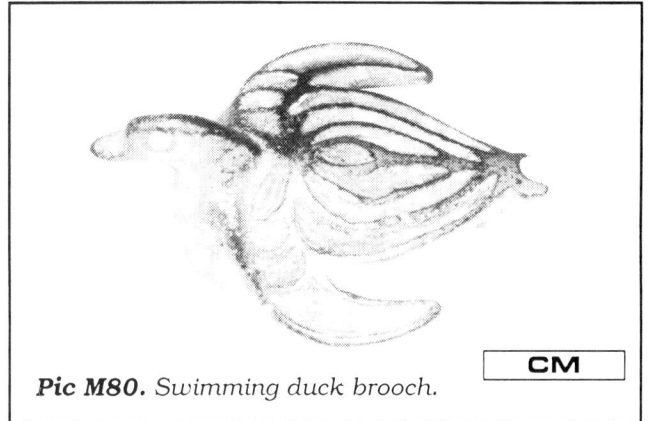
Pic M80. Swimming duck brooch.

wavy comb on its head, a large eye, and an orange enamel cell below representing its wattle. Brooches of this type are generally found in East Anglia.

Birds and animals featured heavily in Celtic mythology and cults, and the wearing of a zoomorphic brooch could have been an expression of this (in the same way that pilgrims wore badges in medieval times to show their faith and as a souvenir of their travels).

Representations of water birds also feature in Romano-British brooch design. **Pic M79** shows a swimming duck, with a slightly curved back and narrow body. The bird is shown with a raised head and extended bill. There are four elongated panels of enamel on the body of the duck, green being the outer colour. The brooch has a chain loop at the rear and a sprung pin.

Pic M80 shows a rarer variation of the above brooch the design being of a swimming duck with wings slightly open as if it is about to take off. This example has a wide, curved, and hollowed-out body. It has a shorter and thicker neck, and the beak is smaller than that of the first type. There are numerous cells on the body which would originally have contained enamel, but sadly none of this survives. The brooch has a chain loop and hinged pin.

Duck brooches may be associated with a Celtic water cult con-

cerned with healing. Lakes and rivers often received votive offerings from the Ancient Britons.

Another rare zoomorphic brooch, shown in **Pic M81** is the frog. Here the tapering body has two enamelled segments with four webbed feet attached. The head has lines incised across it, and there are two recesses for the eyes. The brooch has a chain loop, and was probably made in Gaul.

Of all the animal brooches, the most inspiring group is that of the sea monsters. These brooches may have been associated with mystery cults where some form of initiation was required to achieve a higher divinity.

The first of these (**Pic M82**) is the sea serpent which has an eel-like body in a curved S-shape, ending in a fish-like tail. It has a serrated dorsal fin near the head, and the head itself has a horn on top. Underneath the body is a smooth anal fin. The body is enamelled in blue and green segments, and about half the enamelling has survived. A similar exam-

Pic M81. Frog brooch.

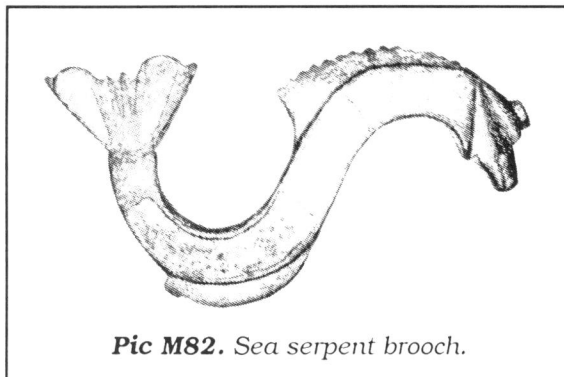
Pic M82. Sea serpent brooch.

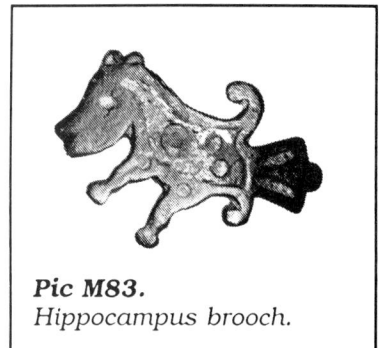
Pic M83.
Hippocampus brooch.

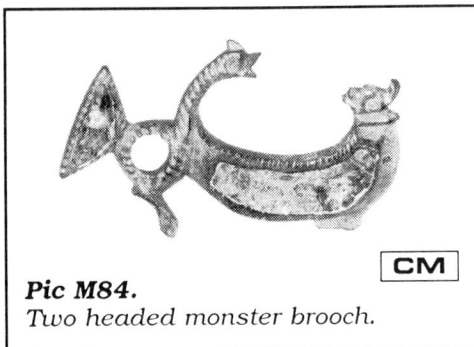

Pic M84.
Two headed monster brooch.

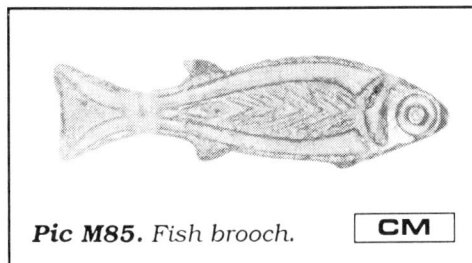

Pic M85. *Fish brooch.*

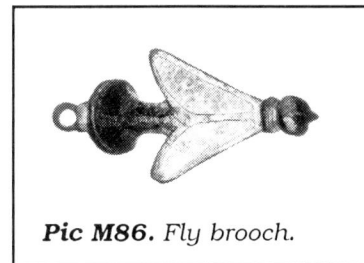

Pic M86. *Fly brooch.*

ple excavated in London was dated to the first half of the 2nd century AD and was thought to be an import from Gaul. This example was found in Gloucester.

The second type of sea monster is the hippocampus, shown in **Pic M83**. This is a fabulous animal comprising the forepart of a horse and the rear of a fish. The body of the horse is enamelled in blue, with a central pellet in red. The horse's head is quite crude having small ears and a single eye coloured red. The horse part of the brooch has two hoofed front legs. The fish tail is coloured blue in the centre with red in each outer panel. There are curved lobes on each side of the tail. The brooch dates from the 2nd century and is almost certainly an import from Gaul, although it was found in South Yorshire.

The hippocampus represents the marine car of Neptune and the Tritons.

An extremely rare representation of a two-headed sea monster is shown in **Pic M84**. The curled up tail ends with a head looking forwards while at the front of the body, another head is looking back. The body of the monster has a large cell with traces of blue enamel, while the tail - which is of triangular shape - shows orange enamel. This brooch is of a continental type.

The water creature shown in **Pic M85** is a fish (probably a salmon). The design has a series of chevrons in the centre. The gills are recessed for enamel and there is a band running along the length of each side. The salmon was regarded as a symbol of wisdom and knowledge. This brooch is a Romano-British type.

The fly brooch shown in **Pic M86** is an interesting derivative of a trum-

pet brooch. The head of the brooch still retains its trumpet form, but the flat bow has developed into a fly with two red enamelled wings, and a moulded insects head at the bottom. The brooch would date late 2nd century AD.

Although I have included a large number of zoomorphic brooches within this chapter, there are several other designs and varieties not shown including the eagle chasing a hare, peacock, owl (very rare), rabbit, three headed dog (extremely rare), and a wasp.

Another type of plate brooch is the skeumorphic which includes designs such as the axe, dagger and sandal sole. The relatively common sandal brooch shown in **Pic M87** has three circular discs, each divided by a cross-shaped leaf pattern, and containing orange enamel. The enamel of these brooches usually exhibits different coloured chips which were intended to represent the iron hobnails. The toe of the sandal is pointed, and there is a chain loop (broken on this example) at the heel. This brooch would date 2nd-3rd century AD.

Pic M88 shows a very rare dagger brooch which has a lozenge-shaped blade with divided enamelled cells of blue with white dots. The handle has a large flat pommel decorated with circles.

Some of the most visually-stunning disc brooches have a type of enamel known as "millefiori". The brooch shown in **Pic M89** is a good example of this; it has an intricate floral pattern of red (which has faded), blue, and white colours set into the surface.

Millefiori enamel was produced in Britain during the mid-2nd century. The process involved arranging glass rods to form a pattern, fusing them

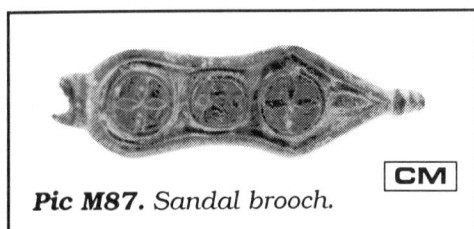

Pic M87. *Sandal brooch.*

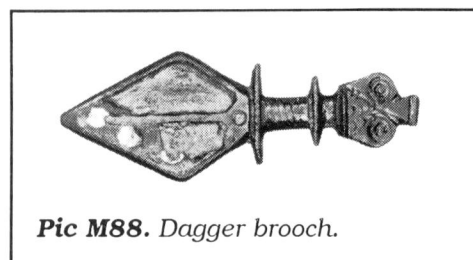

Pic M88. *Dagger brooch.*

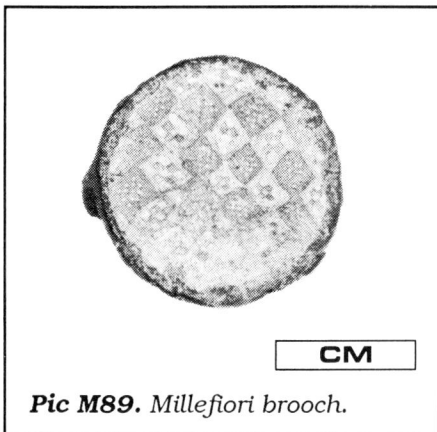

Pic M89. Millefiori brooch.

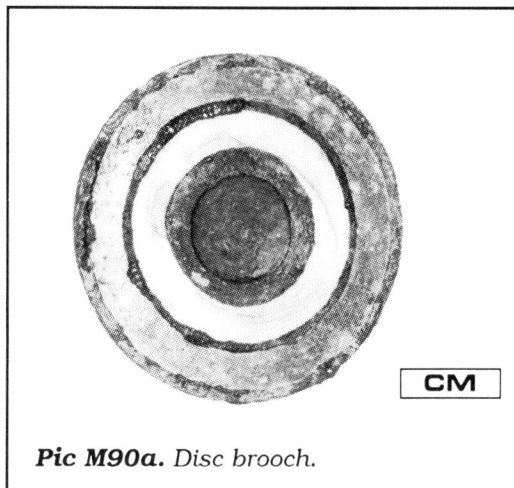

Pic M90a. Disc brooch.

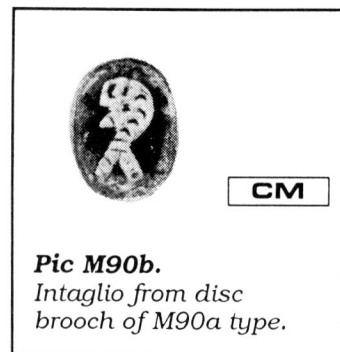

Pic M90b.
Intaglio from disc
brooch of M90a type.

together, and then drawing them out into a single long rod which retained the pattern intact. Slices were then cut from one end of the rod and fused onto the metal of the object to be decorated.

If the original colour is retained and the enamel intact, then the value of such brooches can run into four figures.

During the 3rd century, the Roman Empire experienced a recession accompanied by severe inflation. There was also an increase in civil wars and conflicts which resulted in large hoards of coins being buried. The falling value of money at the time can be seen in the debasement of the silver antoninianus which continued its downward trend until becoming only silver-washed bronze. The debasement is most evident during the reigns of Gallienus (253-268 AD) and Postumus (259-268 AD).

The quality and quantity of excavated brooches from this period are reduced as a result. In addition, an uprising in northern Britain and Wales in 196 AD destroyed many local workshops and created a greater dependence on Roman-made products.

Pic M90a shows a disc brooch. According to the Richborough Archaeological Report published in 1948, a similar example to this was found in a 3rd century deposit.

It is circular in shape and has roundels of enamel: blue on the outer circle, then white, and red in the centre. The dividing strips have remains of silver beading on their surface.

The centre recesses of such brooches can often be mounted with a bronze intaglio (see **Pic M90b**). This carries a curious, Celtic-style bird's head design. It is quite usual for the two parts of such brooches to become separated in the ground.

Fibula design in the 3rd century is marked by the introduction of the "crossbow" brooch. This is a bow type which has developed a terminal knob on the head of the brooch and also on each end of the wings. It has a highly-arched bow and a long catchplate recessed for securing the pin.

As **Pic M91** shows, the crossbow brooch continued to develop in the 4th century, becoming larger and heavier. The knobs on these later brooches became onion-shaped and the catchplate and bow are often gilded.

Towards the end of the 4th century, the crossbow brooch evolved to a hollow construction. This allowed such brooches to retain their large size without excessive weight - important when securing the more delicate fabrics.

Some crossbow brooches were

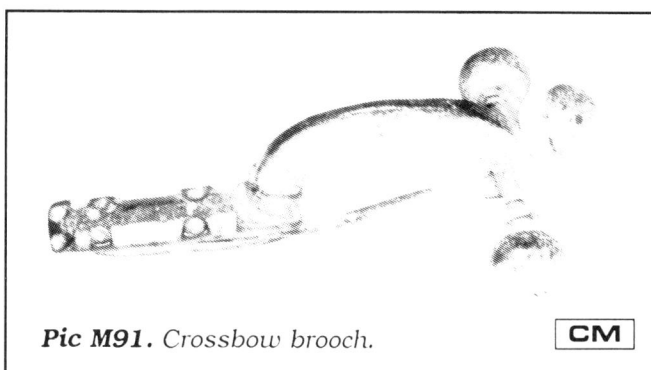

Pic M91. Crossbow brooch.

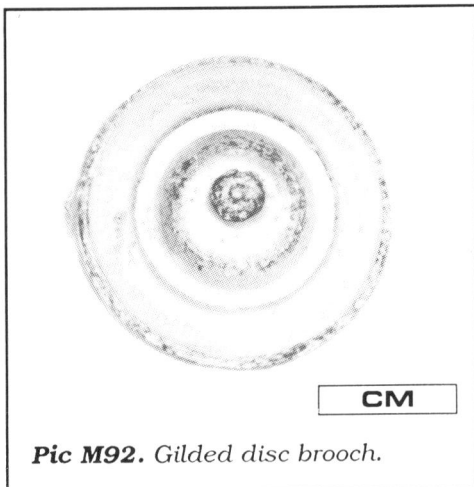

Pic M92. Gilded disc brooch.

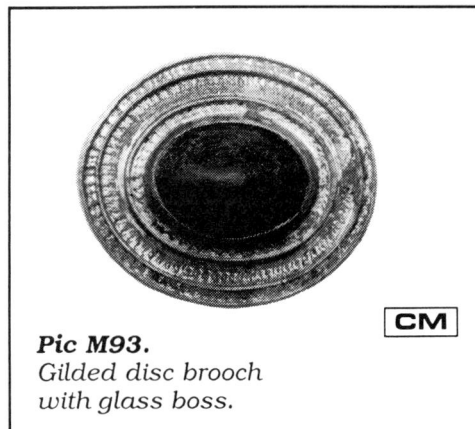

Pic M93.
Gilded disc brooch
with glass boss.

formed entirely of silver, or even made in hollow gold. The chances of finding an example of the latter, though, are fairly remote. Only wealthy people would have worn these, and some are recorded as being gifts bestowed by the emperor.

The crossbow brooch in its various forms has become a very common find. It was popular all over the Roman world and complete examples in bronze - with no gilding present - can sell for as little as £25.

In the latter part of the 3rd and through the 4th century, the disc brooch was usually produced with a gilded surface as with the example shown in **Pic M92**. In the centre is a rivetted boss which usually has four to six radial spokes around it (on this example they are absent). There is a raised circular rib enclosing the central dome. The perimeter of the brooch has punch marks and a raised edge. The underside of the brooch is silvered which is a characteristic feature of the period. The pin is sprung.

Pic M93 shows an oval gilded disc brooch with a conical boss of black coloured glass set in the centre and held in by a raised flange. The flat bronze surface is decorated with three rings of raised ribs which have rows of indented cross-shaped punch marks between them. Again, the underside of the brooch is silvered and it has a sprung pin. These brooches generally survive well in the ground due to their heavy casting, but often come to light with the glass boss chipped or cracked. A few examples have flat moulded glass intaglios set in the centre similar to those found in finger rings. These brooches are all regarded as British types.

It was during the reign of Honorius, in 410 AD, that the last remnants of the Roman legions were withdrawn from Britain and the occupation ended. After this time the economic system crumbled, and with it Roman civilisation. In the first half of the 5th century there was a fairly rapid degeneration from good quality, masonry-built dwellings, to primitive structures of wattle and daub. The citizens of towns, and villa owners, unable to defend their dwellings, abandoned them.

Saxon invaders from Germany landed and advanced from the East Coast and by the middle of the 5th century had taken over parts of East-

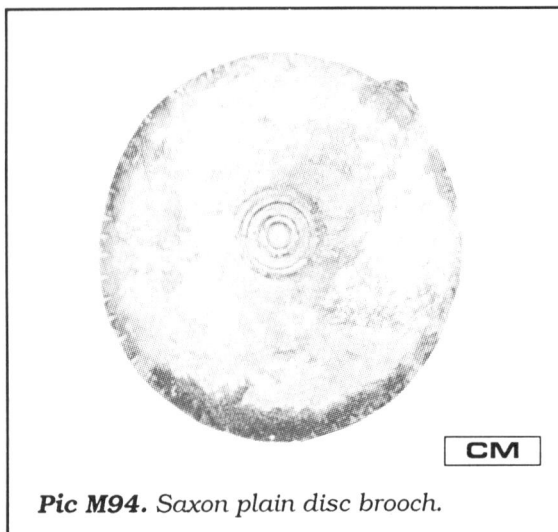

Pic M94. Saxon plain disc brooch.

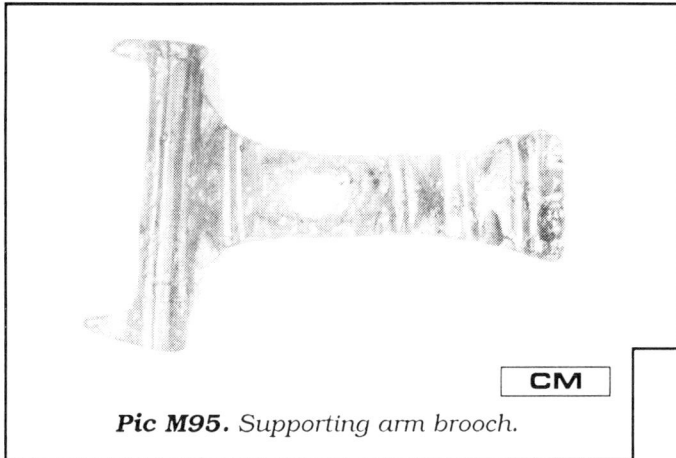

Pic M95. *Supporting arm brooch.*

CM

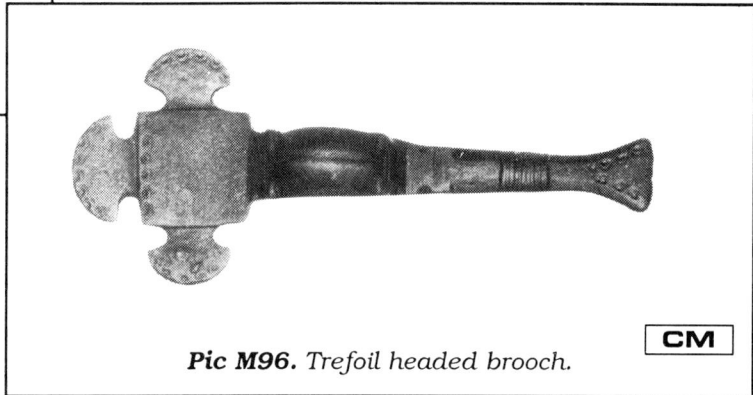

CM

Pic M96. *Trefoil headed brooch.*

ern and Southern Britain. The country reverted to a tribal warrior culture similar to that which existed during the Celtic period before the Roman conquest.

The Saxons brought with them their own language and pagan beliefs, which - by the late 6th century - had taken over from Christianity in many parts of Britain. The brooches of the period reflect these changes.

Pic M94 shows a flat disc brooch which is heavily silvered and has a central design of dot and circles. The edge of the brooch has small notches cut into it. The spring and pin were made of iron rather than bronze, which is an important distinguishing feature between Roman and Saxon brooches. On Saxon brooches, usually all that remains of the pin is a brown rust stain around the hinge on the underside of the brooch. The example shown dates to the late 5th century.

The supporting arm brooch (see **Pic M95**) is a type found in Anglo-Saxon graves. It is Germanic in origin and dates to the 5th century. The brooch has an arched bow, with slightly expanded foot. The spring

and axis bar are held in place by the projecting sides at the head of the brooch. There is lateral grooving on the foot and head. The pin of these brooches can be either bronze or iron, which suggests that a transition period occurred during the mid-5th century.

The crossbow brooch continued to be worn, but the terminal knobs became flattened, the catchplate extended, and a small arched bow introduced in the centre. They eventually developed into the Anglo-Saxon cruciform long brooch.

Pic M96 shows an example of a trefoil headed small long brooch, a diminutive relative of the cruciform. It has a trefoil head with an extended triangular foot. There are crescent-shaped punch marks around the head and foot, which also has additional ribbing. This brooch is 6th century in date.

The equal-armed brooch shown in **Pic M97** comes from East Anglia and is probably of local manufacture, copying continental types. It has two rectangular end plates with lateral grooves and notches. It dates late 5th to 6th century.

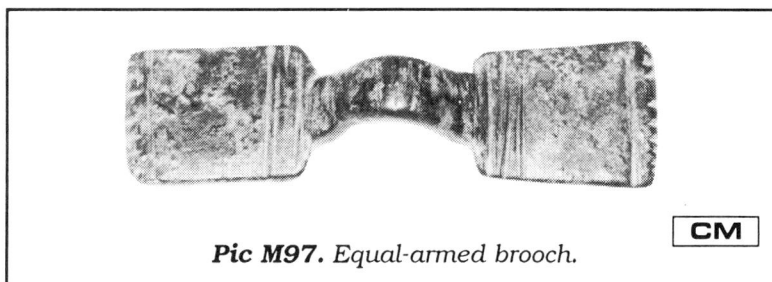

CM

Pic M97. *Equal-armed brooch.*

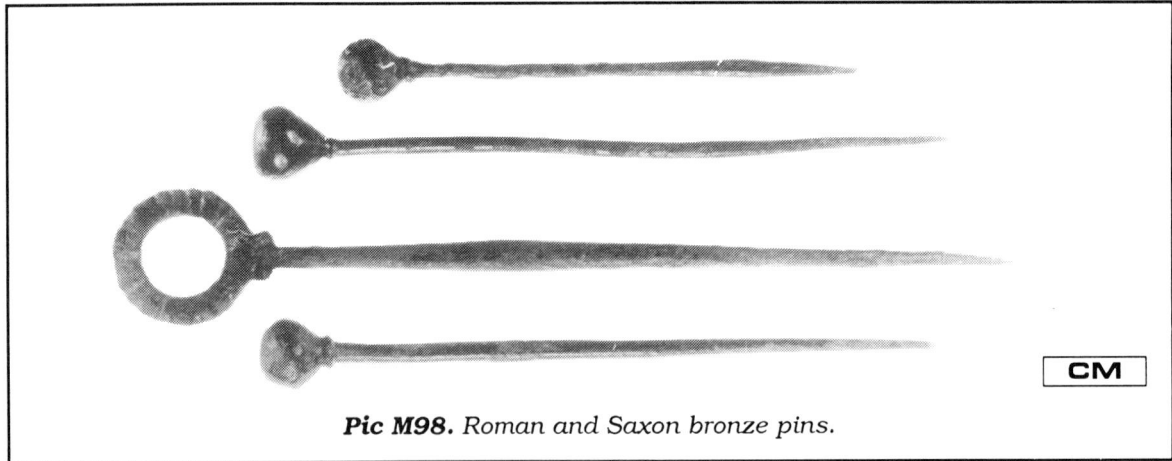

Pic M98. *Roman and Saxon bronze pins.*

A great variety of dress and hair pins were in use during the Roman and Saxon periods (see **Pic M98**). These were made from bone, iron, bronze, silver, and even gold. Roman pins in bronze are usually solid cast with decorated heads. Early Roman pins tend to bulge in the middle of the stem as can be seen in the example illustrated with the open ring head. Saxon pins are more delicate often having faceted heads with a circular dot decoration. The bulge in the stem seen in Saxon pins usually occurs at a lower point as can be seen in **Pic M98**, top example.

Price Guide

		Fine	Very Fine			Fine	Very Fine
M54:	umbonate disc brooch	£30	£90	M74:	lion brooch	£140	£350
M55:	plain disc with centre boss	£20	£38	M75:	stag brooch	£150	£400
M56:	disc with star pattern	£24	£65	M76:	Eros on panther brooch	£200	£600
M57:	triskele disc brooch	£32	£90	M77:	eagle or raven brooch	£70	£200
M58:	piriform plate brooch	£26	£55	M78:	cockerel brooch	£110	£280
M59:	lobed plate brooch	£70	£180	M79:	swimming duck brooch	£55	£160
M60:	lunular or pelta-shaped brooch	£50	£160	M80:	swimming duck brooch	£65	£185
M61:	crescent shaped brooch	£60	£170	M81:	frog brooch	£130	£325
M62:	lozenge-shaped plate brooch	£40	£120	M82:	sea serpent brooch	£140	£350
M63:	disc brooch with side lugs	£30	£75	M83:	Hippocampus	£150	£375
M64:	equal-armed plate brooch	£45	£150	M84:	two-headed monster brooch	£180	£550
M65:	equal-armed plate brooch	£50	£160	M85:	fish brooch	£110	£260
M66:	three cups plate brooch	£30	£80	M86:	fly brooch	£55	£160
M67:	piriform plate brooch	£25	£65	M87:	sandal brooch	£45	£150
M68:	rectangular plate brooch with running dog	£75	£220	M88:	dagger brooch	£110	£260
				M89:	millefiori brooch	£60	£250
M69:	dog brooch	£120	£300	M90:	disc brooch with intaglio	£25	£70
M70:	hare brooch	£70	£200	M91:	crossbow brooch	£25	£55
M71:	horse and rider brooch	£90	£240	M92:	gilt disc brooch	£28	£75
				M93:	gilt disc brooch with glass boss	£40	£120
M72:	horse brooch	£110	£275	M94:	Saxon plain disc brooch	£25	£60
M73:	boar brooch	£85	£230	M95:	supporting arm brooch	£25	£65
				M96:	trefoil-headed brooch	£70	£150
				M97:	equal-armed brooch	£35	£80
				M98:	bronze pin	£15	£30

Chapter IV

Buckles & Military Equipment

The buckle first came to Britain with the Roman Invasion of the 1st century AD. These early buckles were used by the military, principally for securing horse harness and body armour.

The native Celts at this time used bronze toggles as strap fasteners (see **Pic M99**). These are referred to as "button and loop" fasteners and have been dated to the 1st and early 2nd century AD. The example illustrated has a square head with a central circular boss. Projecting from the back is an open triangular-shaped shank which would have been attached to a strap. The head of the fastener would have passed through an eyelet at the other end of the strap.

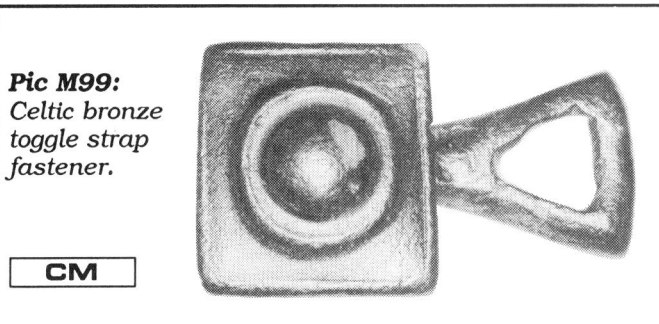

Pic M99:
Celtic bronze toggle strap fastener.

CM

There are several different types, determined by the shape of the head. The most common is the "boss and petal" which has a domed boss set within a petal-shaped head. Other varieties include the double boss and circular headed; enamelling is known on these in red or yellow.

Roman buckles are not common finds in Britain. Many of the plain buckles are very difficult to distinguish from medieval types and for this reason can only be accurately attributed when found in datable deposits.

Pic M100 shows a crescent-shaped bronze buckle which has

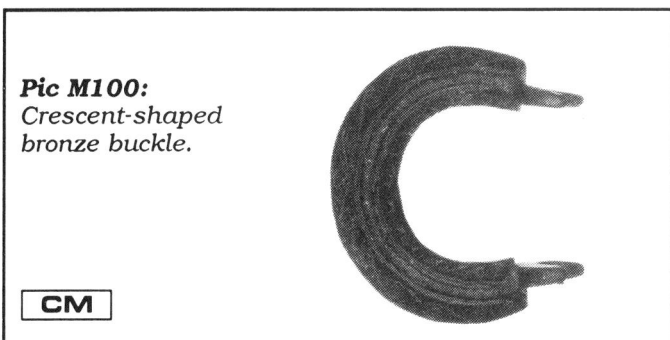

Pic M100:
Crescent-shaped bronze buckle.

CM

looped ends for a separate hinge bar to pass through and connect the pin and plate to the buckle. It has an incised design of scroll work around the outside, with punched dots on the inside.

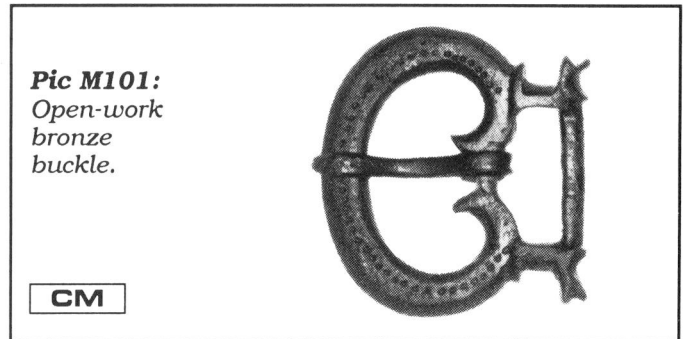

Pic M101:
Open-work bronze buckle.

CM

Pic M101 is an open-work bronze buckle with a crescentic loop and involuted (turned in) terminals. It has an integral hinge bar for the plate, which is separate from the hinge bar for the pin.

An example of a late Roman quoit brooch-style buckle is shown in **Pic M102**. This is a typical form of belt equipment; and the design is of two dolphins facing each other. The connecting plate is open-work with a punched ring and dot design. The central pin is missing.

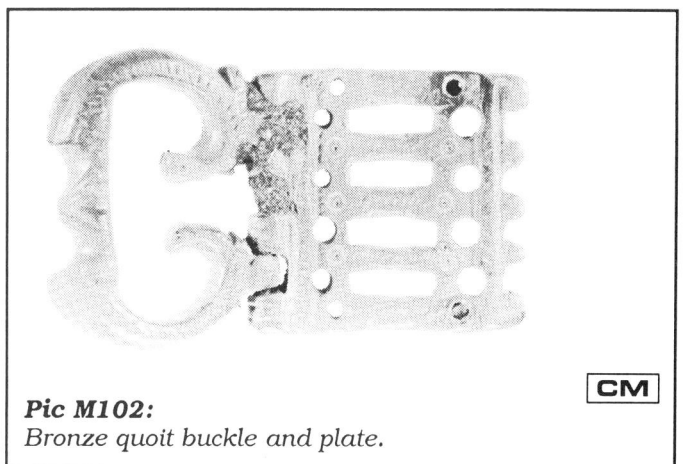

Pic M102:
Bronze quoit buckle and plate.

CM

An unusual buckle is shown in **Pic M103** and this may be a continental type. Both buckle and plate are integrally cast. The plate has a central rectangular panel with an interlaced design. Bordering this is a triangular pattern. The interlaced design occurs on Republican Period Roman equipment, and again, more commonly, in the Saxon era.

Pic M103:
Integrally cast buckle and plate, possibly continental.

CM

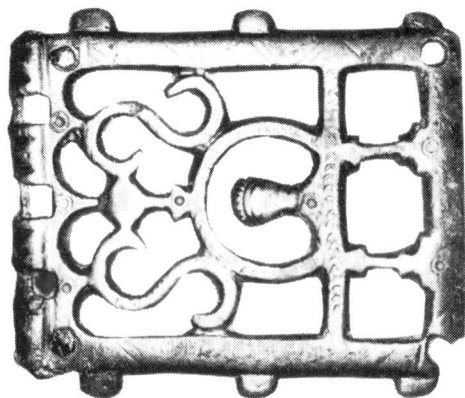

Pic M104:
D-shaped buckle with outward facing horses' heads.

CM

The D-shaped buckle shown in **Pic M104** is a development of the two dolphins design, having two outwardly-facing horses' heads with punched dot eyes and manes marked by diagonal hatching. This buckle dates from the late 4th or early 5th century, and some examples have been found in early Anglo-Saxon graves. The buckle plate may have been finely engraved with a peacock similar to the example found in Warwickshire in 1972.

continental origin, and similar in style to Byzantine examples of the 6th and 7th centuries. It was cast in one piece and carries ring and dot decoration. The pin is quite heavy and extends around the top of the buckle rather like a claw. This feature is prevalent on many Byzantine and Frankish buckles.

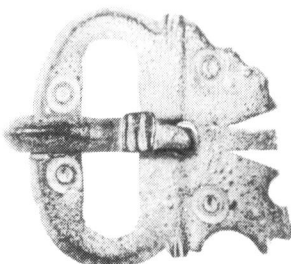

Pic M105: *Open-work buckle plate.*

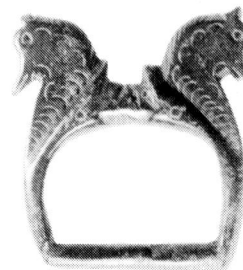

Pic M107:
Tinned bronze Saxon buckle.

CM

A Saxon buckle dating from the 6th or 7th century is shown in **Pic M107**. Note the rounded rectangular form which is characteristic of this period. The bronze has been tinned to give a silver-like finish. There are also a number of small triangular punch marks, containing three dots each, on the plate. This has been folded over the hinge bar and rivetted together.

The open-work buckle plate shown in **Pic M105** may date from the 3rd-4th century. In the centre is a facing head. The details are fairly worn, but the surface was originally decorated with incised lines and crescentic punches.

A buckle from the Saxon era (**Pic M106**), found in East Anglia is of

Pic M108:
Dolphin stud, possibly belt decoration.

CM

Leather belt decorations usually take the form of discs with a single rivet provided at the back for attachment. **Pic M108** is a representation of a dolphin in bronze. Being decorated on one side and having rivets at each end, this may have formed part of a belt decoration.

The belt mount shown in **Pic M109** is probably of late Roman date. It is of gilded bronze with a panel containing a moulded design of two hearts or

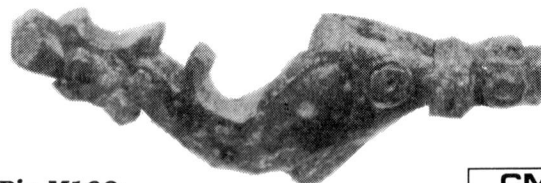

Pic M106:
Saxon buckle with ring and dot decoration.

CM

Pic M109:
Gilt buckle plate, probably late Roman.

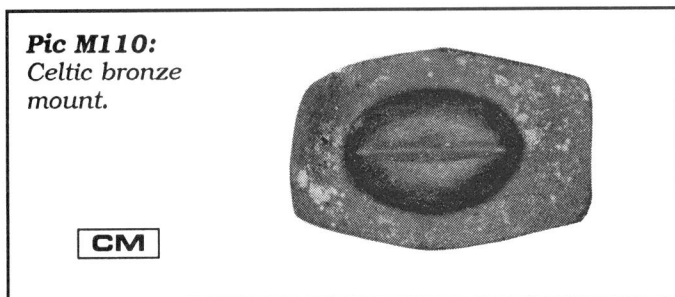

Pic M112: *Roman belt mount.*

Pic M110:
Celtic bronze mount.

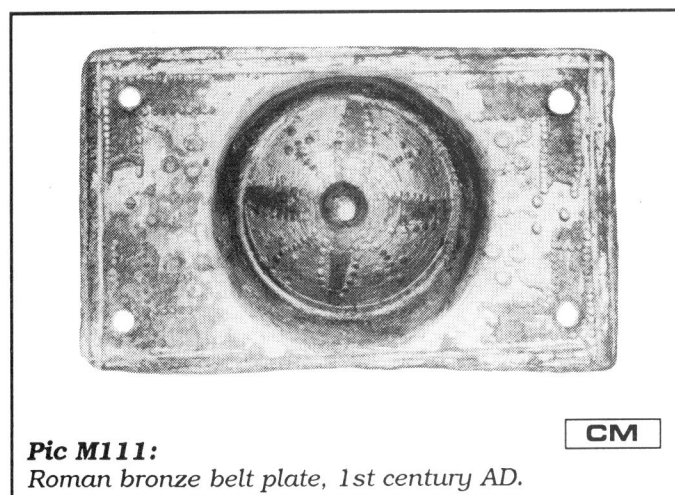

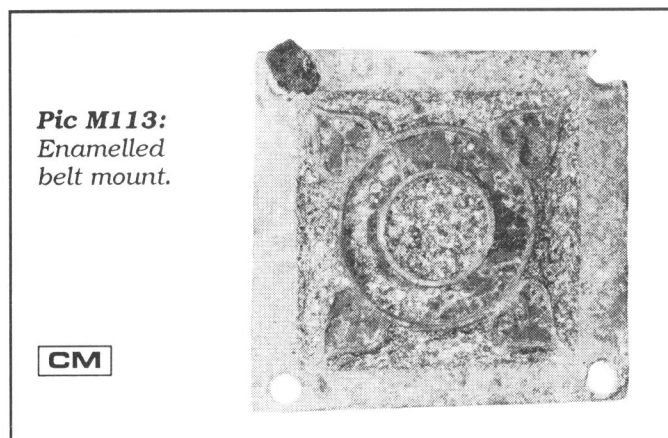

Pic M113:
Enamelled belt mount.

Pic M111:
Roman bronze belt plate, 1st century AD.

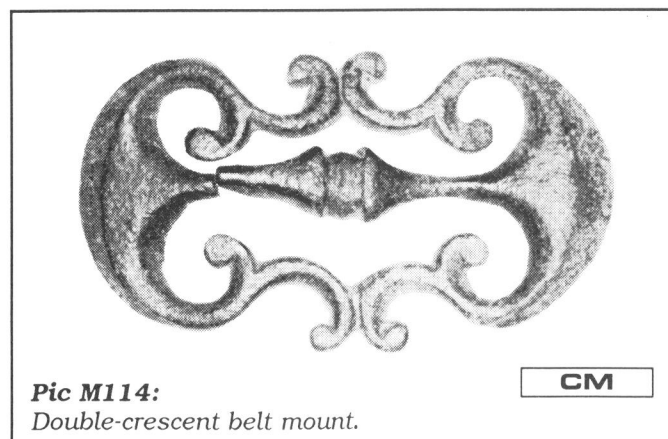

Pic M114:
Double-crescent belt mount.

leaves with a pellet border. A Roman belt, covered in iron or bronze plates, was called a *cingulum*.

Pic **M110** is a bronze mount from a horse harness leather strap. It is hexagonal with a raised oval boss which has a deep median groove. There are two studs at the back. The shape resembles a shield. In date, this mount is likely to be 3rd century.

An example of a bronze belt plate from the 1st century AD is shown in **Pic M111**. It is of flat rectangular form with a raised boss in the centre. It is heavily tinned with niello inlay, a feature of the early Roman period. There are circular punches with a geometric design in the centre re-

sembling a St Andrews cross. The plate is perforated at each corner to take rivets.

Pic M112 is a belt mount which was originally enamelled; traces of blue enamel are still visible. Again of flat rectangular form, this mount has pelta-shaped ends and is likely to date from the 2nd or 3rd centuries.

A larger square-shaped belt plate is shown in **Pic M113**. The centre panel is enamelled red and blue. There is a circular design with a heart shape in each corner. An iron rivet remains in one of the four perforations. This example would date 2nd century AD.

The belt stud shown in **Pic M114** is of open-work design, and has crescent-shaped ends with involuted terminals. It probably dates 3rd century AD.

Pic M105

Pic M112

Pic M113

Pic M119

Pic M142

Pic M151

Pic M152

See text for details

Not to Scale

44

Pic M154

Pic M177a

Pic M174

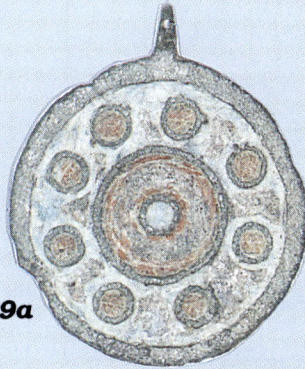

Pic M179a

Pic M179b

Pic M176

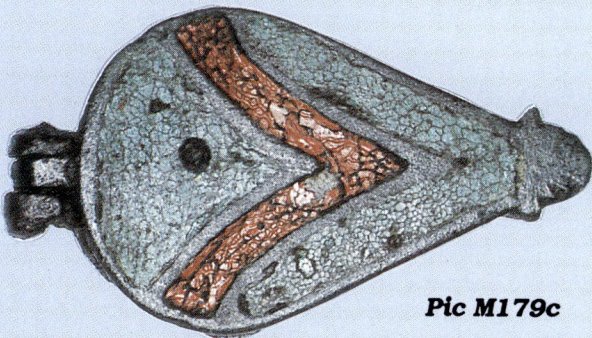

Pic M179c

Pic M179d

Pic M115:
Open-work belt plate, 3rd century.

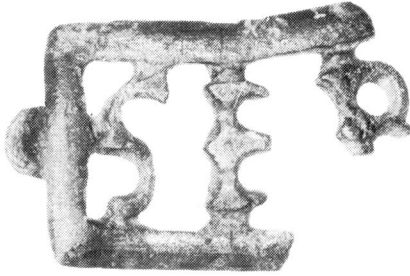

CM

Pic M115 is another open-work belt plate dating from the 3rd century. The example illustrated is incomplete. The lettering in the centre reads "SER", but would originally have been "SERV", perhaps meaning "serve" or "preserve". This might have been linked with another plate stating a god's name such as "IOVIS" (Jupiter).

Pic M116:
Disc belt stud.

CM

A series of heavily tinned discs or studs have turned up in London riverside sites, dating mainly from the 1st century AD. **Pic M116** is an example which has survived from outside London. It has a stamped-out (repoussé) design of a head facing right. There are additional ornaments in the field. It is a fragile item

Pic M117:
Lunular belt mount.

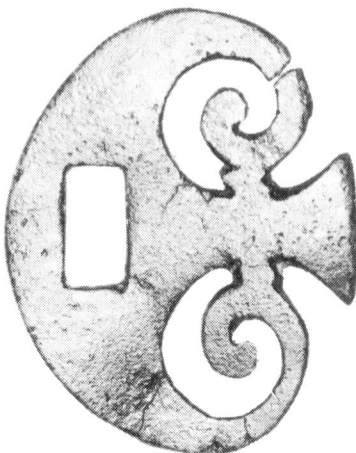

CM

of very thin construction. Some of the busts represented on these discs appear to be emperors.

Pic M117 is an open-work pelta-shaped belt mount, again with involuted ends. Possibly of 3rd century date.

Pic M118:
Hinged buckle, 1st century AD.

CM

The plate armour or cuirass worn by legionaries as protection for the body, required the use of hinged buckles. **Pic M118** is an example of one of these, possibly for use with horse furniture. Attached to an iron sheet, it dates from the 1st century AD. Chain mail was also worn in the 1st century AD, as was scale armour.

Pic M119:
Two-piece lunular bronze pendant.

CM

Horse harness decorations which in more recent times have become known as horse "brasses" were in use in Roman times. **Pic M119** is a two-piece bronze pendant hinged in the centre. It is of lunular design and decorated with rings and dots.

Pic M120: *Leaf-shaped bronze harness pendant.*

CM

Pic M120 is a flat leaf-shaped bronze harness decoration looped at the top for suspension. The surface is tinned, and carries a punched dot decoration. It would date 1st-2nd century AD.

Pic M121: *Horse pendant, 1st-2nd century AD.*

CM

Pic M122: *Terret ring.*

CM

One of the most popular harness pendants in the Roman period is the type shown in **Pic M121** which dates 1st century to early 2nd century AD. There are moulded oak leaves and acorns in low relief on each side, while the surface is covered with silver foil and inlaid with niello. The silver foil covering - of which only traces are visible on this example - is a distinctive feature of early Roman military equipment.

Terret rings are normally associated with the Celts but there is a style of terret or rein guide that might be of Romano-British origin. **Pic M122** is an example, with two loops as opposed to a single loop. The common feature of these terrets is the lower fixing loop which is enclosed beneath a curved and four pointed skirt. This terret would date 1st to early 2nd century AD.

The circular object shown in **Pic M123** has been described as a ferrule from a knife or dagger. These turn up quite frequently on Roman sites and six comparable specimens were found in a tumulus at Lexden, Colchester and were thought to be Roman harness fittings. The shape is always consistent with a raised boss in the centre, circular grooves around this, and a turned up edge. Size varies from 15mm to 40mm diameter. They can be found with either an iron or bronze shank on their reverse.

Pic M123: *Phalera mount.*

CM

A link from a harness fitting is shown in **Pic M124**. This is of 2nd century date and would have been one of four fittings linking the harness strap to the central junction. The fitting consists of three separate

Pic M181

Pic M182

Pic M186

Pic M188

Pic M191

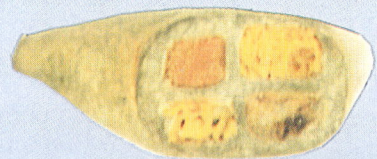

Pic M193

Pic M187

Pic M198

See text for details

Not to Scale

Pic M199

Pic M200

Pic M206

Pic M207

Pic M208

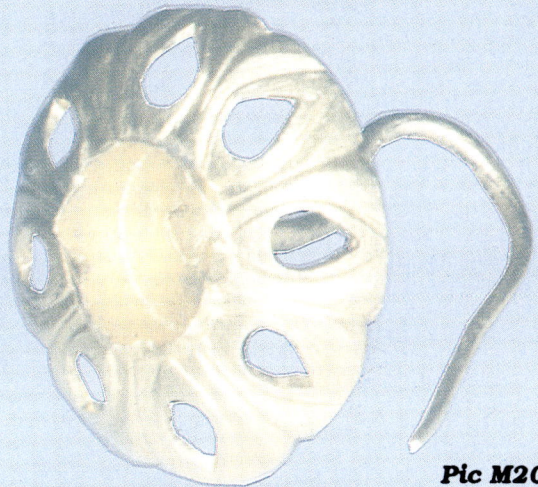

Pic M209

See text for details

Not to Scale

49

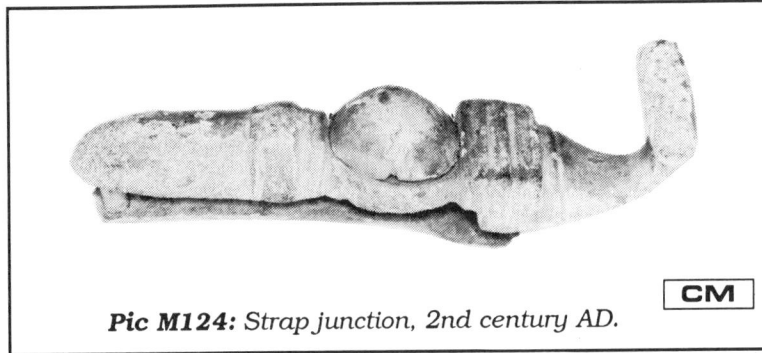

Pic M124: *Strap junction, 2nd century AD.*

components: there is a central stud with a domed top, a back plate connected by two rivets, and a central bar which is looped over at one end.

suggest that it was fixed to a leather strap and that it might have formed part of a cuirass (or plate armour) worn by legionaries.

Pic M125: *Bronze cuirass plate.*

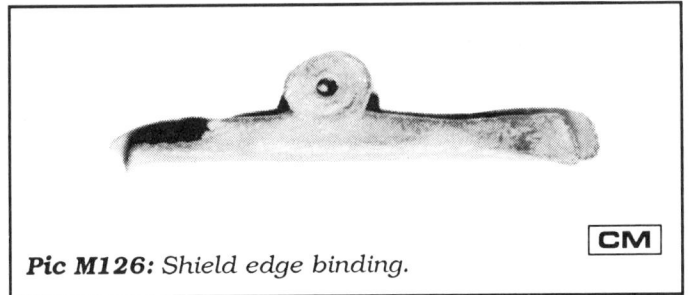

Pic M126: *Shield edge binding.*

An interesting piece of Roman bronze plate is shown in **Pic M125**. This is a fairly heavy duty item, with a decorative pattern of zig-zag lines on one side. The small rivet holes

The cylindrical, V-sectioned strip of bronze shown in **Pic M126** is, surprisingly enough, a piece of Roman shield edge binding. Small sections of this would have been rivetted all around the edge of the shield (which was wooden) to increase its strength and durability.

Price Guide

	Fine	Very Fine		Fine	Very Fine
M99: bronze toggle, square headed	£15	£30	M114: double crescent belt mount	£25	£55
M100: bronze buckle	£10	£20	M115: SERV belt mount	£60	£150
M101: bronze buckle	£18	£40	M116: disc belt stud	£18	£45
M102: bronze quoit buckle and plate	£125	£275	M117: lunular belt mount	£12	£25
M103: bronze buckle	£65	£140	M118: clasp fitting	£15	£30
M104: D-shaped buckle	£25	£55	M119: lunular pendant	£30	£75
M105: open-work buckle plate	£120	£260	M120: hanging pendant	£15	£30
M106: Saxon buckle	£22	£45	M121: horse pendant	£70	£160
M107: Saxon buckle	£16	£35	M122: terret ring	£75	£175
M108: dolphin stud	£25	£45	M123: Phalera mount	£4	£10
M109: gilt buckle plate	£35	£100	M124: strap junction	£15	£30
M110: Celtic belt stud	£8	£15	M125: cuirass plate	£25	£55
M111: Roman belt mount	£65	£180	M126: shield edge binding	£12	£25
M112: Roman belt mount	£35	£120			
M113: enamelled belt mount	£45	£160			

Chapter V

Locks, Keys and Knife Handles

Locks and keys are further examples of artefacts introduced by the Romans into Britain. Two types of locks had been developed by the Romans: the tumbler lock, and the lever lock.

The tumbler lock was made with a perforated bolt which could be slid along, once a suitable key had been inserted to lift the vertical pins out of the bolt and thus release it.

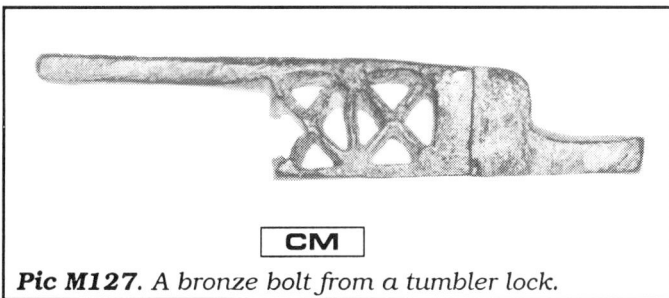

CM

Pic M127. *A bronze bolt from a tumbler lock.*

Pic M127 shows an example of a bolt which is sometimes mistakenly identified as a key. The triangular holes would have matched up to the teeth of a key, which would have been of a similar type to that shown in **Pic M128**. To open the lock, the key would have been inserted and turned, pushing the teeth into the bolt; the interlocked key and bolt could then be moved sideways. The perforations cut into the bolts, can be of circular, square or triangular shape.

The bolts themselves can vary in size, and the example illustrated is quite small, probably having come from a box. It would date 1st or 2nd century AD.

Apart from the bronze bolt, the other parts of the lock would mainly have been made from iron, including a spring to hold the pins in place.

The bronze key shown in **Pic M128** is of similar date to the bolt. It has two vertical rows of three teeth and these

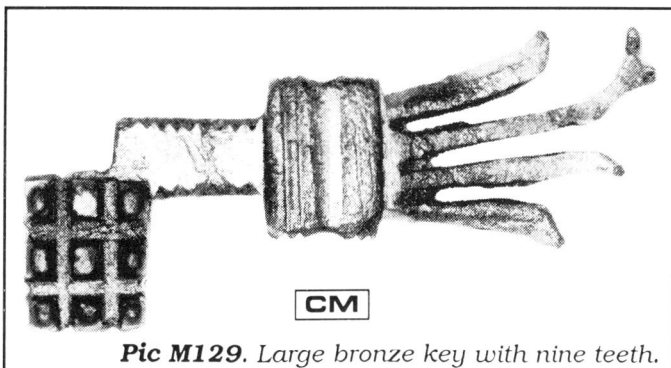

are positioned at right angles to the shank to give maximum leverage in use. The small circular bow is for suspension from a chain, while the narrow square-sectioned shank is notched at each end and has a large incised "X" on one side.

Most keys of this type appear to be marked in this way, with a varying number of Xs used to aid identification.

Pic M128. *Small bronze key with six teeth.*

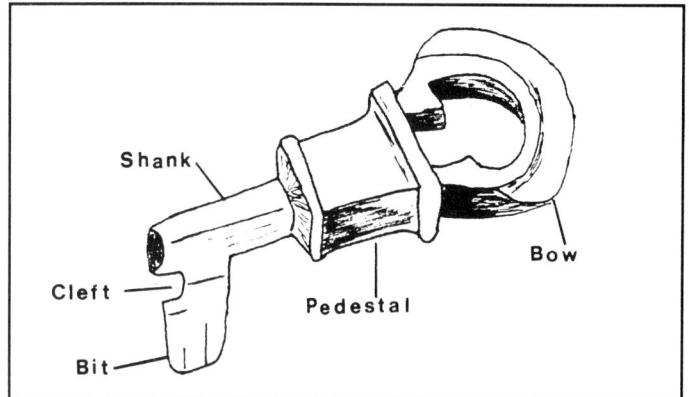

CM

A much larger bronze tumbler key was found in Hampshire (**Pic M129**). This has a total of nine teeth set in three rows, and could well have come from a lock fitted to the door of a villa. It is quite elaborate, having an openwork trifoliate bow (part of which is missing). Beneath the bow is a rectangular pedestal decorated with grooves, and the shank is notched at each end.

The second type of lock design developed by the Romans is the lever lock. The working principle is that obstructions are built into the lock to prevent the wrong shape of key from working the mechanism, and similar designs of lock are still in use today (although it has been suggested that the Romans were not able to invent a lock that could be operated from both sides of a door).

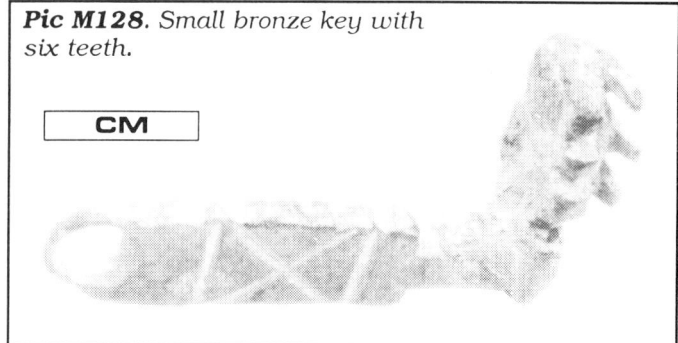

CM

Pic M129. *Large bronze key with nine teeth.*

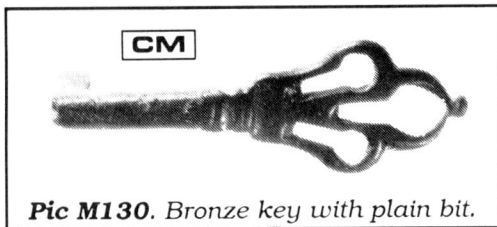

Pic M130. Bronze key with plain bit.

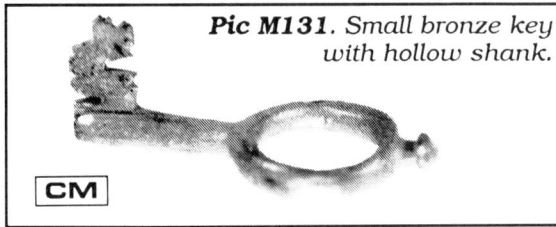

Pic M131. Small bronze key with hollow shank.

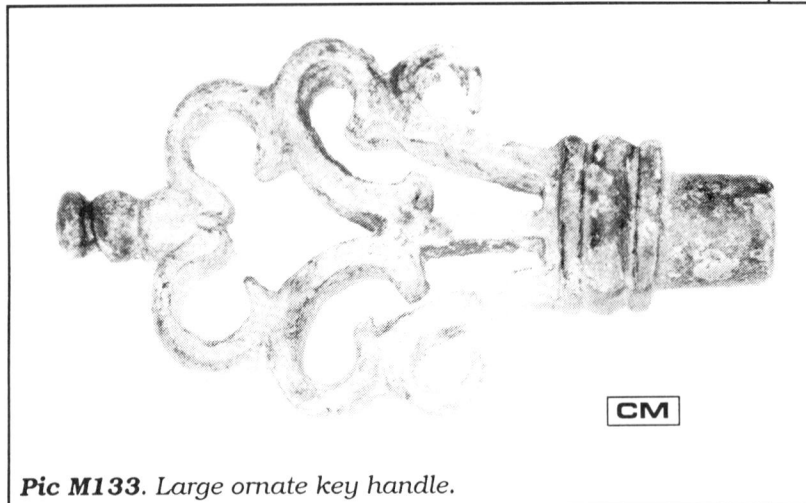

Pic M132. Two bronze key handles.

Both tumbler and lever locks were in everyday use quite early in the Roman period, as excavations at Pompei have shown. The lever lock, however, was more favoured in late Roman times.

Pic M130 shows an example of a lever lock key in bronze with a simple bit to open the lock. The bow is of the same openwork trifoliate design but with a small knob mounted on the top. The shank is slightly rounded in section and, in fact, all Roman lever keys have a tubular shank, sometimes hollowed out.

The lever lock key shown in **Pic M131** has a hollow tubular shank, and a large circular bow with an extended knob at the end. The bit has various clefts cut out and would have served quite an intricate lever lock. Judging from this and its unusual style, the key could be late in period (3rd or 4th century AD) although I have no hard evidence to support this view.

Many of the keys used in Roman Britain had a bronze bow or handle combined with an iron shank. As might be expected, the iron section of these rarely survives apart from where the keys have existed in waterlogged or very dry conditions.

Pic M132 shows two bronze handles with some remains of the iron shanks. The larger trifoliate bow has an acorn finial. These attractive and ornate handles, apart from aiding identification of a key, could be re-used if necessary.

I have seen one example of this type of key that had an iron shank of over 9cms length.

The smaller key shown in **Pic M132** has an unusual handle which consists of a single bow with double fluted sides. The iron shank is quite short and rather delicate, and the key has a small part of the bit surviving.

A very large and ornate bronze key handle (**Pic M133**) was found near to a temple site and this could indicate its use. It certainly would have served a substantial lock.

Another elaborate version of a bronze key handle, moulded in the round in the form of a hound's head, is shown in **Pic M134**. The animal's long ears are pinned back as if it were running, and a means of suspending the key is provided by a hole through the hound's mouth. This handle was found near Wroxeter, in Shropshire. An example of similar design to this was excavated at Richborough and dated 50-80 AD.

A further example of a cast bronze handle is shown in **Pic M135** and is in the form of a seated lion. It also dates 1st century AD and could have been intended as either a key or a knife handle (although the fact that it has a circular socket favours its use as a key handle).

Keys made entirely of iron were

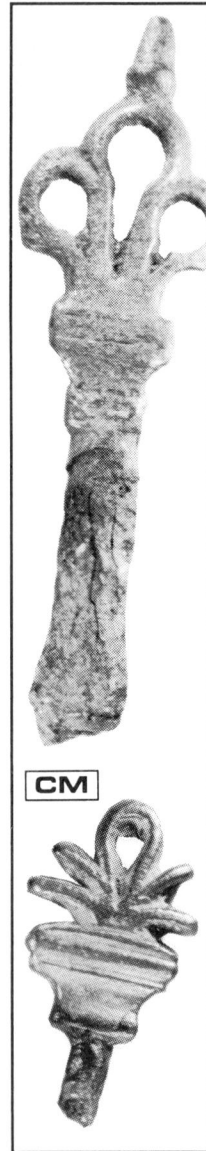

Pic M134. Bronze key handle in the design of a hound.

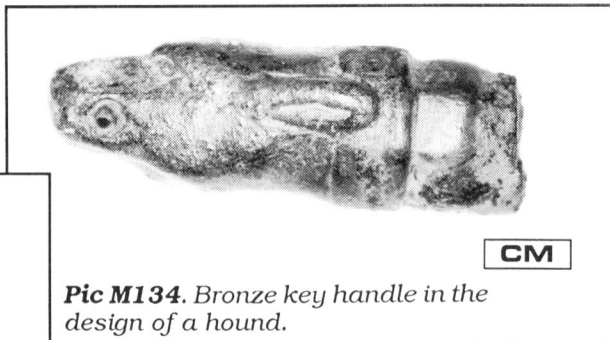

Pic M135. Bronze key handle in the design of a seated lion.

Pic M133. Large ornate key handle.

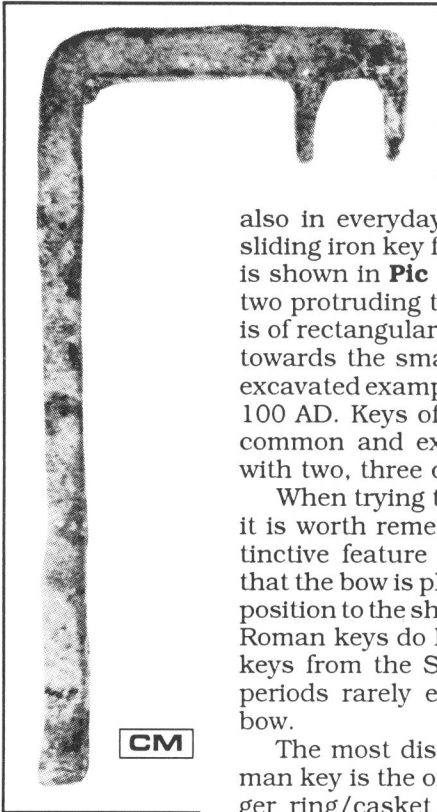

Pic M136. Iron L-shaped key.

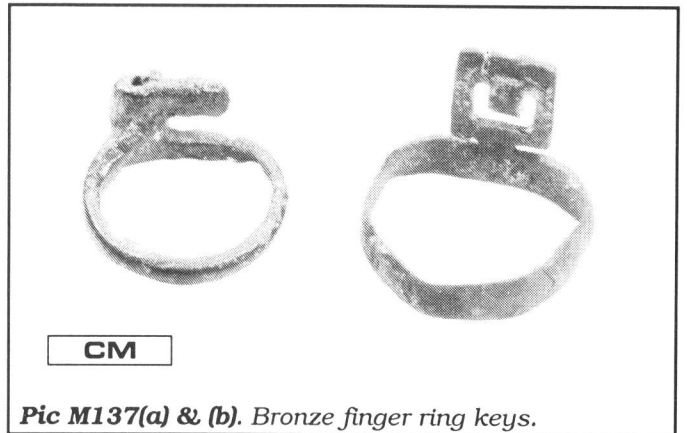

Pic M137(a) & (b). Bronze finger ring keys.

also in everyday use. An L-shaped sliding iron key found in East Anglia is shown in **Pic M136**. The key has two protruding teeth and the shank is of rectangular section, thickening towards the small circular bow. An excavated example has been dated to 100 AD. Keys of this type are fairly common and examples are known with two, three or four teeth.

When trying to date an early key, it is worth remembering that a distinctive feature of a Roman key is that the bow is placed in a horizontal position to the shank. Although some Roman keys do have a vertical bow, keys from the Saxon and medieval periods rarely employ a horizontal bow.

The most distinctive form of Roman key is the one-piece bronze finger ring/casket key combination - see **Pic M137(a) & (b)**. Here two plain banded rings have been attached at right angles to the bit of a key. Obviously the ring had to be designed so that it was not uncomfortable to wear, but at the same time the key part needed to be intricate enough to serve a lock.

The example shown on the left in the photograph has a rectangular plain bit with a short hollow shank. The hoop of the ring is square in section. The other finger ring/key on the right has a slot cut out of the bit, with notches on the end. On this example the ring hoop is wider and flatter in section.

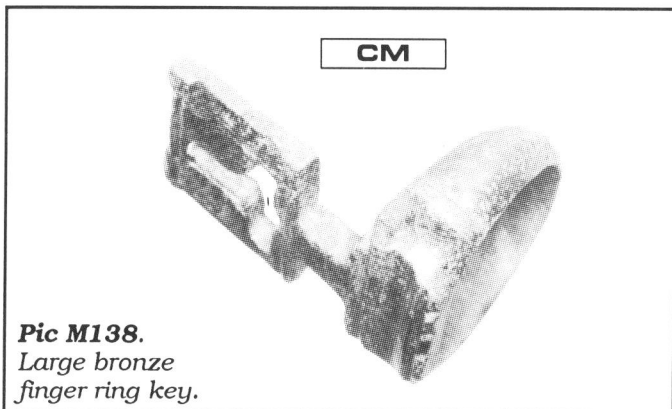

Pic M138. Large bronze finger ring key.

Pic M138 shows a larger, more solid example. The ring has a fluted bezel with a side projection containing a key bit which has a T-shaped slot cut out of it.

From the large numbers found in this country 'key rings' must have

been both popular and fashionable items; they also served a practical purpose for at the time pockets were unknown. From the various sizes of key rings found, and the fact that some are quite delicate while others are heavy duty, it is likely that they were worn by both sexes.

Interestingly, the use of key rings is confined solely to the Roman period.

A few examples have been found made from silver, but I have not seen any in iron, which was a metal commonly used for finger rings in the 1st century AD. Most, therefore, probably date from the 2nd century AD. (Another curious suggestion I have heard is that these rings were worn as a souvenir of marriage).

Other methods of keeping keys safe were also employed by the Romans, a good example being a bronze wrist bracelet found in Cambridge which had a key suspended on it.

Knives are another class of object which were in widespread use in Roman times. They are rarely found complete as the blades were generally made of iron which has rusted away down through the centuries. The handles, however, were usually made of bronze and were often highly decorated.

Pic M139 shows the handle of a folding knife, in the form of a hound chasing a hare. Modelled in the round, the knife blade slots into the underside of the two animals between the two bars forming the ground line.

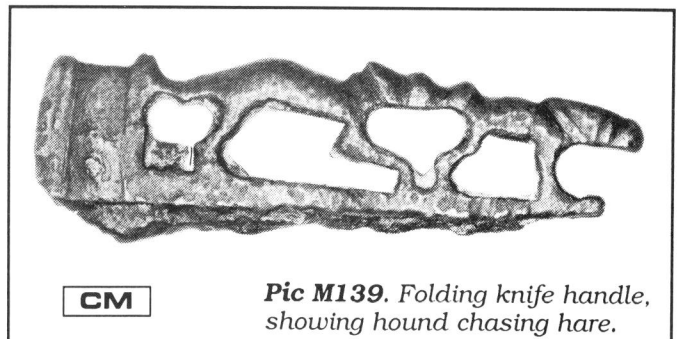

Pic M139. Folding knife handle, showing hound chasing hare.

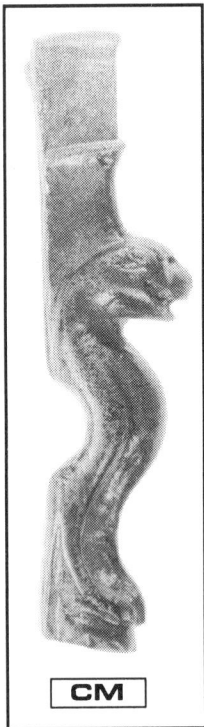

Pic M140.
Folding knife handle, panther design.

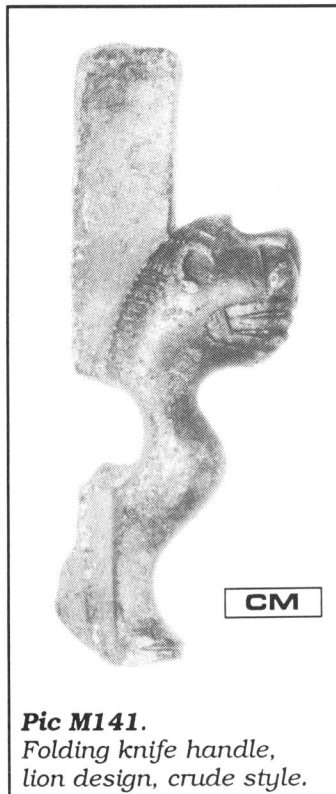

Pic M141.
Folding knife handle, lion design, crude style.

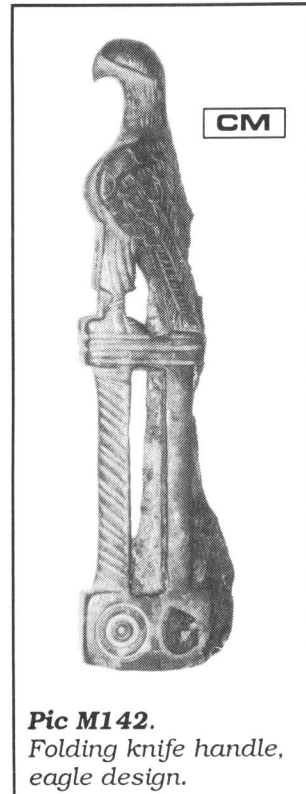

Pic M142.
Folding knife handle, eagle design.

Behind the hound there is a rectangular plate containing an iron rivet. The rivet passes through the tang of the triangular-shaped plate and would have acted as a pivot.

The 'hare and hound' is the most common style of folding knife to have been used in Roman Britain. The Celtic style of the animals indicates Romano-British workmanship, and dates the knife to 1st-2nd century AD.

The folding knife could have been used as a razor, if it was sharp enough, or as a penknife for shaping reed pens. In fact, the high quality of iron ore available to the Romans in Britain, combined with the use of charcoal fuel in the smelting process, meant that such knives could have been produced with a very hard and sharp blade.

There are many other varieties of folding knives known to have been produced during the Roman period, but most of these other types are rarely found in Britain.

Pic M140 shows a bronze folding knife handle in the design of the forepart of a panther, mounted on a solid pedestal base (slotted to take the blade). The curved opening behind the body of the animal may have been intended to allow easy gripping of the blade when opening it out. The panther design itself was also used on lamp stands and casket legs.

Pic M141 shows a much cruder version of the same design found in Essex, and which is probably of local workmanship. The animal represented is a lion. It has an oversized head in proportion to its body, which is a Celtic feature.

Another example of a folding knife handle, of Roman workmanship, is shown in **Pic M142**. This design is of an eagle looking ahead with wings closed, and perched on an extended rectangular pedestal. The iron knife blade has survived in its closed position, concealed neatly within the framework of the handle. This is a very elegant example of a folding knife.

A quite small example of a folding knife is shown in **Pic M143**. Here the hollow handle is oval in shape, has a pointed finial, and is divided into five equal segments. A slot runs along the top of the handle and even the finial is grooved to receive the tip of the blade.

The Romans sometimes used handles to combine a number of different implements ... much like the Swiss Army knives of today. **Pic M144** shows a bronze handle in the design of a leaping dolphin. The underside of the handle is slotted to receive a knife blade which was rivetted at the dolphin's tail. Across the mammal's back are the remains of an iron tool which was rivetted to the upper part of the tail. Through the mouth there appears to be the remains of a chain link from which the knife would have

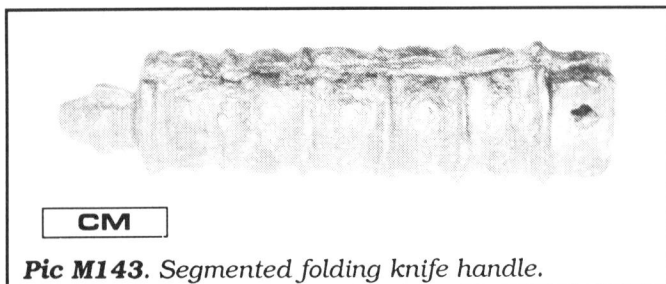

Pic M143. *Segmented folding knife handle.*

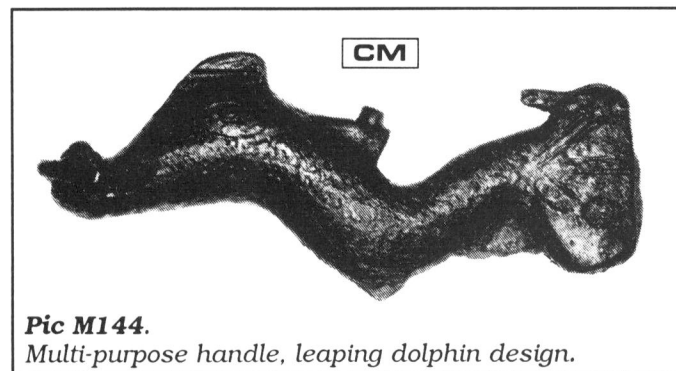

Pic M144.
Multi-purpose handle, leaping dolphin design.

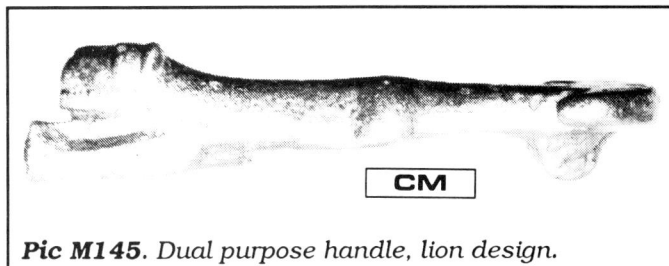

Pic M145. *Dual purpose handle, lion design.*

been suspended. The dolphin's body is decorated with incised, semi-circular punch marks, imitating fish scales. This knife handle was found in Colchester and may have been used by a Legionary.

Pic M145 shows a dual-purpose knife handle in the form of a stretched out lion holding its prey in its paws. The back paws of the lion are crescent-shaped containing a slot on one side for a small blade. Underneath there is a recess for another, larger blade fixed to a lug extending below.

During the 1st and 2nd centuries AD, knife handles were often made in the form of animals. Each Legion adopted an animal as its emblem, and the animal designs may have been purely military symbols. (In the case of Legion XX, which was stationed in Britain, the symbol was a boar).

It is also possible that the animals had other significance. Devouring animals (eg lions, griffins, dolphins, snakes and panthers) symbolise the triumph of death over life. The dolphin can also be regarded as a symbol of rebirth into the afterlife, as it reflects the journey of the soul across the ocean.

Another fascinating knife handle shown in **Pic M146** depicts an erotic scene involving three figures. The handle is modelled in the round with a man engaged in sexual intercourse with a woman who is positioned on the shoulders of a kneeling figure. The rear of the standing male is slotted vertically to take the folding iron blade (now missing). The figures are mounted on a square pedestal which still contains the iron rivet for pivoting the blade.

All three figures are naked, except for a single strap or bikini-like harness running across the woman's chest. She is supported by the man's hands on her legs, and has her left hand on the man's shoulder; her right hand is placed on the head of the kneeling figure. This figure is quite small, almost dwarf-like, and has an oversize ape's head (probably a mask).

There is a faintly engraved inscription or dedication on each side of the pedestal, but sadly this has worn off. All that can be made out is the letter "S", then possibly an "E", followed by another letter which is possible a "C". This could mean "withdraw" which would be a suitable description. On the other side there appears to be "N A" with "IRI" underneath.

According to Catherine Johns, at least four parallels are known from Britain, but none from the Continent. She suggests the design may refer to some kind of public performance or entertainment, especially as one example was excavated from the theatre at Verulamium. The illustrated example was found in Hertfordshire, and dates from the late 1st or early 2nd century AD.

The female figure on the knife handle appears to resemble Aphrodite or Venus, the goddess of love. A comparison can be made to a group of marble figures recovered from a brothel in Pompei. Here Aphrodite is shown with her hand on Priapus (god of fruitfulness) and she has a tiny figure of Eros sitting below her feet.

Another unusual variation for a folding knife handle (**Pic M147**) is moulded in the round and shows a female monkey feeding her infant

Pic M146. *Folding knife handle, showing erotic scene.*

Pic M147. *Folding knife handle, showing monkey feeding infant.*

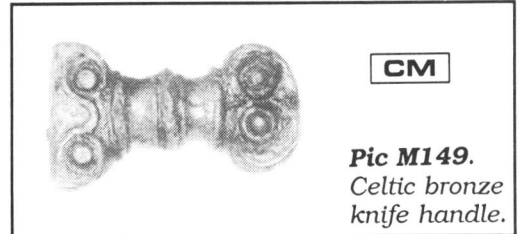
Pic M148. Bronze dagger handle, stallion's head design.

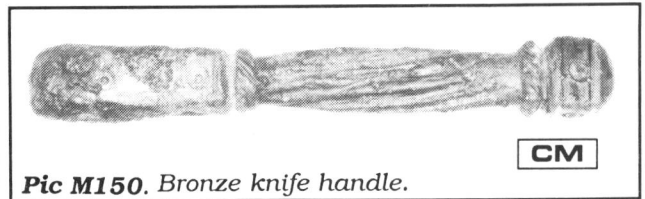
Pic M150. Bronze knife handle.

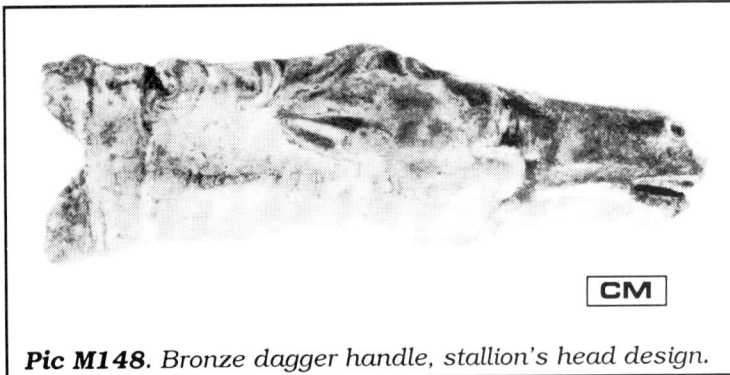
Pic M149.
Celtic bronze
knife handle.

which is sitting on her left leg. There is a circular pedestal base through which the knife is pivoted. A slot runs down the back of the monkey for the knife to fold into.

Apart from their use on folding knives, bronze handles were also commonly used on conventional knives and daggers. **Pic M148** shows the beautifully-moulded head of an unbridled galloping stallion. Of classical style, this piece was certainly an import and it reveals the high quality of Roman art. The flattened, rectangular section behind the neck contains traces of a large iron blade, possibly a double-edged dagger or short sword.

In contrast, **Pic M149 & M150** show two small knife handles. **Pic 149** is Celtic in origin and is solid bronze. In the centre is a circular sectioned baluster moulding and at the top an oval moulding which is decorated with a pair of deeply recessed ring and dot designs. At the lower, flattened end the design is repeated but the cells are petal boss shaped. The handle has an elliptical-shaped opening which is 14mm in depth, by 3mm at its widest point; this contains part of the iron blade. From its size, the knife must have had a very specific use and may even have been a surgical instrument.

Pic 150 The second bronze handle is Roman in style and quite delicate in form - possibly indicating use as a scalpel. The handle is squared and flattened at the end which could mean that it was used as a pestle for grinding. The stem is circular in section, with a twisting, grooved design. There are ring and dot punch marks on each end, and the iron blade would have slotted between the rectangular-shaped panels.

Pic M151 shows a standing female figure on a square, pedestal base which is socketed to receive either a knife or a key. The surface is highly tinned and the figure is quite crude, perhaps representing a lar.

Pic M152 shows a very crude knife handle, found near Wroxeter, and is certainly of Romano-British workmanship. Again it shows a standing female figure, and she has her arms around her waist.

The item shown in **Pic M153** is from Essex. It has a long rectangular panel surmounted by a bust of what appears to be Venus, wearing a diadem and with her hair tied back. The inscription on the front reads "Felix" (standing for "good luck"), and this is usually combined with "Utere" to mean good luck to the user.

The small bronze handle shown in **Pic M154** has a lion's head as a decorative terminal, and a square pedestal base slotted to receive the iron blade.

Pic M155 shows a small handle for a knife that may have had quite

Pic M151.
Bronze knife
or key handle,
female figure.

Pic M152.
Bronze knife handle,
crude female figure.

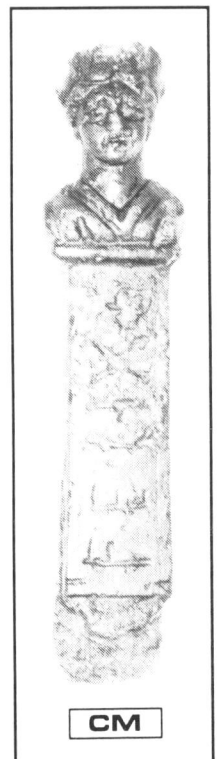
Pic M153.
Bronze knife
handle
showing
female bust.

56

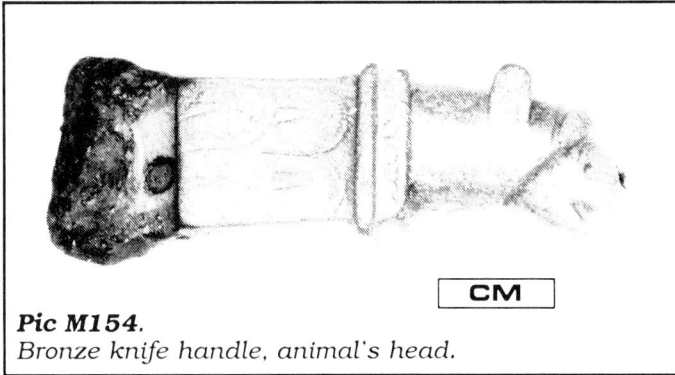

Pic M154.
Bronze knife handle, animal's head.

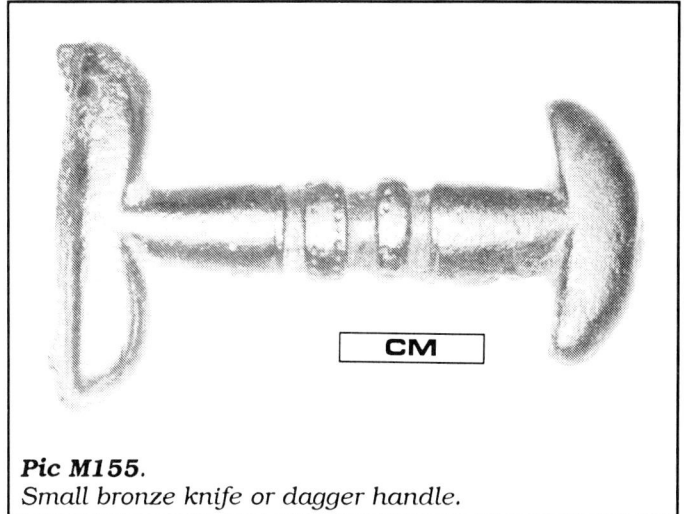

Pic M155.
Small bronze knife or dagger handle.

specialised uses. It is similar in shape to a dagger handle and may have been used in rituals.

The use of enamelled decoration on knife handles was rare during the Roman Occupation but the handle shown in **Pic M156** has a moulded design with piriform cells showing traces of blue enamel. It is a hollow tube, slotted to receive the blade. Other examples exist with red and blue enamel in lozenge-shaped cells. They date to the 2nd century AD, as do the knives previously listed.

Pic M157 shows a knife handle of later date, having a gilded bronze surface. The decorative moulding of a lozenge with a circular punch, resembles an eye. This handle could be as late as 4th or 5th century AD in date.

Price Guide

	Fine	Very Fine
M127: bronze bolt from tumbler lock	£6	£14
M128: small bronze key with six teeth	£20	£45
M129: large bronze key with nine teeth	£75	£160
M130: bronze key with plain bit	£40	£90
M131: small bronze key with hollow shank	£18	£40
M132: bronze key handle	£8	£18
M133: large ornate key handle	£45	£110
M134: bronze key handle in the design of a hound	£45	£120
M135: bronze key handle in the design of a seated lion	£70	£175
M136: iron L-shaped key	£18	£50
M137(a) & (b): bronze finger ring key	£25	£60
M138: large bronze finger ring key	£35	£85
M139: folding knife handle, hound chasing hare	£75	£160
M140: folding knife handle, panther	£80	£180
M141: folding knife handle, lion, crude style	£85	£190

	Fine	Very Fine
M142: folding knife handle, eagle	£100	£225
M143: segmented folding knife handle	£25	£60
M144: multi-purpose handle, leaping dolphin	£110	£250
M145: dual-purpose handle, lion	£65	£140
M146: folding knife handle, erotic scene	£600	£2,200
M147: folding knife handle, monkey feeding infant	£150	£375
M148: bronze dagger handle, stallion's head	£350	£1,000
M149: Celtic bronze knife handle	£55	£130
M150: bronze knife handle	£30	£65
M151: bronze knife or key handle	£120	£275
M152: bronze knife handle, crude female figure	£75	£160
M153: bronze knife handle with female bust	£130	£325
M154: bronze knife handle, animal's head	£55	£130
M155: small bronze knife or dagger handle	£30	£65
M156: enamelled bronze knife handle	£45	£120
M157: gilded bronze knife handle	£55	£130

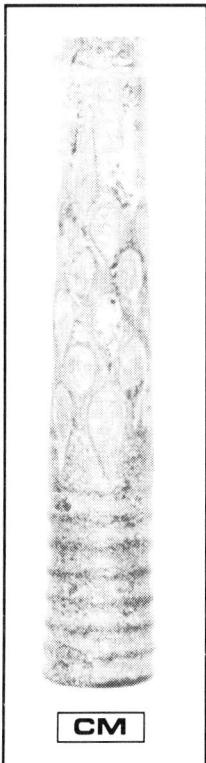

Pic M156.
Enamelled bronze knife handle.

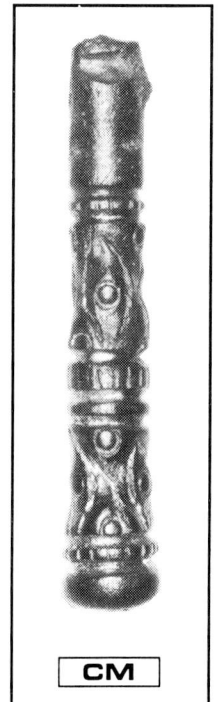

Pic M157.
Gilded bronze knife handle.

Spoons, Cosmetic Grinders, Medical Implements & Seal Boxes

K nives were rarely used by the Romans at the dinner table, for food was generally prepared for eating beforehand; forks were also virtually unknown. Spoons made of bronze or silver, however, were in use in most households. These had differing shapes of bowls depending on their intended function.

Pic M158 shows an example of a tinned bronze spoon, having a pear-shaped bowl and a straight tapering handle ending in a point. Several grooves have been cut into the stem by way of simple decoration. A distinctive feature of many Roman spoons is that the bowl is stepped or lowered from the handle by an off-set which can be sometimes ornamented with an animal's head. On this example it is solid, curved on the under-side, and has three circular perforations.

A side view of a silver spoon found in Surrey - **Pic M159(a)** shows more clearly the stepped junction between the bowl and the handle. This example has an onion-shaped finial knop decoration on the end of the handle.

cluding dishes, bowls, spoons and goblets) and the Water Newton treasure (again thirty items, including bowls, jugs, a cup and strainer, and a number of silver plaques in the design of leaves).

The most recent and spectacular hoard is the Hoxne treasure found by Eric Lawes in November 1992. Apart from 569 gold solidi and 14,205 silver siliquae coins, the tableware of silver included twelve vessels, twenty ladles, seventy-nine spoons, and four strainers.

Britain has now become one of the richest sources of 4th-5th century Roman silver hoards. Comparisons between the hoards reveal many items with Bacchic motifs. Parcel gilt decoration showing a running panther or a Triton blowing a horn on the bowl of the spoon, are some of the features.

The Hoxne treasure was concealed around 410 AD and would represent the considerable wealth of an estate buried during troubled times. The Romans were never able to return to Britain and their treasure, in many

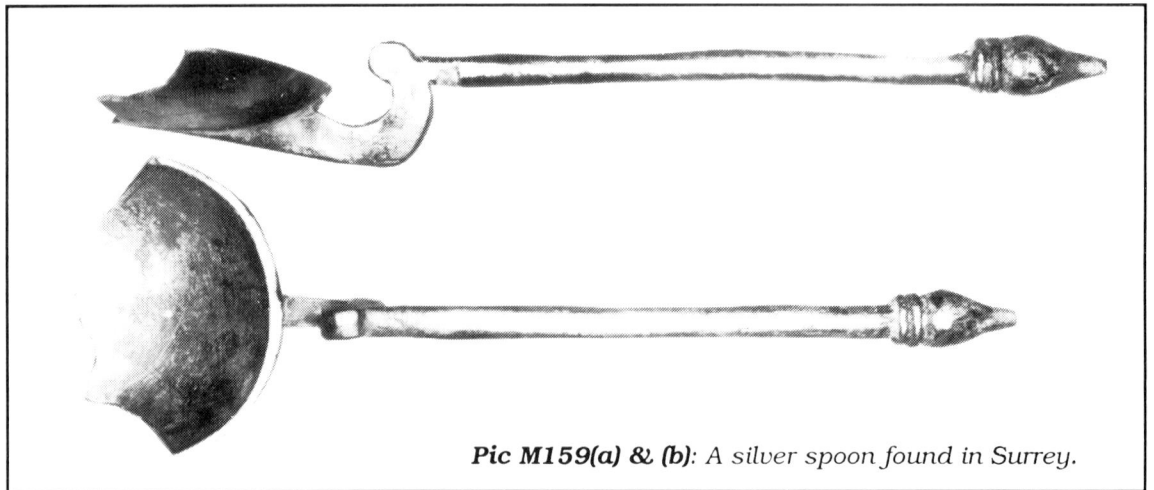

Pic M159(a) & (b): A silver spoon found in Surrey.

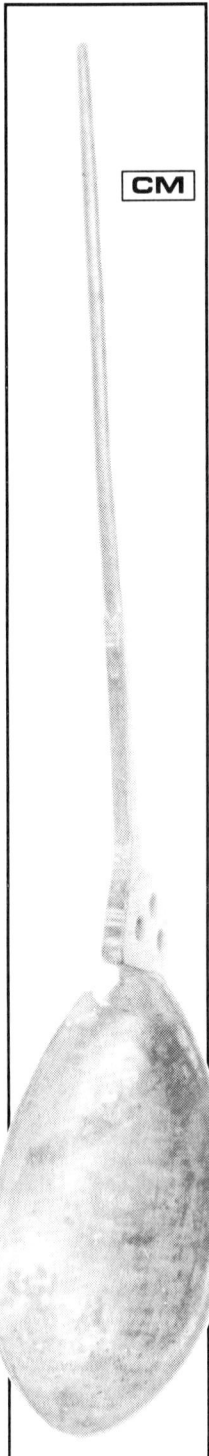

It is difficult to give an accurate dating on any individual spoon used within the Roman period. However, the Thetford treasure included thirty-three silver spoons amongst its jewellery, all dating to the late 4th century. Half of these had oval bowls containing inscriptions, and a tapering handle. The others had a coiled duck handle, which is a design solely confined to this late period.

Other hoards of silver tableware include the Mildenhall treasure (which consisted of thirty items, in-

cases, still lies buried in our soil.

Silver spoons with parcel gilding as those of the Hoxne treasure are, by the way, very rare.

A common type of spoon in use during the 1st and 2nd centuries was the 'cochlear' (**Pics M160 and M161**). This had a small round and dished bowl which is assumed to have been intended for eating eggs and certain types of shellfish. The pointed end was used for prising out shellfish and snails, hence the Latin name for the spoon. Both spoons shown in these

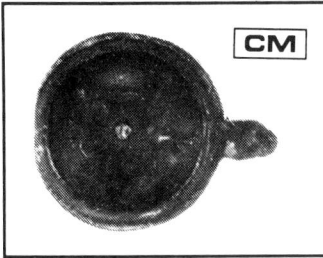

Pic M160: A pewter spoon, possibly used for dispensing medicaments.

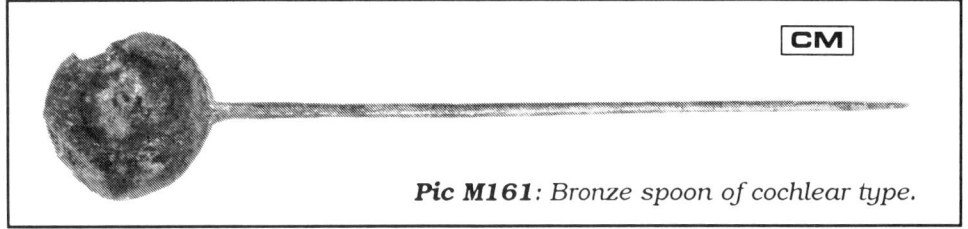

Pic M161: Bronze spoon of cochlear type.

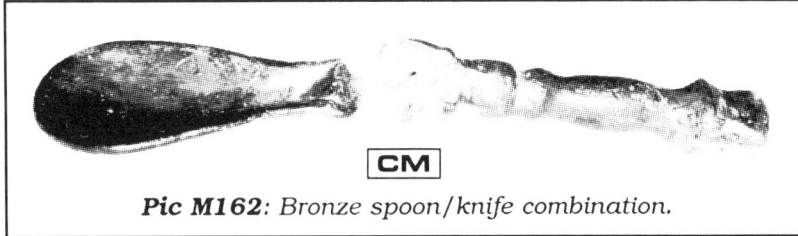

Pic M162: Bronze spoon/knife combination.

photographs were recovered from the Billingsgate spoil heaps and have been well-preserved by the silt of the River Thames. The bronze example in the right photograph still retains its colour, and often spoons were tinned to give them a brighter, silvery appearance.

The left example is of pewter but the handle is missing. The bowl itself is decorated in the centre with a floral pattern surrounding a raised pellet. The rim is stepped, possibly to serve as some form of measure, so this spoon may have been used for the dispensing of medicaments.

Spoons combining other utensils also exist as shown in **Pic M162**. This example is of tinned bronze, is of fairly heavy-duty construction and was found in Surrey. The bowl is mandolin-shaped, rather like a small shovel. The handle has moulded decoration while the off-set is in the outline of an eagle's head with an open beak (quite an aggressive posture). At the rear of the handle is a slotted square panel which would have held an iron blade, either for use as a knife or scalpel.

A very specialist utensil is shown in **Pic M163**. This was found in East Anglia and is made of silver. It dates from the 4th century and has a curious flat, comma-shaped terminal. The stem is square sectioned and is moulded with a spiral groove for half of its length. The opposite end has a small angled and flattened head. These utensils would appear to have been an important addition to any tableware of the period and are often combined with strainers. Many suggestions have been made as to their intended use, the most likely being for the eating of shellfish or snails.

Strainers with perforated designs were used for clearing wine and other liquids.

Another specialised form of spoon is the bronze ligula shown in **Pic M164**. This has an elongated narrow bowl which was used for extracting cosmetics or sweetmeats from the narrow glass phials in which they were stored. The stem is quite thin and ends in an olive-shaped probe or pestle.

The object shown in **Pic M165** is an example of a bronze ear scoop; like the ligula it was found at Billingsgate. The ear scoop, with its small, circular bowl was used for removing wax but also served for

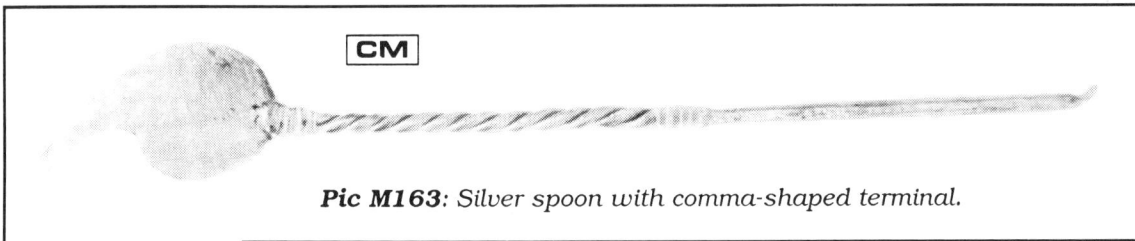

Pic M163: Silver spoon with comma-shaped terminal.

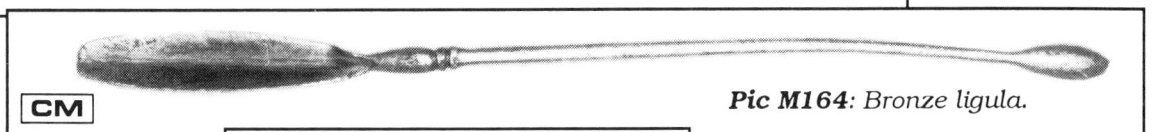

Pic M164: Bronze ligula.

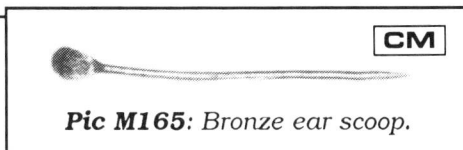

Pic M165: Bronze ear scoop.

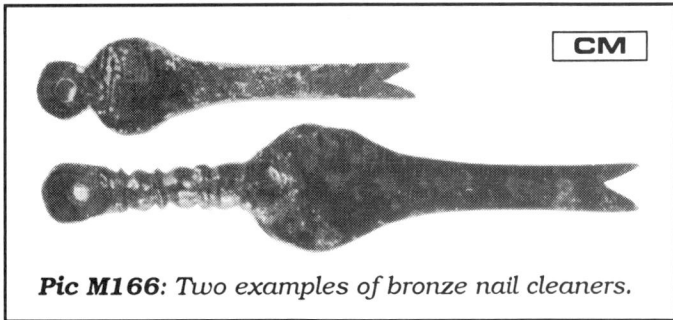

Pic M166: *Two examples of bronze nail cleaners.*

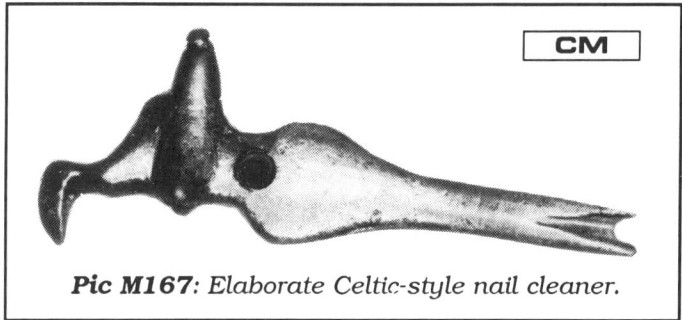

Pic M167: *Elaborate Celtic-style nail cleaner.*

applying medicaments, especially to the ears or eyes.

The scoop would have formed part of a toilet instrument set also comprising: nail cleaners, tweezers, and pick. Large numbers of these manicure sets were in use in Roman Britain, and they were often hung together on a chatelaine from a belt. **Pic M166** shows two examples of bronze nail cleaners which would have formed part of a toilet set; both examples have a suspension loop at one end. The flattened stem bulges out for gripping between the thumb and finger, while the device has a forked tip used for the actual cleaning.

A more elaborate nail cleaner is shown in **Pic M167**. This has a bird with a curved bill at one end, perched on a phallus. Moulded in the round, this piece is Celtic in style and possibly dates from the 1st century AD. It is of heavier construction than the nail cleaners described above, and has its suspension hole below the ornamentation.

Military amulets were often phallic, the symbol representing fertility and good luck, and serving to ward off the evil eye. The use of this design on a nail cleaner, is intriguing.

Nail cleaners were certainly in use during the Celtic period. A discovery has recently been made of a La Tene III (Nauheim) brooch with its pin missing. The brooch had been adapted into a nail cleaner by using the coiled spring as a suspension loop and filing the bow at one end into a forked tip. This adaptation would

date from the first half of the 1st century AD.

Tweezers (Latin name *vulsella*) were made in bronze and used mainly for removing body hair; two examples are shown in **Pic M168**. Depilation was quite fashionable amongst women at the time.

Roman tweezers are usually plain but fairly sturdy; their end grips curve inwards and a suspension loop is provided by bringing the arms into a waist.

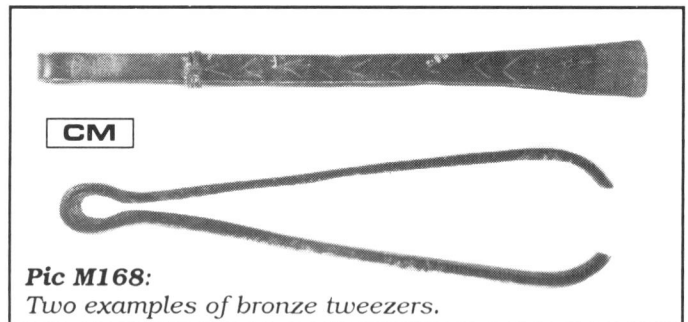

Pic M168:
Two examples of bronze tweezers.

The top pair of tweezers shown in **Pic M168** carries a decoration of incised "V" marks along the length of the arms (a ring and dot pattern would be more usual). This pair of tweezers also has an adjustable coiled band that is intended to be slid along the jaws and to hold the ends together. Roman tweezers are also found with wider ends which may indicate that they were used for holding parchments (a prevalent use for tweezers in the late Saxon and medieval periods).

Cosmetic sets have also been ex-

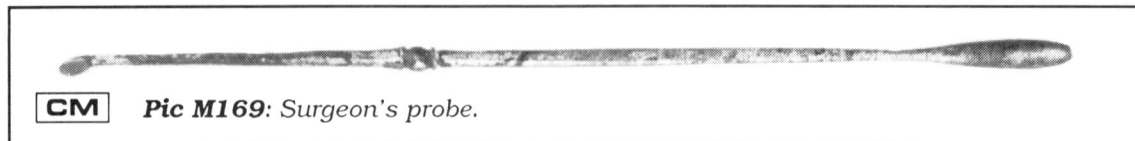

Pic M169: *Surgeon's probe.*

Pic M170: *Combined spatula/ligula medical instrument.*

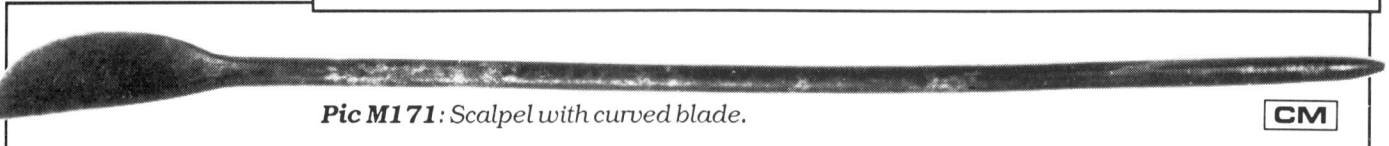

Pic M171: *Scalpel with curved blade.*

Pic M172: *Writing stylus.*

CM

Pic M173: *Bronze chisel.*

cavated alongside more specialised medical instruments. The Romans developed a whole range of surgical tools for operations and treatments and **Pics M169, M170** and **M171** illustrate three such bronze instruments which were found in Britain. **M169** (top) is a *specillum* which is a surgeon's probe. It has a circular flat head which is angled, and an olive-shaped probe is provided at the other end. A few examples of these are known in gold or silver but none have been found in Britain made from precious metal.

The centre item, **M170**, is a spatula with a flattened blade combined with a ligula at the other end (it was quite usual for medical instruments to serve two purposes in this way). The final item, **M171**, found at Billingsgate, is a scalpel with a curved blade.

Some Roman medical implements even use a screw thread in their construction, although these are rare.

The Romans often improvised in the uses to which they put their tools; for example the back of ear scoops were often employed for the treatment of haemorrhoids.

The stylus (**Pic M172**) is also mentioned as serving a surgical purpose besides that intended. This is an implement with a point at one end used for writing on a wax-filled recess in a block of wood. The broad, flat end of the stylus was used for erasing any mistakes made by smoothing out the wax. Styli were usually made of iron inlaid with brass strips, but some examples are of bronze.

Writing on parchment (papyrus or animal skins) was carried out by means of a reed pen or quill with a split nib. Lead tablets were also often engraved with curses which could be hung from doors or walls. The curse was usually an inscription relating to a grudge against another person with the aim of inflicting injury. When excavated, these pieces of lead are often rolled or folded up, so it is always worth checking lead fragments for signs of any such lettering.

Triangular silver plaques, with leaf decoration, can also be found

folded up. These carry dedications to gods, and were originally fixed to the walls of temples.

The bronze implement shown in **Pic M173** is similar to a stylus but is described as a chisel by most sources.

Pic M174 shows a pair of intriguing items previously believed to be perfume or cosmetic grinders. They date from the 1st century BC to the 1st century AD and are essentially Celtic in form. Examples are known decorated with animal terminals and some even have enamel work on their sides. Their distribution is confined to Britain and their purpose is, I believe, now clear. (However, it should be pointed out that the British Museum is strongly opposed to the suggestion; the debate will continue).

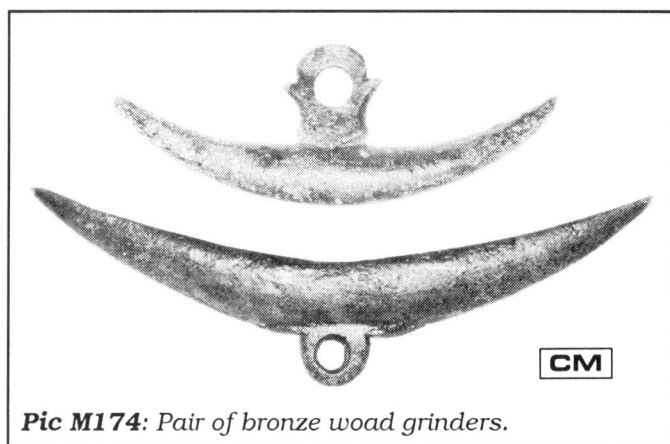

Pic M174: *Pair of bronze woad grinders.*

During the Celtic period in Britain a biennial herb *Isatis Tinctoria* was cultivated for the blue dye that could be obtained from it by crushing. The plant is more commonly known as woad and the ancient Britons painted their bodies with the dye which was obtained by grinding parts of the plant between the pestle shown at the top and the mortar, shown beneath it (there is a channel within the mortar for receiving the pestle).

Once the blue dye was obtained the pestle could serve to apply it to the skin; lines could be drawn using the pestle one way, while the ends would serve for inscribing circles.

The use of woad was an important ritual for all Celtic warriors of the time and this is signified by the cult symbols (bull and human heads)

61

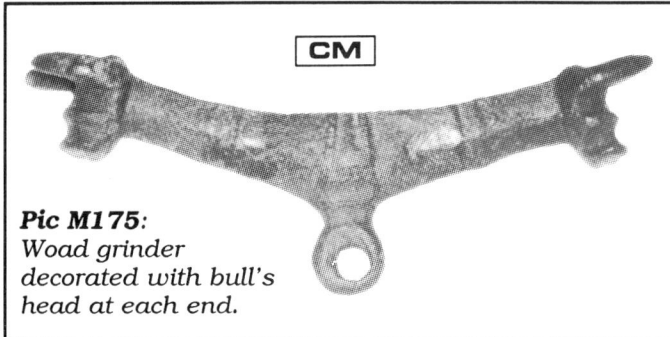

Pic M175:
Woad grinder decorated with bull's head at each end.

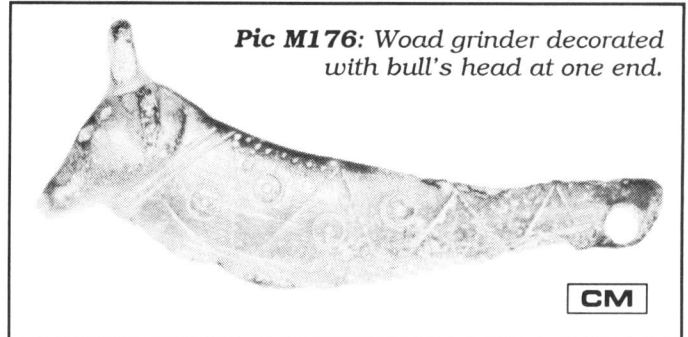

Pic M176: Woad grinder decorated with bull's head at one end.

sometimes appearing on the terminals of the mortar (see **Pic M175**). The fact that provision is made for the two implements to be suspended, meant that they could be carried by a warrior on his person and probably used before going into battle.

Interestingly enough, the most richly ornamented of the woad grinders are those with a loop at one end as opposed to a central loop (see **Pic M176**). The pestle to match would also have had a loop at one end. The decorated examples are rarer and may have different tribal connections. The example shown in **Pic M176** carries a beautifully-moulded bull's head with large horns which appear to have been knobbed. The bull was an emblem of strength and was regarded as one of the masters of the animal world. The sides of the mortar are decorated with ring and dot punch marks placed within a zig-zag formation of lines.

Another very interesting type of Romano-British artefact that detector users might find are the small bronze and enamelled seal boxes with hinged lids - see **Pic M177(a)**. These were used as a simple form of security during the transportation of written messages or of packages. The base of the box was fixed to the package either by nails or by means of a cord passed through the four holes in the bottom (as shown in the half of the box on the left). On each side of the base there is a small slot cut out for another cord to pass through, which would then be placed around the receptacle to be secured. The cord would then have been tied in a knot within the seal box itself, and held in place by wax stamped with a seal (possibly from a ring intaglio). Once this was done, it would have been impossible to remove the cord without breaking the seal.

Most seal boxes have been dated to the 2nd century by a comparison of their decorated lids to designs of Romano-British brooches.

The example shown in **Pic M177(a)**, however, appears to be of an earlier date than this. The box is

rectangular and the lid decorated with an enamelled pattern in Celtic style. In the centre are two discs, enamelled yellow. The geometric patterns around the discs show traces of blue enamel, while traces of red enamel appear in the outer field. (These twin petal designs are referred to as "swash Ns").

The seal box was found intact in East Anglia, and upon being opened a Celtic silver coin was found inside (the outline of the coin is still visible in the corrosion on the underside of the seal box lid). This coin - the reverse side is shown in **Pic M177(b)** - according to Van Arsdell is number 754.1 of the Iceni tribe, and is a silver unit of the Ecen symbol type (c40-45 AD). It has a double crescent emblem on the obverse and a Celticised horse of the reverse with three pellets below.

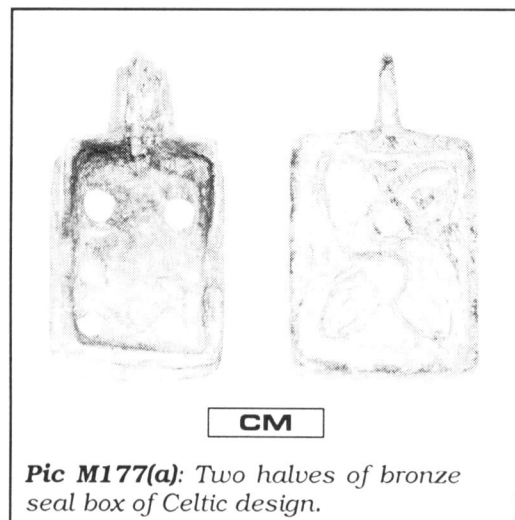

Pic M177(a): Two halves of bronze seal box of Celtic design.

The coin is unlikely to have circulated after the Boudicca rebellion of 61 AD, so the seal box must have been in use prior to that date. The Celtic imagery of the design may indicate an Iceni use and perhaps both Romans and Celts used their own seal boxes when communicating between each other. (The Iceni had been independent allies of the Romans, so there must have been considerable interplay between them).

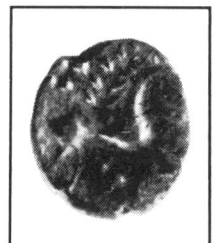

Pic M177(b):
Silver Celtic unit found inside M177(a).

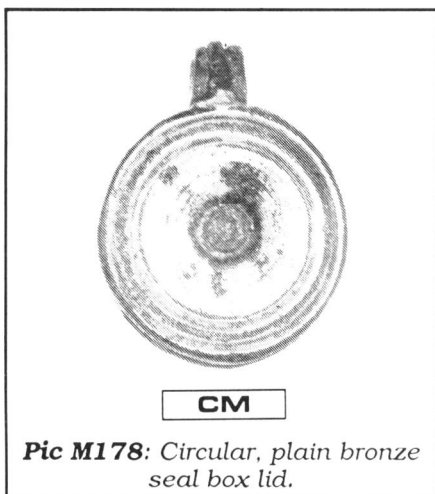

Pic M178: Circular, plain bronze seal box lid.

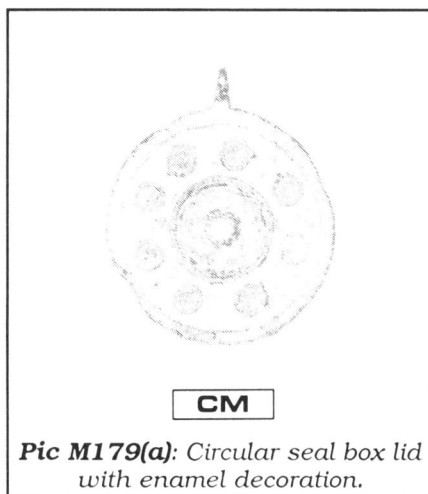

Pic M179(a): Circular seal box lid with enamel decoration.

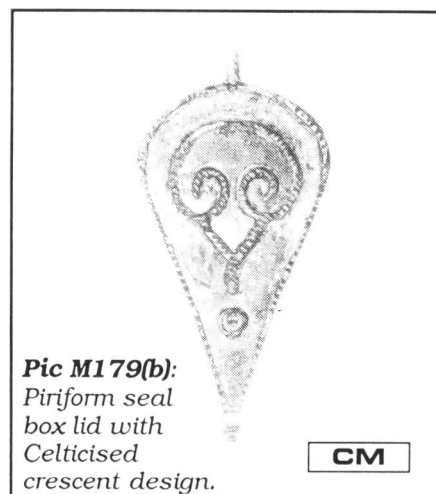

Pic M179(b): Piriform seal box lid with Celticised crescent design.

The shape of seal boxes varies and some examples are plain as that shown in **Pic M178**. This box is circular and has a heavily tinned finish. The base has the usual four holes, but two are large and irregular, indicating use.

Two lids, one circular and one piriform are shown in **Pic M179(a)** and **M179(b)**. The circular example is decorated with eight small circles clustered around a larger circle; traces of enamel remain and the style is Roman. The piriform lid is of a slightly Celticised crescent design. The enamel is yellow but has become stained, while the borders of the design are grooved and heavily tinned. This example comes from Billingsgate in London.

Pic M179(c) shows a piriform seal box lid with a red enamel chevron, and a green enamel background. Pic **M179(d)** shows a lozenge-shaped seal box lid with twenty-five lozenge cells which would originally have contained enamel.

The design of seal box lids varies enormously. A few have even been found with portraits (possibly of emperors) and some have phallic ornamentation. Three examples excavated from the fort at Richborough were all circular and carried animal designs of a bird, frog and hare. I have also seen a seal box found intact, even down to the wax inside.

Price Guide

	Fine	Very Fine
M158: bronze spoon	£125	£275
M159: silver spoon	£300	£750
M160: pewter spoon	£35	£90
M161: bronze egg spoon	£35	£75
M162: spoon/knife combination	£130	£280
M163: silver pick	£250	£600
M164: bronze ligula	£30	£60
M165: bronze ear scoop	£14	£25
M166: bronze nail cleaner	£15	£28
M167: erotic nail cleaner	£60	£175
M168: bronze tweezers	£15	£28
M169: bronze specillum	£30	£55
M170: bronze spatula	£25	£45
M171: bronze scalpel	£25	£45
M172: bronze stylus	£40	£75
M173: bronze chisel	£25	£45
M174: pair bronze woad grinders	£90	£200
M175: woad grinder bull's head decoration at each end	£140	£325
M176: woad grinder, bull's head at one end	£160	£375
M177: seal box, Celtic design	£60	£150
M178: seal box, plain	£30	£65
M179 (a), (b), (c) & (d): seal box lids with decorative designs	£15	£35

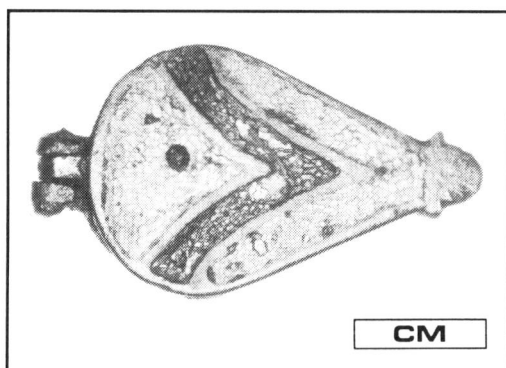

Pic M179(c): Piriform seal box lid with red enamel chevron.

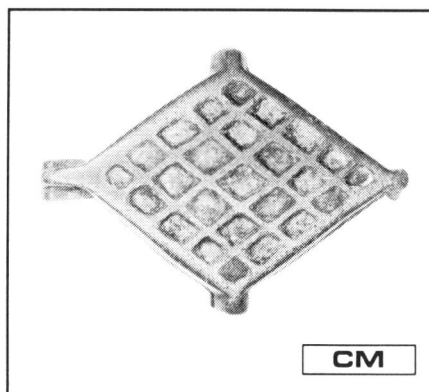

Pic M179(d): Lozenge-shaped seal box lid.

Jewellery

The survival of artefacts in the ground is not only dependent on the type of environment they are buried in, but also the durability of the object itself. This can be affected by the type of metal the artefact is made from, or - in the case of most jewellery from the Roman period - the fragility of design. With most rings, earrings, necklaces and even bracelets, any disturbance of the ground (such as ploughing or erosion) can reduce such artefacts to mere fragments in a very short space of time.

As a result, Roman jewellery is very difficult to find in near-perfect condition, which is a vital prerequisite in terms of high intrinsic value. Any finger ring which is broken or badly cracked will lose up to 80% of its value; this is simple because the object is no longer wearable.

In the Roman period the wearing of jewellery was a significant feature of class distinction, and also served as an indication of rank. In the early years of the Roman Empire severe restrictions were placed on the wearing of gold rings. Gold was used for special occasions and by those in high office only. Up until the end of the 1st century AD, iron was the metal employed for everyday use. Bronze was not popular at first and the large seal rings worn by men were usually of silver or iron.

The problem so far as detectorists are concerned, is that iron is a ferrous metal which most metal detectors now have the ability to reject. Even when iron rings are found and have survived intact, the metal has usually expanded as a result of rust, causing the intaglio or seal in the bezel to crack.

Bronze and silver rings were used extensively throughout the Occupation of Britain. Most Roman gold rings found, however, date from the 3rd or 4th century when cost was the only restriction placed on their use. The prestige value of gold rings can be appreciated from the fact that it was not until 197 AD that the Emperor Septimius Severus granted permission for all soldiers to wear a gold ring. (It is also believed that some military awards would have included the wearing of a large gold ring with a gold coin mounted in the bezel).

For jewellery, the Romans used

Pic M180.
Bronze ring
with coils.

CM

high carat, almost pure gold which is very soft and a vivid yellow in colour. This often distinguishes such finds from later rings where the quality of the gold is more varied and debased.

Accounts tell us that in the late 3rd century wealthy Roman citizens wore an abundance of jewellery and one man was noted for having six rings on every finger. This would mean that both the upper and the lower joints of each finger would have been used to retain the rings. Many of the small rings that are found were probably intended for the top joint, otherwise they would have only fitted the fingers of children. Also, rings that have a flattened bezel and shoulders (which is a distinctive Roman fashion) would seem intended for wear on the top finger joint.

It is difficult to accurately date many of the simple types of bronze rings as many will have seen a long period of use, and some were quite crudely made.

Pic M181.
Celtic bronze ring.

CM

Pic M180 shows a small bronze finger ring which was found in London in a 1st century context. However, this conflicts with other reports which point to a 4th century date. There are also rings, in a very similar style, dating from the medieval period. The ring is decorated with two parallel lines of four flattened coils, with the ends wound around the shank.

Another early bronze ring (see **Pic M181**) features a Celtic design. The circular bezel has four piriform enamelled cells around a central ring and dot design. Two of the cells retain their blue enamel. The design ap-

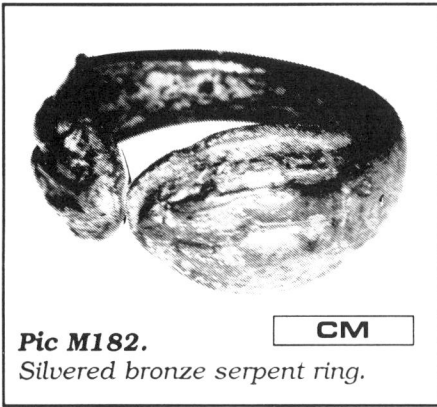

Pic M182.
Silvered bronze serpent ring.

Pic M183.
Bronze snakes head ring.

Pic M184.
Bronze snakes head ring of crude style.

pears to be based on a swastika motif with four arms radiating out and curving back.

Pic M182 is an example of a serpent penannular ring in bronze which has been tinned or silvered. The two large and flattened snakes' heads face each other in a similar way to those on the Roman bracelet shown in **Pic M212**.

The bronze ring shown in **Pic M183** is of a more usual form with the snakes' heads being situated alongside one another and facing in opposite directions. The hoop of the ring is flattened at the top, and then each end is bent around.

The use of snakes in jewellery design is widespread which must be partly due to the association of the snake with the Roman healing god Aesculapis. The snake was thus thought to have regenerative properties and the wearing of a snake ring was believed to bring good health. The snake also has underworld symbolism and was often used as a means of warding off evil spirits. Finally, the snake was looked upon as a symbol of fertility.

Snake rings were at their most popular in the late 1st and early 2nd centuries AD. They were usually made from silver or bronze, and sometimes had ornamental decoration between the snakes' heads.

Pic M184 shows a very crude ring from East Anglia. It has simple, flattened terminals resembling snakes' heads and was probably of local manufacture.

Roman rings are often set with an intaglio or have an engraved bezel. This acted as a seal for the wearer which was a customary form of security and signature. Each seal had to be different to prevent forgery or confusion, while the quality of the engraving or the type of stone used would again be an indication of rank.

In Britain, the use of blue or green glass set into a bronze ring would appear to have been the commonest form of intaglios. **Pic M185** shows the top half of a bronze ring with an oval green glass intaglio. This is moulded with the impression of a standing figure which resembles Hercules brandishing his club. Dating from the 3rd century it represents the general poor quality of intaglios used in Britain at that time.

Many different stones, as well as glass imitations, were used as seals and most would have been imported into Britain. The stones you are most likely to come across are: carnelian (a translucent orange-red colour); jasper (opaque, often red, green or brown); nicolo (layered onyx in blue); amethyst (mauve); and onyx (a form of agate banded white and blue-grey, but can also be black banded).

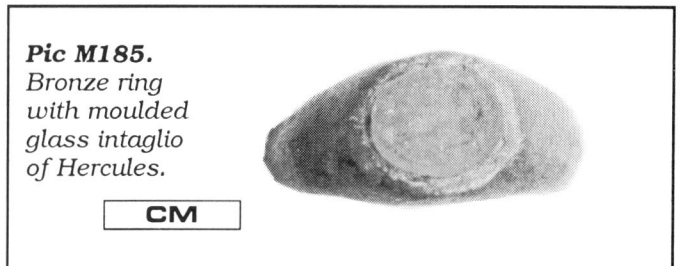

Pic M185.
Bronze ring with moulded glass intaglio of Hercules.

The first three stones were those most commonly used in Britain and were generally used in gold or silver settings; in contrast, the glass imitations were set in bronze rings.

Representations of many different deities, animals, birds, or even groups of figures occur in the design of intaglios. In the 1st and 2nd centuries AD the style of engraving was very delicate with fine detail, while the ring itself was normally plain.

From the 3rd century onwards the fashion changed and the ring itself became more ornamental, sometimes with filigree (open work) or elaborate decoration. The stones used were more colourful but not so finely engraved, although earlier stones were reused and even re-cut in the 4th century. There was also less distinction at this time between glass and precious stones owing to the emphasis on colour.

The bronze ring shown in **Pic**

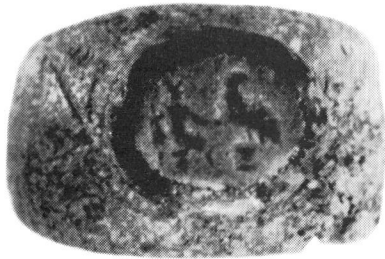

Pic M186.
Bronze ring with moulded blue glass intaglio of Jupiter with an eagle.

CM

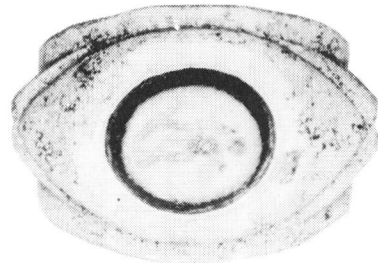

Pic M187.
Bronze ring with moulded blue glass intaglio.

CM

M186 (probably 2nd century) has a blue glass intaglio imitating nicolo. The intaglio is moulded rather than hand-cut which would have been the case had the stone been genuine nicolo. The design is of a seated figure (possibly Jupiter) with a bird in front (either a raven or eagle). The eagle was associated with Jupiter and was normally shown with its wings folded and its head turned (as in this case). Jupiter was the sky god and the chief Roman deity to be invoked before any undertaking.

The ring shank is narrow at the back but widens at the shoulders to create a much larger and ostenta-

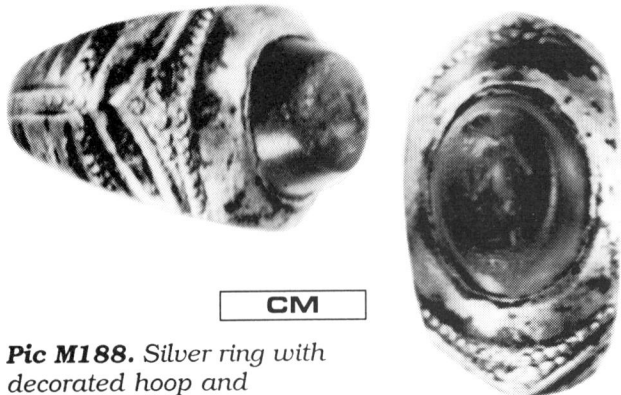

CM

Pic M188. *Silver ring with decorated hoop and carnelian intaglio.*

tious appearance. The shoulders of the ring are also decorated with incised dots and lines, unusual for this date. It is thought that the ring may have had military significance.

Pic M187 is another bronze ring, having a large pointed oval bezel which is raised up from the hoop of the ring. The glass intaglio is blue and moulded with a standing figure which appears to have a rudder beside it (which could indicate Fortuna). She also looks to be holding a cornucopia. The intaglio is raised and the ring may be late 2nd to 3rd century AD in date.

The silver ring shown in **Pic M188** has its shank decorated by a series of grooves and circular punches. The bezel, which again expands at the shoulders, is set with a carnelian intaglio (a replacement, not the origi-

nal) with the standing figure of Victory, left. The raised nature of the stone is common to rings dating from the 3rd century onwards. The ring itself possibly dates late 2nd century.

Pic M189 shows a silver ring set with a very attractive red jasper intaglio representing a bird with two seed pods hanging from its beak. The way to distinguish jasper from carnelian is that the former is opaque and does not allow light to pass through it. The colour of jasper is also usually much darker and richer than that of carnelian, which is translucent.

The design of a bird holding something in its beak is quite common to Roman Britain and represents fruitfulness or prosperity.

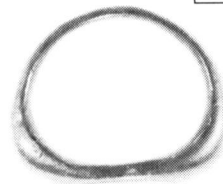

CM

CM

Pic M189. *Silver ring with red jasper intaglio.*

The ring dates from the early 2nd century and has a plain shank with a flattened, slightly expanded bezel. Notice how the intaglio has been tailor-made for the ring, being carefully concealed in its setting and blending perfectly with the overall shape of the ring. This distinctive style and shape is normal for silver rings of this period.

Pic M190 shows another silver ring with a larger intaglio (in blue nicolo) of a female head facing left. As nicolo is layered, different shades of colour can be revealed when engraving the stones, thereby highlighting the design. This is a typical feature of Roman gem cutting. The intaglio takes up virtually the whole width of the bezel of the ring and is only slightly raised from the surface. This example is mid-2nd century in date.

Another silver ring is shown in **Pic M191**, this time with a well-cut

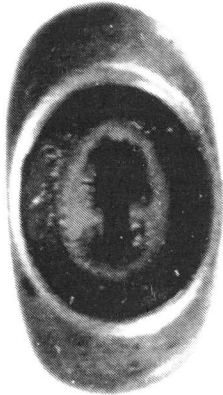

Pic M190.
Silver ring with nicolo intaglio.

CM

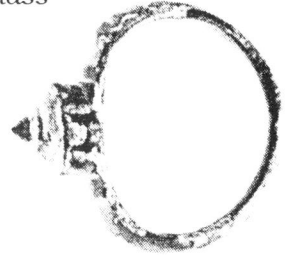

Pic M191.
Silver ring with red carnelian intaglio.

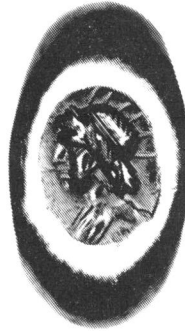

Pic M192.
Bronze ring with glass cone.

CM

carnelian intaglio representing the head of Sol, the sun god. His head is shown radiate, the lines representing the rays of the sun. The intaglio has a slightly ragged edge and is also cracked, so it is probably one that has been re-used from another ring. It has been deeply set into the ring, possibly to protect it from further damage. This ring dates early 2nd century AD.

When the intaglio is cracked in this way it does, unfortunately, reduce the overall value of the ring. There are many other types of rings from the Roman period other than seal rings and some of them are quite simple in design.

Pic M192 shows a bronze ring with a raised bezel set with a piece of moulded green glass in the shape of a cone or pyramid. Sometimes diamonds were inverted in this way to form a writing instrument like a stylus, but in this example the design may be purely decorative.

A number of Romano-British rings have a bezel inset with enamel, as with the example shown in **Pic M193**. Here the flat, rectangular bezel has been divided into four equal segments inlaid, alternately, with red or yellow enamel (one of the segments is missing). The ring probably dates 2nd century and compares in design with some Romano-Celtic dress fasteners. The hoop on this ring is quite thin and has broken, while the solid bezel is quite thick and heavy.

Pic M194 shows an unusual

bronze ring which has a very delicate shank. This is thin and flat in section with a lozenge-shaped bezel, decorated by means of a series of nodules. This ring is difficult to date with any accuracy.

Besides the metals already mentioned of gold, silver, bronze and iron, jewellery made from pewter or lead was certainly worn by the Romans. **Pic M195** shows a base pewter ring dating to the 3rd or 4th century. There must have been many such rings made in the Roman period but few have survived, having suffered the corrosive effects of burial in dry soil. The ring has a small raised circular bezel with wide, sloping shoulders and a fairly thick hoop.

Rings, amulets and bracelets were also carved from bone and jet (a black, fossilised wood) while ivory, shale and glass were amongst the materials used for bracelets worn by women. Jet was a popular material in the making of amulets and was regarded as having mystical qualities for women.

Finds of these materials require a keen eye on the part of the searcher if he is to stand any chance of recovering them during fieldwalking.

The designs used on rings can reflect the superstitions and beliefs prevalent at the time. **Pic M196** shows a silver ring set with a single gold stud in the bezel. This was intended to act as an "eye" to keep away evil

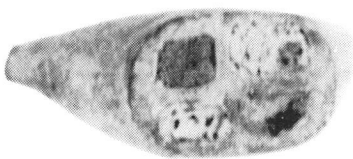

Pic M193.
Bronze ring with quartered panels.

CM

Pic M194.
Bronze ring with lozenge-shaped bezel.

CM

Pic M195.
Pewter or lead ring.

CM

Pic M196.
Silver ring with gold stud.

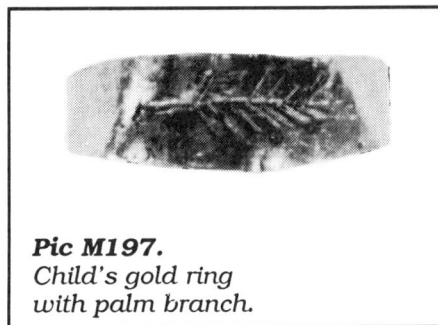

Pic M197.
Child's gold ring
with palm branch.

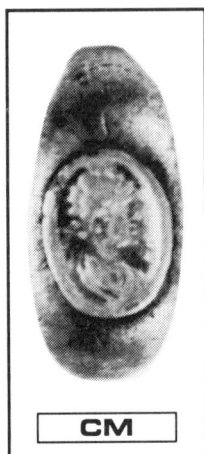

Pic M198.
Silver ring
with inset bust
of man.

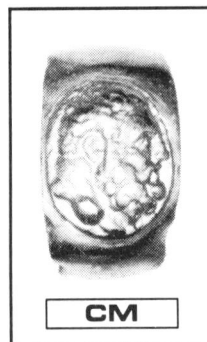

Pic M199.
Gold ring
with inset of
Hercules head.

spirits and thereby bring good luck to the wearer. Such rings are rare finds in Britain.

Other symbols, such as the phallus, were also used to ward off the evil eye, principally for children. The gold ring shown in **Pic M197** was recovered from a Thames-side spoil heap and is so small that only a child could have worn it. The ring has a simple engraved leaf or palm branch on the slightly expanded bezel and this may have been intended to protect the child from disease. This ring dates 3rd or 4th century and is again a rare find for Britain, although examples are common in the eastern part of the Roman Empire.

A few Roman rings are known with metal inserts in their bezels rather than stones, as the example shown in **Pic M198**. This silver ring has an oval silver bezel of a higher purity inserted into the ring. It shows a young male bust in relief, and resembles the depiction of an emperor in style. The ring is 2nd century in date although the silver mount may be a later replacement (perhaps no suitable gems were available at the time).

Another example of this style of ring is shown in **Pic M199** which is in gold. It has a finely moulded oval bezel with the bearded and muscular head of Hercules in relief.

Pic M200 shows an interesting silver ring with eight lozenge-shaped panels. It also has a raised central band, which is ribbed. This ring was found in Suffolk in association with 4th century Roman coins. It is worth noting that Roman rings often have

eight sides, while medieval rings are more usually ten-sided (the sides standing for ten Hail Marys, or prayers).

Another small ring, intended for wear by a woman or child is shown in **Pic M201**. This is a wide-banded plain gold ring with an oval green enamel inlaid bezel, which again may represent an eye to ward off evil spirits. It would date 3rd-4th century.

Inscriptions on rings of the period usually refer to love, good luck or long life. **Pic M202** shows a small bronze ring with the lettering AMO AMA standing for "My Love".

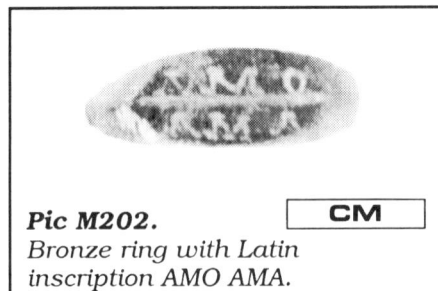

Pic M202.
Bronze ring with Latin
inscription AMO AMA.

The silver ring shown in **Pic M203** has a raised circular bezel with a retrograde inscription which is difficult to read, although I think the interpretation of PCN or PON to be likely. This could be the abbreviation of a motto, or the initials of somebody's name. This ring is 3rd century in date.

An enigmatic series of rings in silver and bronze bear the inscription TOT on their bezels (**Pic M204**). This is believed to be a corruption of the word VOTIS which appears on many Roman coins representing a

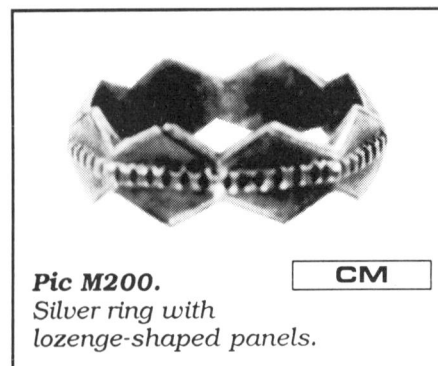

Pic M200.
Silver ring with
lozenge-shaped panels.

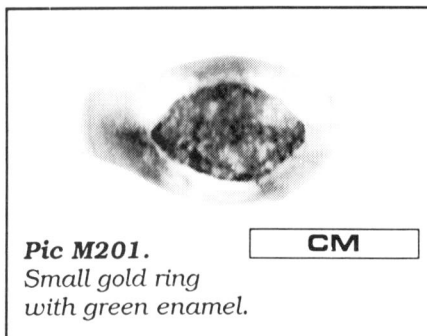

Pic M201.
Small gold ring
with green enamel.

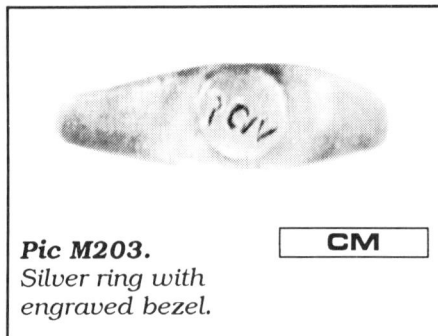

Pic M203.
Silver ring with
engraved bezel.

Pic M204.
Silver ring with TOT inscription.

Pic M205.
Silver ring with UTERE FELIXB inscription.

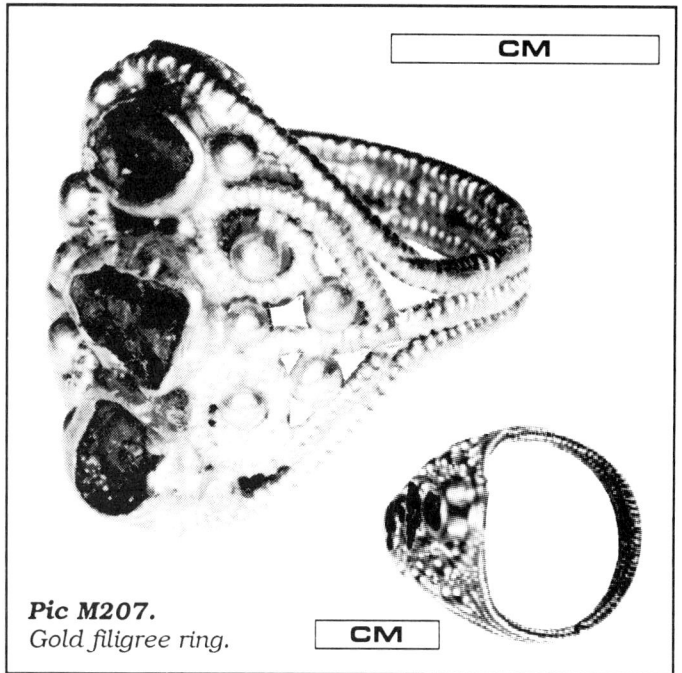

Pic M207.
Gold filigree ring.

pledge or vow from the Emperor. The word also appears on early Saxon sceats incorporated into the reverse design, although this may not have a connection to the ring inscription as the coins are 7th century in date.

The TOT rings are of late-Roman or Saxon and date from the 5th century. Coming from Lincolnshire, one example has DLO over TOT. This could be a dedication or pledge by the wearer.

A popular inscription that occurs repeatedly throughout the Roman period is used on the silver ring shown in **Pic M205**. It reads UTERE FELIXB meaning "Good Luck to the User". Other inscriptions include AVE MEA VITA ("Hail My Life") and MIHI VIVAS ("Live For Me").

Roman gold rings of continental origin are often hollow and filled with sulphur. This acts as a packing for the ring while keeping down its weight. The ring also benefits from this packing in that it keeps its shape

and the intaglio is kept in place.

Many of these rings may have been votive as their durability is suspect. They are rarely found in Britain and such examples that come to light are usually in a squashed flat or broken condition.

Examples of late Roman gold rings made in Britain are chiefly represented by the Thetford Treasure which dates to the 4th century. The Thetford style of workmanship is to be seen on many rings found in East Anglia and which also date to this period.

Pic M206 shows a fine quality gold ring of the 4th century. It has a flat, wide-banded hoop with a raised oval box setting surrounded by a projecting rope flange. Eleven small globules have been added to the shoulders each side to form a triangular shape (a bunch of grapes). The layered brown and white intaglio is possibly agate, and the design of the intaglio is that of an amphora.

Another example of a 4th century Romano-British gold ring is that shown in **Pic M207**; this is of open-work or filigree design. The hoop is formed from solid beaded bands while

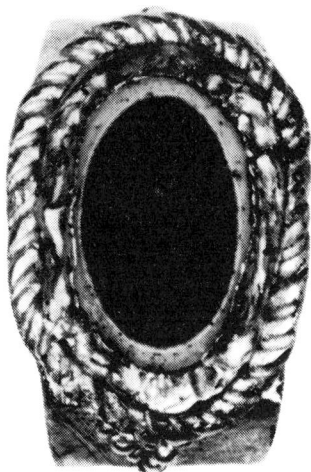

Pic M206.
Gold ring with agate intaglio.

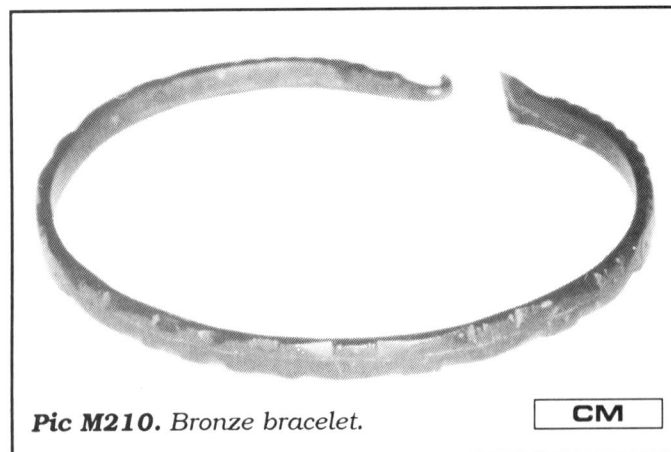

Pic M209.
Gold earring.

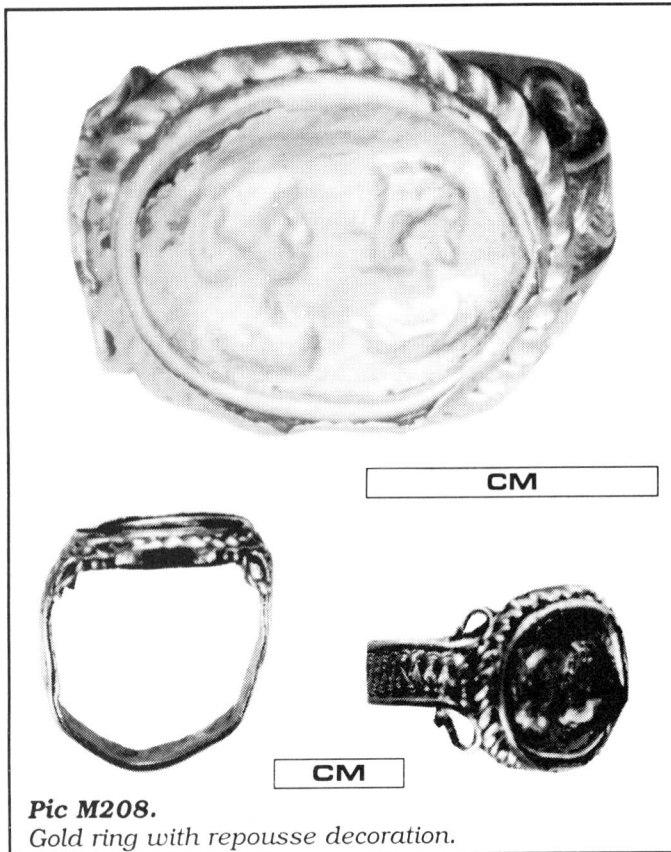

CM

Pic M208.
Gold ring with repousse decoration.

around the bezel. The oval box setting is flatter than that of the previous example and has a rope flange border. Inset into the bezel is a gold plaque punched in repousse with the design of a male and female bust facing one another.

This is a betrothal ring, more commonly represented by clasped hands. It may date from the 5th or even 6th century.

Earrings were in use throughout the Roman world but are rare finds in Britain. **Pic M209** shows an example in gold. The design is circular with eight piriform perforations. In the centre is a deep recess which may have held either a pearl or stone which is now missing. It would date 3rd or 4th century AD.

Bronze and silver bracelets deriving from the Roman period are not rare finds in Britain but usually come to light damaged. Most were worn by women on their arms, wrists or ankles and different Latin names were given to them such as *compes*, *dextrale* or *spathalium*. Those found in Britain are usually of simple design. **Pic M210** shows a square section bracelet, with faceted edges and carrying a ring and dot design.

A slightly more elaborate example is shown in **Pic M211**. This has a ring and dot design, interspersed with grooves. Both of these bracelets date

the bezel has filigree spirals with pairs of globules in each centre. Across the width of the expanded bezel are three box settings in a line, each of which contains fragments of green glass.

During the 4th-5th centuries repousse decoration was used, as **Pic M208** exemplifies. Here the hoop is flat with bands of plaited gold wire fixed to it, and bordered each side by thick bands which are coiled back

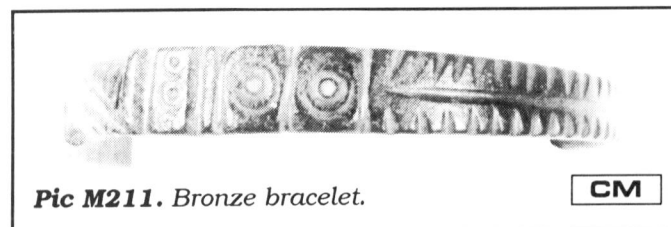

Pic M210. Bronze bracelet.

CM

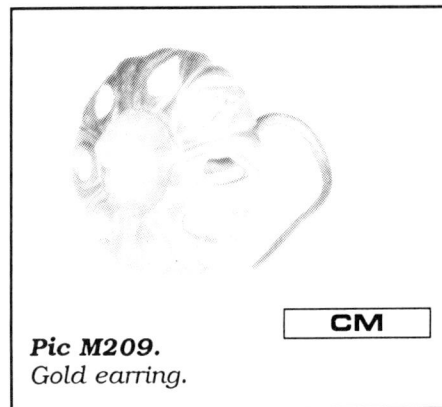

Pic M211. Bronze bracelet.

CM

Pic M212.
Bronze snake headed bracelet.

CM

3rd-4th century, while the simple serpent-headed bracelet shown in **Pic M212** is earlier. This is decorated with three lines of punched dots.

The unusual silver bracelet shown in **Pic M213** was found in Kent. It is made of silver wire, with four silver globules concealing the catch. On either side are two twisted rope design loops for additional fastening or attachment. This example would be 4th century in date.

The other most common type of bracelet is made up of twisted strands, while some have a spiral fastening.

Pic M213.
Silver bracelet with globule decoration.

CM

Price Guide

	Fine	Very Fine		Fine	Very Fine
M180: bronze ring with coils	£35	£85	M195: pewter or lead ring	£20	£45
M181: Celtic bronze ring	£100	£240	M196: silver ring with gold stud	£120	£250
M182: silvered bronze serpent ring	£55	£140	M197: child's gold ring with palm	£65	£140
M183: bronze snake's head ring	£75	£180	M198: silver ring with inset bust of man	£130	£285
M184: crude style bronze snake's head ring	£25	£65	M199: gold ring with inset of Hercules head	£450	£1,100
M185: bronze ring with moulded glass intaglio of Hercules	£45	£120	M200: silver ring with lozenge shaped panels	£100	£220
M186: bronze ring with moulded glass intaglio of Jupiter and eagle	£65	£150	M201: small gold ring with green enamel	£110	£240
M187: bronze ring with moulded blue glass intaglio	£70	£165	M202: bronze ring with inscription AMO AMA	£55	£140
M188: silver ring with decorated hoop and carnelian intaglio	£120	£260	M203: silver ring with engraved bezel	£80	£175
M189: silver ring with red jasper intaglio	£100	£225	M204: silver ring TOT inscription	£120	£250
M190: silver ring with nicolo intaglio	£110	£250	M205: silver ring UTERE FELIXB inscription	£125	£250
M191: silver ring with carnelian intaglio	£125	£275	M206: gold ring with agate intaglio	£650	£1,300
M192: bronze ring with glass cone	£35	£85	M207: gold filigree ring	£675	£1,400
M193: bronze ring with quartered panels	£45	£125	M208: gold ring with repousse decoration	£1,500	£3,500
M194: bronze ring with lozenge shaped bezel	£25	£60	M209: gold earring	£70	£150
			M210: bronze bracelet	£40	£100
			M211: bronze bracelet	£50	£120
			M212: bronze snake headed bracelet	£60	£130
			M213: silver bracelet with globule decoration	£125	£275

Chapter VIII

Cube Matrices & Lead Seals

In 1982, a metal detector user in Shropshire found a curious cube-shaped object. The find was made in a field which - in the past - had produced Roman coins. Upon his arrival home, he washed the dirt from the object and noticed that each side carried an engraved design resembling the obverse or reverse of a silver coin of the 2nd century AD.

Thinking that the cube may have been a form of Roman coin die, the finder sent it to London where a contact took it along to the British Museum. Unfortunately, they were unable to supply any further information and eventually dismissed the cube as a "piece of Victorian jewellery". Despite this, the finder still believed the cube to be Roman, and as I knew him fairly well it eventually came into my possession.

Pic M214(a).
Roman bronze
cube matrix.

CM

The cube is 25-28mm square, and has been cast from solid bronze with circular incised designs on each of its six faces. These resemble three obverse and three reverse designs used on the coins of Antoninus Pius and Marcus Aurelius. They are as follows:-

1. ANTONINUS AUG PIUS PP
   (Laureate head right).
2. ANTONINUS AUGUSTUS PP
   (Laureate head right).
3. M AURELIUS CAESAR ANTONINI
   (Bare head right).

In the case of 2 and 3, the obverse legends are not to be found on any contemporary coins. The designs date from 138-161 AD with the Marcus Aurelius legend dating to 149-152 AD. This side has been re-engraved because it is set much deeper in the cube, and it may have replaced another portrait of Antoninus Pius.

Pic M214(b).
Side 1 of the
matrix reading
"Antoninus
Aug Pius PP"

Pic M214(c).
Side 2
reading
"Antoninus
Augustus II"

Pic M214(d).
Side 3
reading
"M Aurelius
Antonini"

Pic M214(e).
Side 4,
"Cos III",
Fortuna
standing left

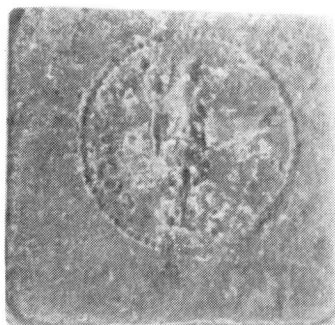

Pic M214(f).
Side 5,
"Imp II Cos II".
Mars walking
left.

Pic M214(g).
Side 6,
"Cos III",
clasped
hands.

The three reverse designs are as follows:-
4. COS III
   (Fortuna standing left).
5. IMP II COS II
   (Mars walking left).
6. COS III
   (Clasped hands).

The engraving is of a very high quality and could have been carried out by an official die cutter. The cube, however, could not have been used to make coins as the force of the strike needed for their production would have damaged the opposite side. The cube would therefore have been held and used by hand to form an impression. The material receiving the impression would have needed to be soft and perhaps clay, wax or even lead was used.

This would mean that the cube was a form of seal matrix employed for security purposes by an official or merchant.

Interestingly enough, two other similar cube matrices have been found in this country, and both have been classified as Roman. One is in the British Museum. The other, found at Kingscote in Gloucestershire, has been well-documented by Martin Henig in "Chesalls Kingscote Excavations, 1975-76 Season".

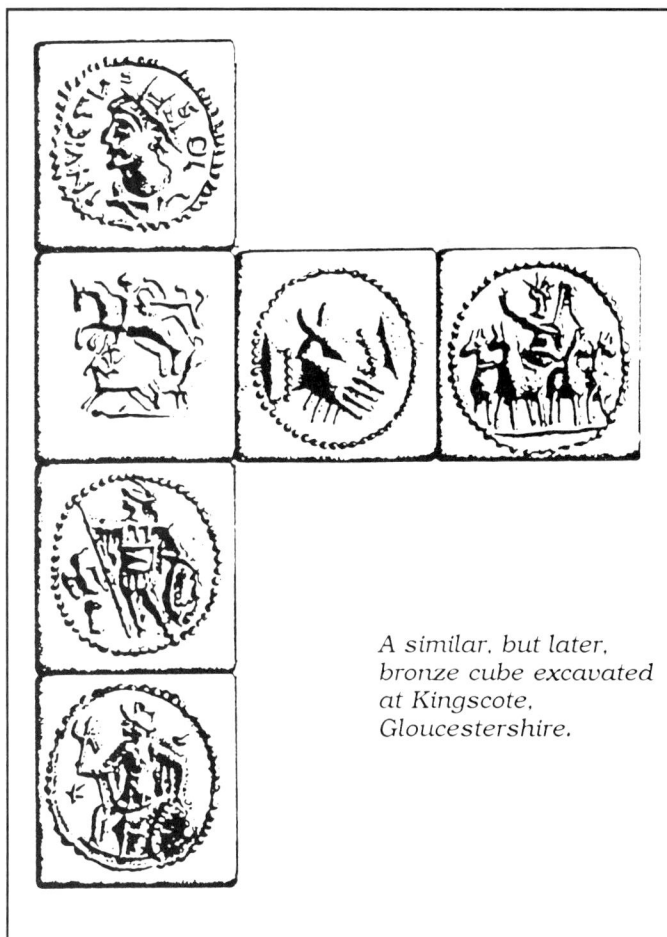

A similar, but later, bronze cube excavated at Kingscote, Gloucestershire.

The latter cube is smaller than my example (15-19mm square), but is again of bronze. The designs are more barbarous in style, one side carrying the legend INVICTUS SOL with a bust of Sol facing left. The other devices are Roma seated, Mars, Sol in quadrigu, the clasped hands of

73

Concord, and a hunting scene. The last face has no beaded border.

The dating on this cube, based on the context in which it was found and from the designs, is suggested as being 270-280 AD.

An element of mystery still surrounds these cube matrices. All three known examples are undoubtedly Roman, but who actually used them? Whether they were used to produce official or unofficial seals is also unclear (at this period certain documents or even storage bags, would have been secured by seals to prevent unofficial tampering).

So far as I am aware, no further examples have been unearthed since 1982, but I am sure than sooner or later another cube matrix will turn up and lead us to a greater understanding of their use.

Lead Seals

The use of seals - whether of clay, wax or lead - was an important part of Roman trade, and they helped prevent merchandise being tampered with either during transportation or while being stored.

Only the lead seals have survived the ravages of time, and from a number of different sites in Britain over 300 Roman lead seals have been found. They would have been used as a form of security on cargoes or supplies mainly intended for the Legions or important officials; very few Roman lead seals found in Britain derive from private merchants.

Roman lead seals are usually quite thick, of rectangular or circular shape, and have designs stamped on one or both sides of them. Through the middle of the seal is an opening, where a cord would have been passed to enable the device to be secured to a parcel or package.

A number of lead seals have been found in London on Roman sites at the side of the Thames where boats would have been unloaded. Other seals have been found near Roman fort sites where stores of merchandise would have been kept.

Pic M215 shows a Roman lead seal carrying the pictorial design of a Roman emperor holding a spear and charging on his horse. Two other seals with this have been found: one at Richborough, and the other at

Pic M215.
Lead seal showing mounted emperor.

CM

Felixstowe (both Roman forts). The dating has been given as 3rd-4th century AD, and the design resembles coin reverses showing the emperor spearing a fallen soldier.

Pic M216 shows an oval lead seal with a standing figure of Genius holding a cornucopia and patera. The

Pic M216.
Lead seal depicting Genius.

CM

legend around it reads STAREL INP. ST(ationis) AREL(atensis) INP which translates as "Seal of the Office at Arles". The seal is in excellent condition, having been found at Billingsgate in London, and shows that official taxation had been paid on a cargo imported from the Mediterranean (possibly wine).

The much cruder seal shown in **Pic M217** also depicts a figure holding a cornucopia, but no legend is visible.

Pic M217.
Lead seal showing standing figure.

CM

Pic M218. *Lead seal reading "LIIA" and "FIT".*

Pic M221. Lead seal showing three busts of emperors.

A number of seals are not pictorial but instead carry letters and numbers referring to Legions that were operating in Britain. An example is shown in **Pics M218(a)** and **(b)**. On one side of the seal is L II A, which stands for "Legio II Augusta". On the other side are the letters FIT, possibly standing for *Fictor* or "made this".

Some of the Legion seals carry the letters EXP standing for *Expedivit* or "despatched". Seals for the 2nd, 6th, and 20th Legions have all been found in Britain.

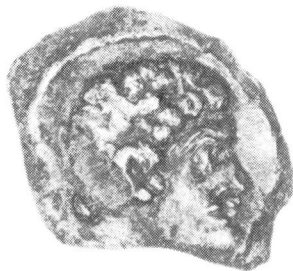

Pic M219. Lead seal showing bust.

Pic M220. Lead seal showing walking Victory.

Pic M219 shows a seal depicting an emperor of the Constantine family, while **Pic M220** shows a standing figure of Victory with the letters C.V. in front. These letters might mean *Cohortis V*, a cohort being a division of infantry.

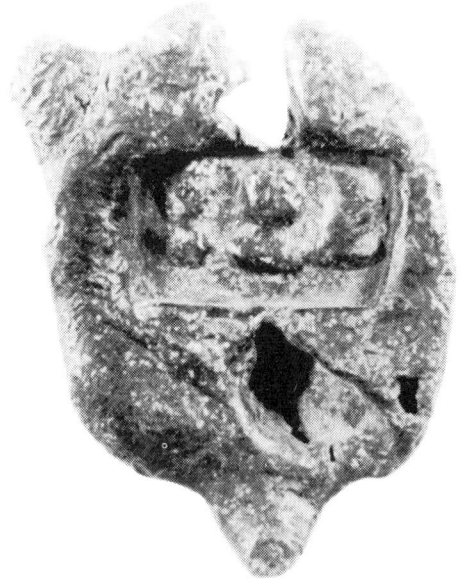

Another group of pictorial seals (see **Pic M221**) feature the busts of three emperors (Septimus Severus, Caracalla, and Geta) side by side; this would indicate that the seals had an official or civic use.

A curious lead plaque is shown in **Pic M222** which may have been a weight, decorative fitting, or even some sort of seal. Recovered from the Billingsgate spoil heaps, London, it features a man and women in an amorous posture.

Most of the lead seals found by detector users will date from the 16th to 18th centuries when they were used to seal bales of wool (at that time, one of England's most important exports).

Very often such seals will show symbols associated with the merchant concerned and sometimes Roman numerals indicating the length of material in the bale. However, if you have some of these seals it is worth carrying out a careful check of them. It is possible that amongst them you may have a seal from the Roman period.

Pic M222. Lead inset showing man and woman.

Price Guide

	Fine	Very Fine		Fine	Very Fine
M214: Roman bronze cube matrix	£550	£1,800	M219: lead seal, of bust	£20	£45
M215: lead seal of mounted emperor	£20	£45	M220: lead seal, walking Victory	£12	£30
M216: lead seal of Genius	£30	£65	M221: lead seal, three busts of emperors	£25	£55
M217: lead seal, standing figure	£12	£25	M222: lead inset showing man and woman	£12	£25
M218: lead seal, LIIA, FIT	£10	£20			

Chapter IX

Pottery and Bronze Utensils

Finding pot shards is an important part of fieldwalking, for even small fragments can be identified and dated, thus revealing a lot of interesting information about an area.

Plain and coarse Roman pottery can be quite difficult to differentiate from pottery of the Saxon and medieval periods unless you have the necessary expertise; but some pottery from the Roman period, such as Samian ware, is quite distinctive.

Samian ware was mainly produced in Gaul during the 1st to 3rd centuries AD and is of a red gloss colour with a smooth and shiny appearance. If this surface chips or wears off then a duller and rougher texture is exposed underneath.

Pic M223 shows a Samian conical cup made during the 2nd century AD. It is plain, having had most of its red gloss rubbed off.

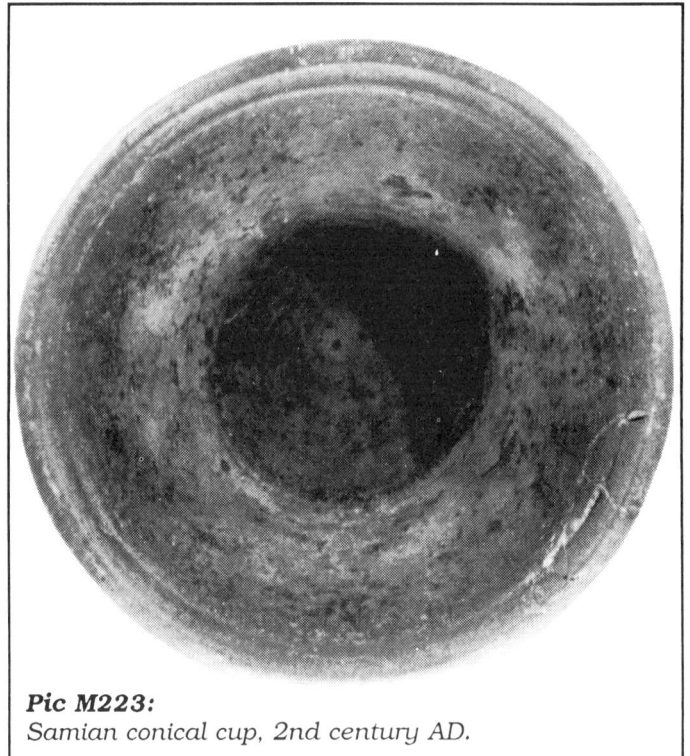

Pic M223:
Samian conical cup, 2nd century AD.

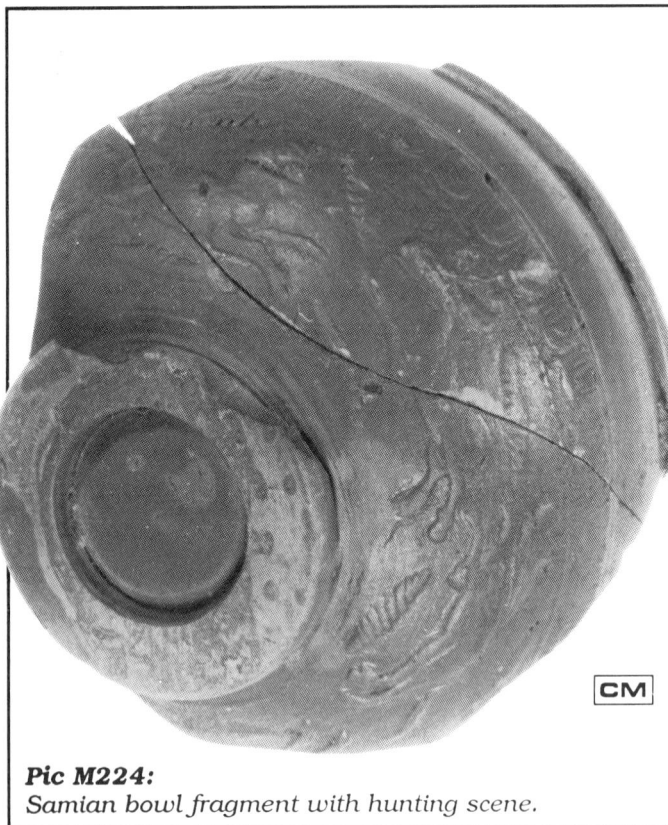

Pic M224:
Samian bowl fragment with hunting scene.

Many Samian vessels are stamped with the potter's name in a regular panel on the base. **Pic M224** shows part of a decorated Samian bowl portraying a hunting scene involving running dogs. Above this is an ovolo pattern which is a common design to be found on Samian pottery. Panels containing figures and animals were a decorative feature of Samian ware which was regarded as the best tableware.

Castor ware, which is slate coloured, is another type of pottery dating to the 2nd century AD and was also sometimes decorated with hunting scenes.

Pic M225 is a beaker with a dark grey slip; it has white over-painted strips of zig-zag form around the centre.

Bowls, dishes, flagons, and amphorae were all in everyday use in Roman times, as were pottery lamps which contained oil and had a wick protruding from their spout. They are also sometimes found decorated with designs in the middle and maker's marks. Virtually all of the examples that are on open sale in Britain originate from North Africa or the Middle East.

Bronze vessels of British origin are rare, and are often damaged when found. **Pic M226** shows a bronze oil flask or *balsamarium* found in the Fens. It has survived intact with only slight damage to its body, which is globular. The vessel has been moulded in two halves, which were then joined together around the mid-

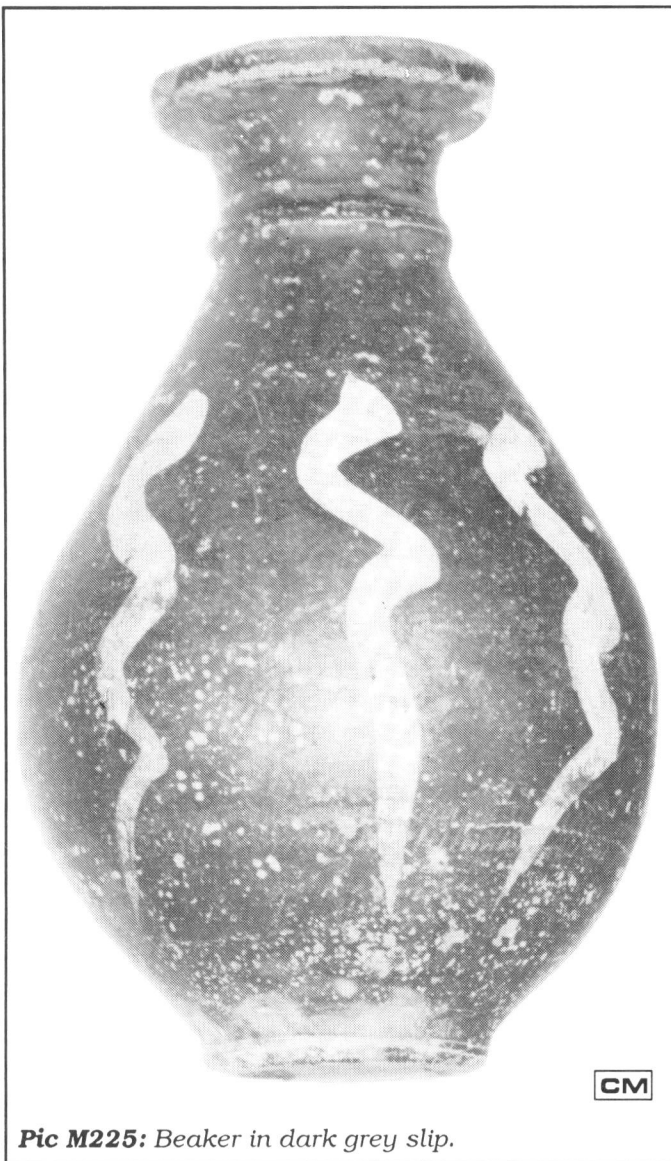

Pic M225: *Beaker in dark grey slip.*

Pic M226:
*Bronze oil
flask or
balsamarium.*

dle. The narrow neck opens out into a flattened top which is fitted with a hinged lid with a moulded acorn thumb-piece in the centre. The handle, which is of circular section, is attached to the flask by vertical rings which are fixed through holes in the main body.

The *balsamarium* would have contained oil which the Romans would have rubbed on their skin after bathing. Excess oil would then have been scraped off using a curved bronze *strigil*.

Handle attachments are often found separated from the objects to which they were originally attached. **Pic M227** shows a diamond-sectioned bronze handle with hooked terminals. It may have been fixed to a glass flask for suspension or as it has also been suggested it may have been a bronze helmet handle.

Pic M228 is more likely to have been used for this latter purpose as it is far more robust. The design, in crude style, is of two facing dolphins

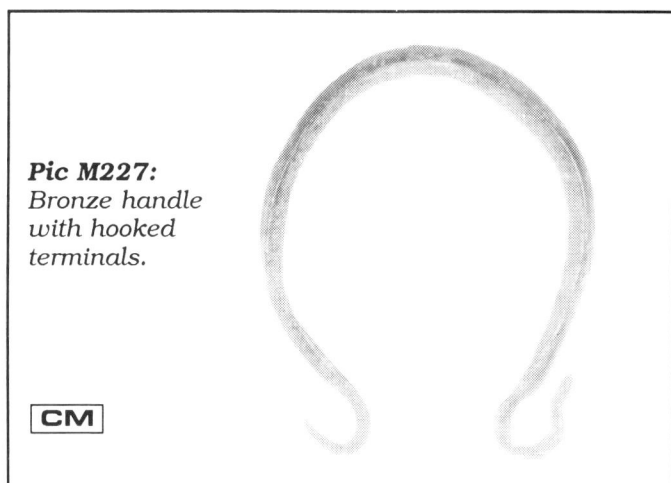

Pic M227:
*Bronze handle
with hooked
terminals.*

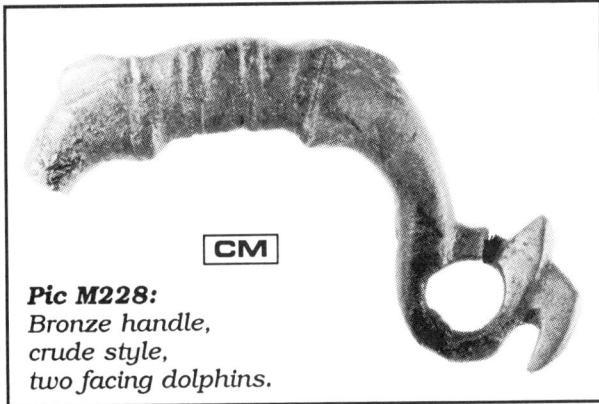

Pic M228:
*Bronze handle,
crude style,
two facing dolphins.*

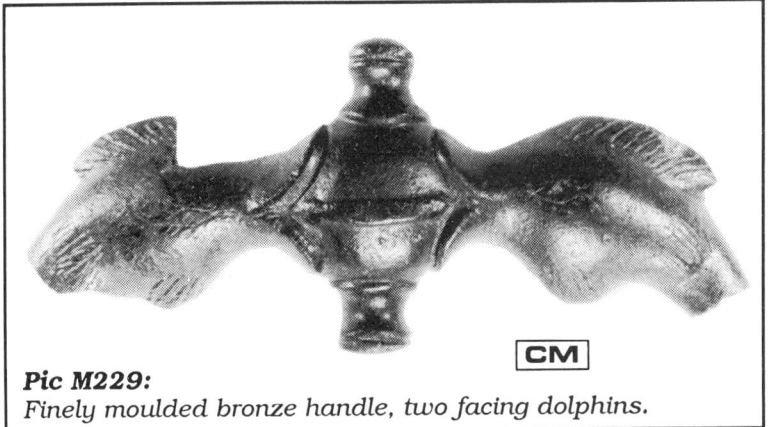

Pic M229:
Finely moulded bronze handle, two facing dolphins.

with simple incised decoration. The back of the handle is flattened with the tails of the dolphins forming loops for attachment.

Pic M229 shows a much more finely moulded bronze handle or mount, again in the form of facing dolphins; the device between them is knobbed. The back of the handle is hollowed out and this could have been used on a bucket or casket.

An interesting bronze handle and spout combination is shown in **Pic M230**. This dates from the 2nd century and would have been originally attached to a bronze jug. From the shape of the handle and the angle at the bottom, it is clear that the jug was quite bulbous in shape. The solid casting of the handle is in contrast to the jug itself, which would have been

of lightweight construction.

Another bronze spout, shown in **Pic M231** would also have been attached to a bronze vessel. It may have been purely ornamental, with its comic actor's theatre mask style face which represents a slave (a character in contemporary comedy). Other representations of theatre masks include tragedy and satyr forms.

Other vessels in bronze used by the Romans include *paterae* and skillets (see **Pic M232**). These are shallow, circular vessels which were used to contain liquids for sacrificial or domestic purposes. The example illustrated has a flat horizontal handle which has been pierced for suspension. This is attached to the rim of the bowl which has a flattened base and a ring foot which is deco-

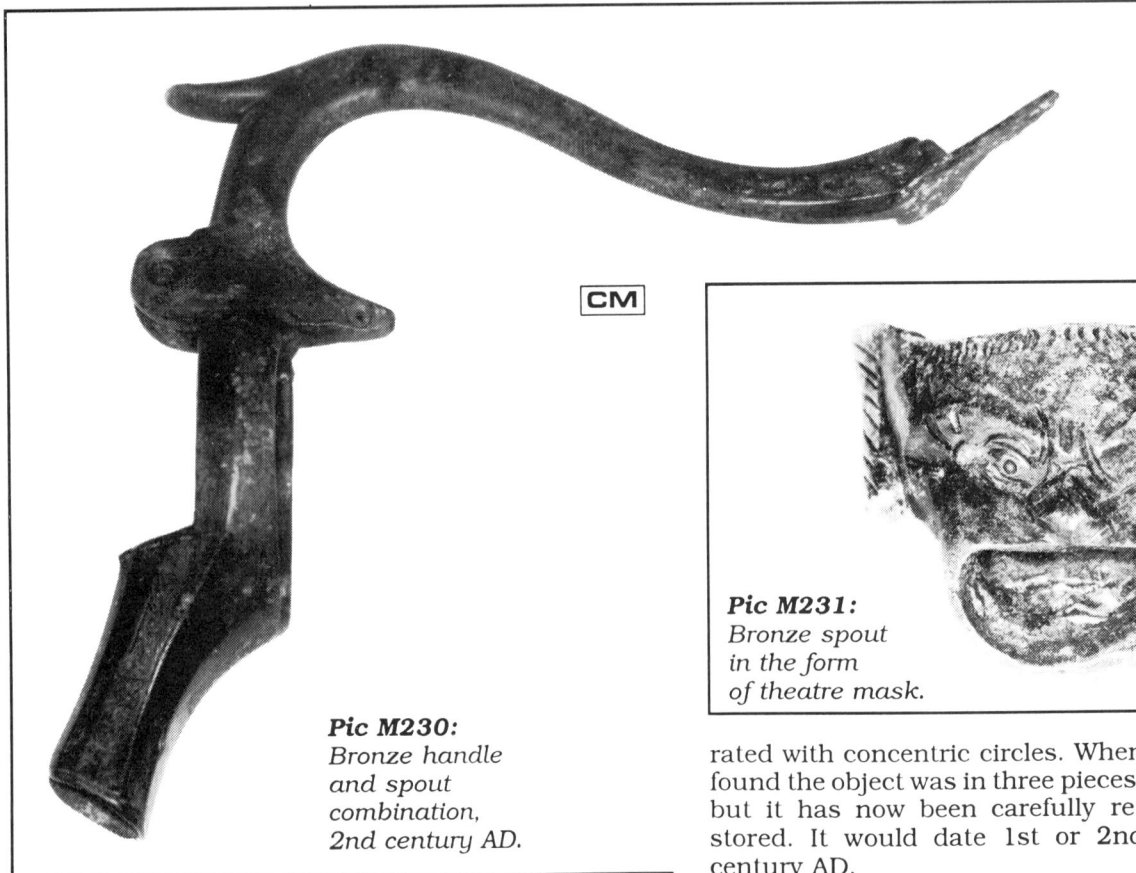

Pic M230:
*Bronze handle
and spout
combination,
2nd century AD.*

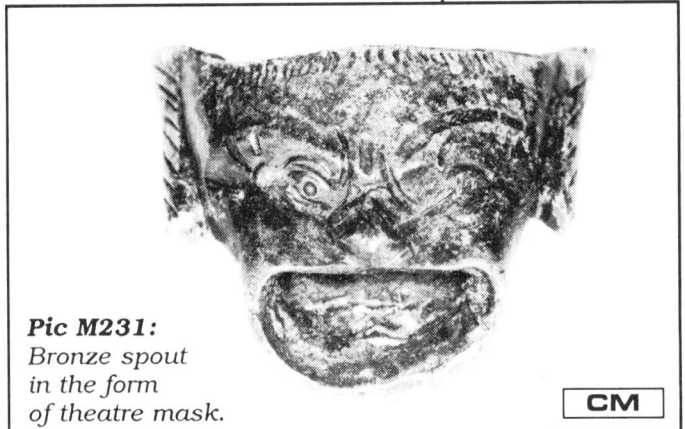

Pic M231:
*Bronze spout
in the form
of theatre mask.*

rated with concentric circles. When found the object was in three pieces, but it has now been carefully restored. It would date 1st or 2nd century AD.

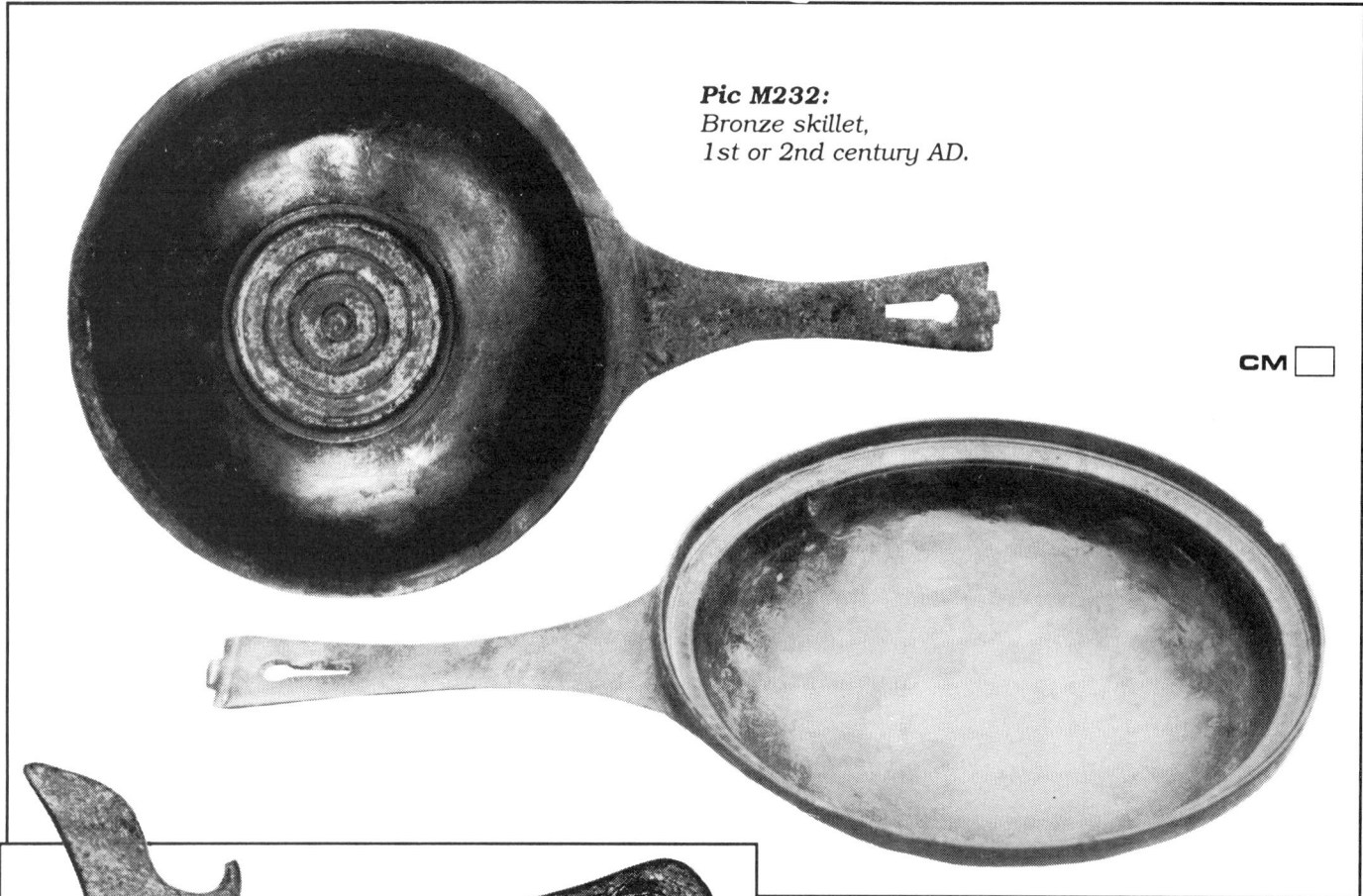

Pic M232:
Bronze skillet,
1st or 2nd century AD.

CM

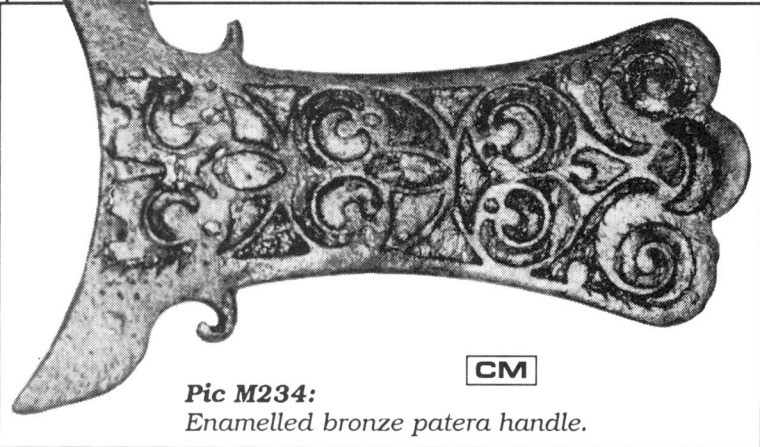

Pic M234:
Enamelled bronze patera handle.

CM

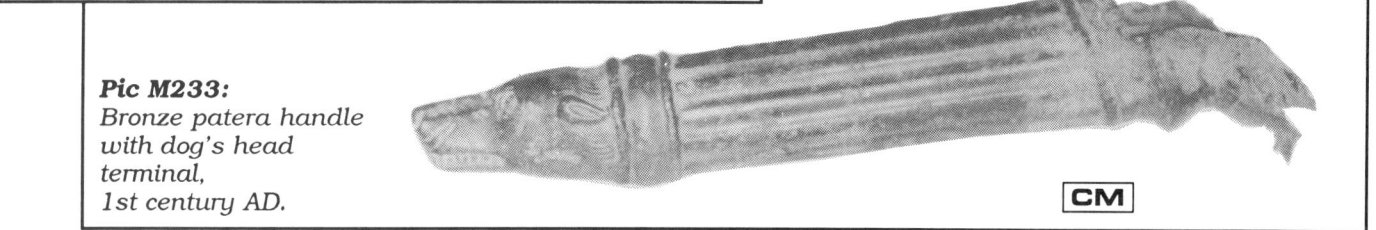

Pic M233:
Bronze patera handle
with dog's head
terminal,
1st century AD.

CM

A typical bronze patera handle is represented by **Pic M233**. This is moulded with a dog's head terminal and has a cylindrical ridged stem. Found in Suffolk it has separated from the bowl. The patera was used for ceremonial purposes and for receiving wine; again, it is 1st century AD in date.

The ram's head is another common form of terminal used on handles.

Pic M234 shows a Romano-British bronze patera handle. It is flat with a richly decorated surface design of crescents and leaf shapes enamelled in red and blue. The arms for attachment often take the outline of cranes' heads with long bills.

The bronze lamp shown in **Pic M235** is in the design of a cloaked male figure standing to reveal an oversize phallus, which serves as the nozzle to hold the wick for burning. The lamp is hollow and there is a filling hole at the top of the figure's head. This would have been originally fitted with a hinged lid, which is

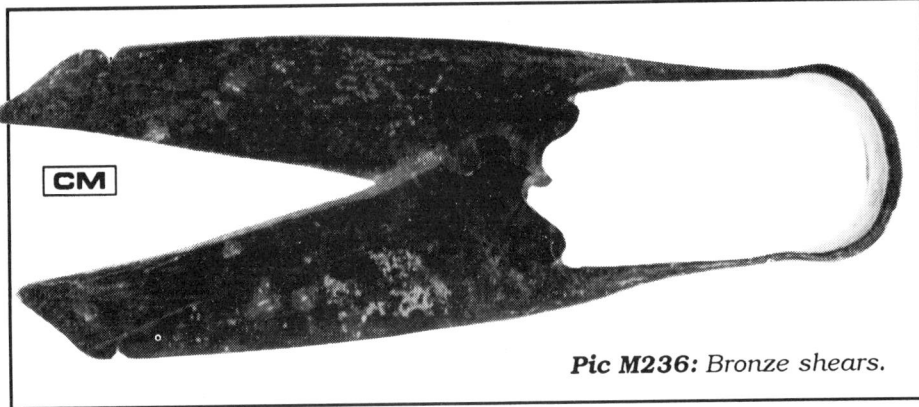

Pic M236: Bronze shears.

Pic M235: Bronze oil lamp in the form of standing figure.

now missing. Hooded figures found in Britain are usually exposing themselves in this way. The figure may be a localised version of Priapus, the Roman god of fruitfulness and the protector of flocks. Figures such as these were thought to bring good luck and ward off evil spirits.

The bronze shears shown in **Pic M236** are the same pair recorded by Hattatt, and were found near Leeds. Shears are rare finds from the Roman period. They are far more common finds from medieval times, when they were made of iron. Roman shears were principally used for cutting hair, although Hattatt suggests that they could also have been used for nail trimming.

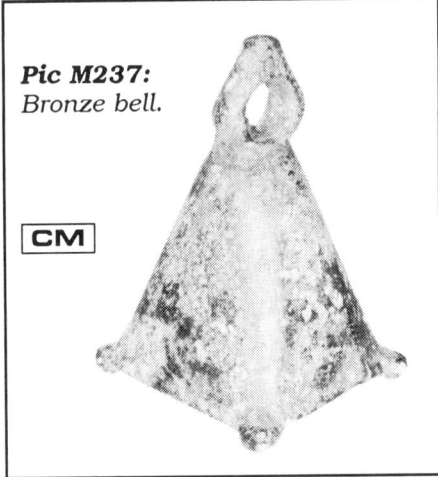

Pic M237: Bronze bell.

Bronze bells similar to that shown in **Pic M237** are of Roman date. They were hung in doorways, together with lamps, as a protection against evil spirits. The example illustrated is pyramid-shaped with a loop at the top. Another example I have seen was circular with triangular cut-outs; this may have been late Roman or Saxon in date.

Pic M238 shows an attachment from the base of a Roman vessel. Three or four of these were used and served as feet for the vessel to stand on. It resembles a cosmetic grinder in shape, but is flat on one side and of heavier construction.

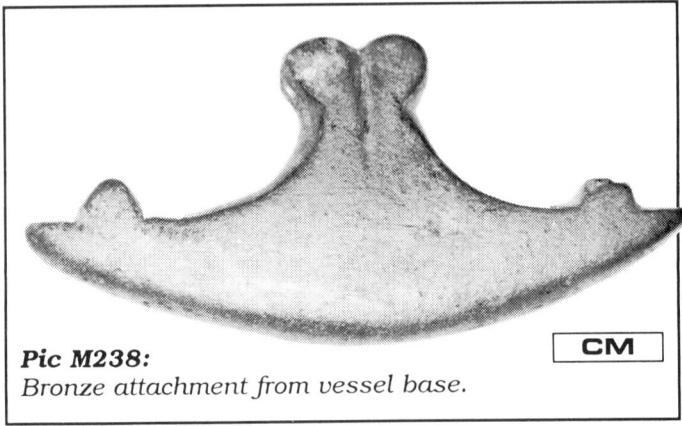

Pic M238: Bronze attachment from vessel base.

Price Guide

	Fine	Very Fine		Fine	Very Fine
M223: Samian conical cup	£70	£300	M230: bronze handle and spout	£75	£160
M224: Samian decorated bowl fragment	£30	£75	M231: bronze spout	£160	£400
M225: beaker with dark grey slip	£60	£250	M232: bronze skillet	£375	£950
M226: bronze oil flask or balsamarium	£550	£1,200	M233: bronze patera handle	£130	£300
M227: bronze handle	£8	£16	M234: bronze patera handle	£140	£325
M228: bronze handle, two dolphins	£35	£75	M235: bronze lamp	£325	£900
M229: bronze handle, two dolphins	£120	£280	M236: bronze shears	£120	£275
			M237: bronze bell	£18	£40
			M238: bronze base	£6	£12

Steelyard Weights & Bronze Mounts

Most Roman sites in Britain contain large numbers of lead fragments. Most of this lead will be waste, but occasionally lead weights can turn up.

Pic M239a shows two plain lead weights from the Roman period. These can vary in shape although oval or conical are the most common designs. In actual weight they can vary from a few ounces up to several pounds. Most of the weights found are plain apart from a single iron loop at the top for suspension, but some have an additional iron loop underneath.

The Romans used a system of weighing based on the pound or *libra*

allows different scales to operate using a single weight.

The steelyard was used throughout the Roman world and, being portable, was employed by many street sellers and merchants.

The bronze steelyard weights used in Britain in the Roman period were often in the form of busts of deities or other personifications.

Pics M241a & M241b show a hollow cast bronze steelyard weight in the form of a bust of a male wrestler. The head is shown shaved except for a small tuft of hair at the back. At the top of the weight can be seen the remains of a bronze loop that would have been used for sus-

Pic M239a. Two lead Roman steelyard weights.

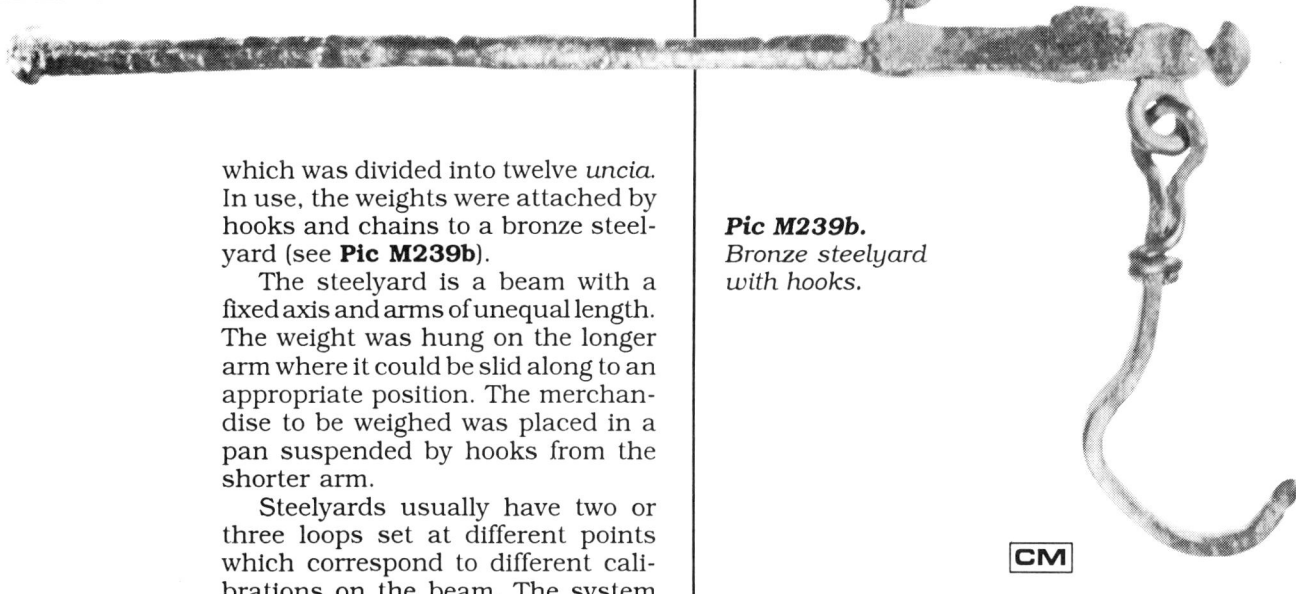

Pic M239b.
Bronze steelyard
with hooks.

which was divided into twelve *uncia*. In use, the weights were attached by hooks and chains to a bronze steelyard (see **Pic M239b**).

The steelyard is a beam with a fixed axis and arms of unequal length. The weight was hung on the longer arm where it could be slid along to an appropriate position. The merchandise to be weighed was placed in a pan suspended by hooks from the shorter arm.

Steelyards usually have two or three loops set at different points which correspond to different calibrations on the beam. The system

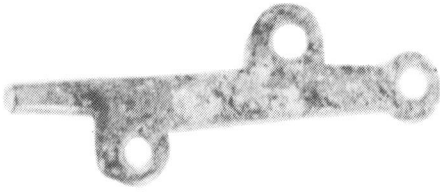

Pic M240. *Component parts of a steelyard.*

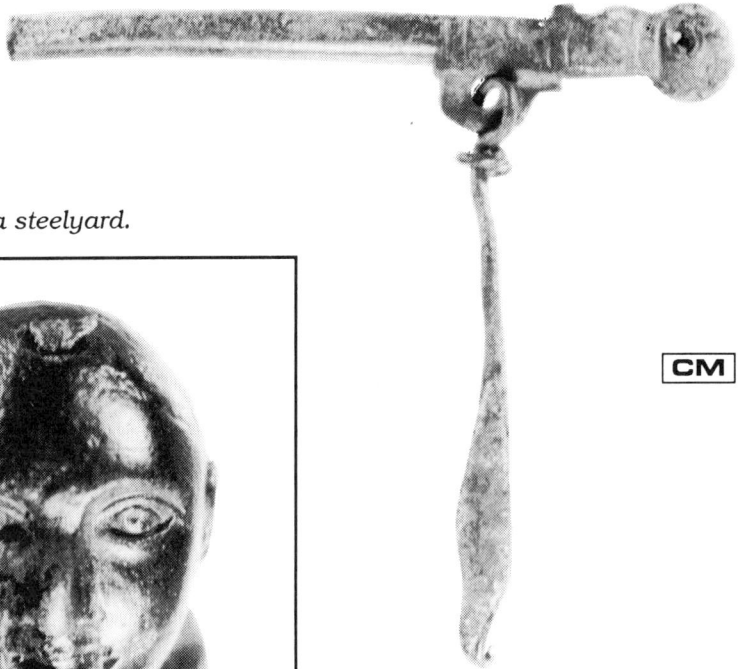

Pics M241a & M241b.
Two views of a bronze steelyard weight in the form of a wrestler's head.

Pic M242.
Romano-Celtic bronze weight.

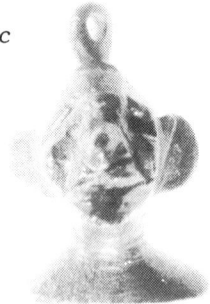

pension. At 1lb 2oz, this weight is quite heavy and the hollow centre is entirely filled with lead which has been rounded off at the base so that the weight does not stand up.

Although a British find this weight is probably Germanic in origin, and would date 2nd century BC.

The crudely-designed bronze steelyard weight shown in **Pic M242** is probably of East Anglian manufacture as several have been found in that area. It has a flat oval base with an integral loop at the top. The head is oval in section with Celtic-style facial features and large pointed ears. The head also appears to have been shaved as in the case of the wrestler, but this example weighs only 1oz.

The steelyard weight shown in **Pic M243** has been cast with an opening at the back of the hollow head for the lead filling (most of which is now missing).

From a more complete example I have seen recently, this weight would have had a bronze moulded backplate attached to it by an iron rivet, and the plate would have enclosed the lead and concealed it from view. It is extremely rare to find weights of this type with the plate still in position.

This weight is in the design of a

Pic M243.
Bronze steelyard weight representing Victory.

female figure, apparently winged Victory, and weighs 11ozs. Victory represents loyalty and success, and is normally depicted standing on a globe. She is wearing a garment fastened on the shoulders with a V-shaped opening at the neck. The head is of good style, suggesting that this weight is an imported item.

The steelyard weight shown in **Pic M244** is of solid bronze and is a representation of a male head with a very thick and elongated neck. This is perhaps intended to be Mercury as the figure is wearing a cap on his head. The loop at the top is integrally cast and there is a small piece of chain remaining. The female head shown in **Pic M245** is another lead-filled bronze steelyard weight. The iron loop, originally provided at the top, has rusted away. The head is that of Venus, goddess of beauty and love. Her hair is swept back into a bun and she is wearing a diadem. The wedge-shaped nose suggests Roman-British workmanship. This weight was found in Essex.

The impressive bronze weight shown in **Pic M246** is in the form of a hare. Possessing fine detail and style, this weight would be 2nd century in date and is certainly an import. The suspension loop (now missing) would have been at the top of the head which is filled with lead.

The hare was found in Cambridgeshire and unfortunately was harshly

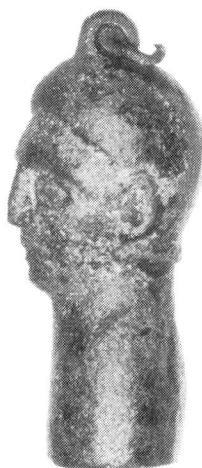

CM

Pic M244.
Bronze steelyard weight in the form of a male head.

CM

Pic M245.
Bronze steelyard weight depicting the head of Venus.

cleaned when found due to a heavy encrustation covering it. The cleaning process removed all traces of the original patina and this made the weight very difficult to authenticate as Roman. In fact, every authority on the subject dismisses it as being Georgian or Victorian. It took several years for it to be declared Roman, and this illustrates the danger of over-cleaning an artefact.

A much smaller, but more common Romano-British weight or mount is shown in **Pic M247** and is in the form of a sleeping dog wearing a collar. This has a flat underside and the design shows simple detailing. In Roman times different animals or

CM

Pic M246. *Steelyard weight in the form of a hare.*

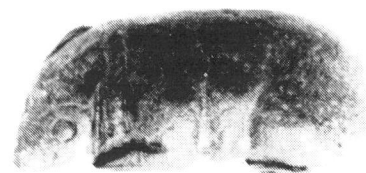

CM

Pic M247.
Mount or weight in the form of a sleeping dog.

Pic M232

Pic M231

Pic M226

Pic M234

Pic M254

Pic M252

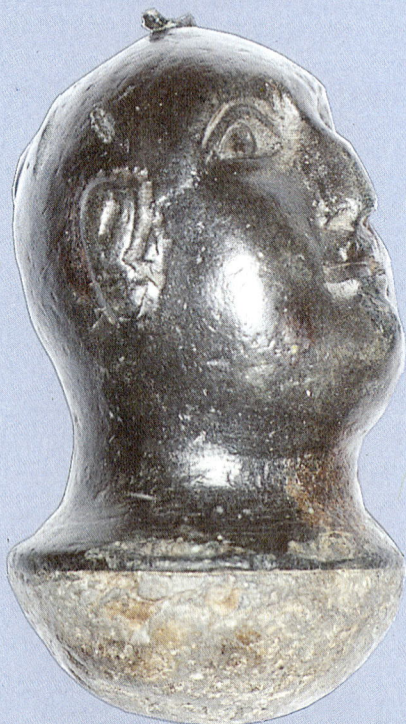

Pic M241a

See text for details

Pic M244

Pic M245

Not to Scale

Pic M255

Pic M257

Pic M261

Pic M248

Pic M250

Pic M266

Pic M265

See text for details

Not to Scale

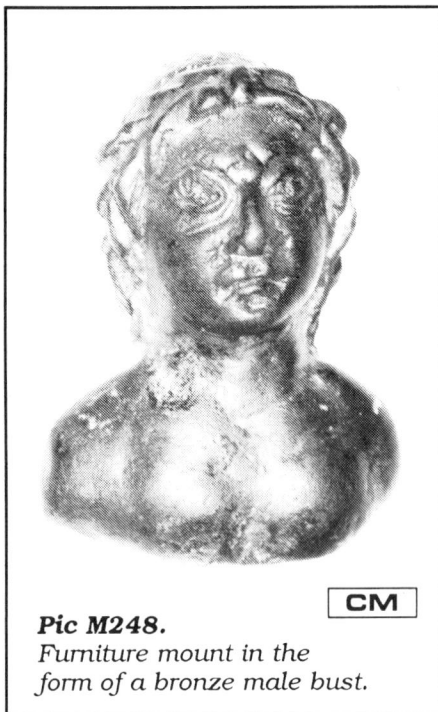

Pic M248.
Furniture mount in the form of a bronze male bust.

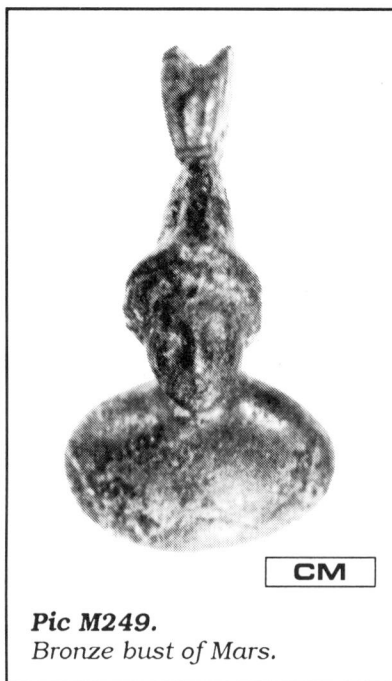

Pic M249.
Bronze bust of Mars.

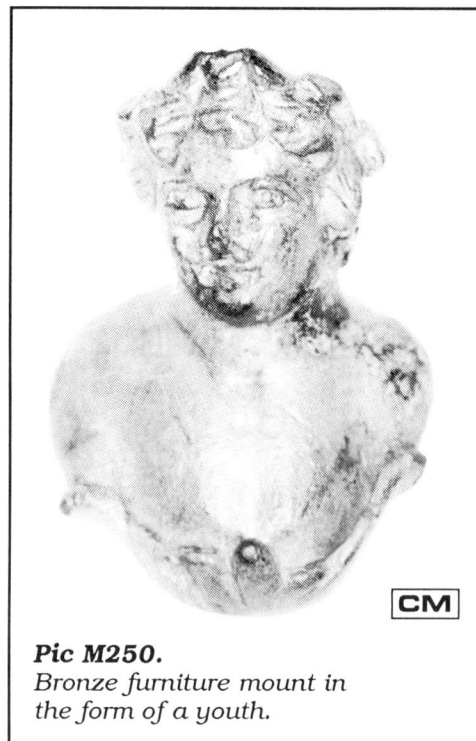

Pic M250.
Bronze furniture mount in the form of a youth.

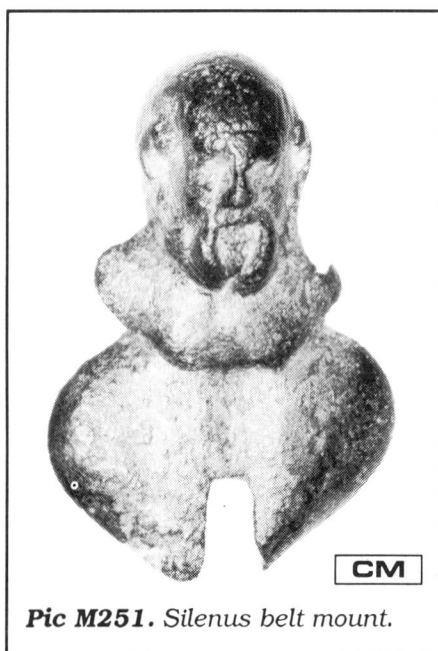

Pic M251. *Silenus belt mount.*

busts were used to represent the various weights and thus avoid confusion.

Some of the bronze heads or busts that have been found are not weights. These would originally have been fastened to poles or sceptres used for religious purposes or as part of civil regalia. The difference between these and weights is that the staff decorations will have hollow necks with rivet holes; they will also lack the suspension loop.

A considerable number of small heads have also been found which are mounts or appliques for vessels.

Pic M248 shows another hollow-cast bust representing a young man wearing a laurel wreath (possibly Bacchus, god of wine). This has no suspension loop but does show the remains of its lead filling. Moulded in the round, there is an opening behind the shoulders indicating that this object was fixed onto something, perhaps as part of a furniture ornament.

This bust is in an excellent state of preservation with a chocolate-coloured patina. The facial features are slightly crude with oversized eyes. The hair is represented by a series of "V" incised marks.

Pic M249 shows another mount in the design of a youthful bust of Mars wearing a Corinthian helmet. Some sources suggest that this might be a weight, but I feel this to be doubtful. The bust is Romano-British in style and has fairly simple features. Mars was the Roman god of war although in Celtic belief his role could be more peaceful, such as that of healer.

Minerva, the female counterpart of Mars, is very similar in appearance and representations of this goddess were commonly used as mounts or even knife handles.

Another bronze furniture mount is shown in **Pic M250**. This is the bust of a male youth - perhaps a young Bacchus or Dionysus. He is shown naked and rising out of a whorl of leaves (calyx). The head is moulded in the round but the breast is open at the back and has a bar behind for attachment. The figure is shown with his head slightly inclined to the right, and he is wearing a wreath of leaves around his head.

86

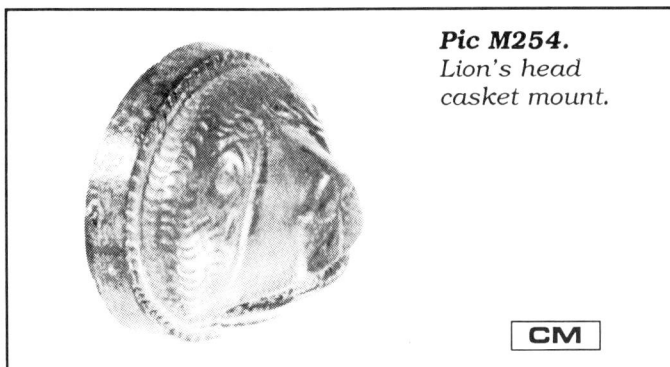

The hair is modelled in thick, wavy locks. The eyes have the pupils shown by small circular indentations and the chin is receding. On this example there is slight damage to the nose.

Pic M251 shows a bronze fitting with a rectangular opening at the bottom and a square shaped fixing loop behind the shoulders. The figure represented is Silenus. He is shown bald-headed with a snub-nose, pointed ears and a moustache and beard, giving him an Oriental appearance. Silenus was the son of Pan and teacher of Bacchus. He was regarded as having the power of prophecy and imparted wisdom in a drunken state. This included the statement that the secret of human life was that the best thing for man is not to be born at all; the next best thing is to die as early as possible.

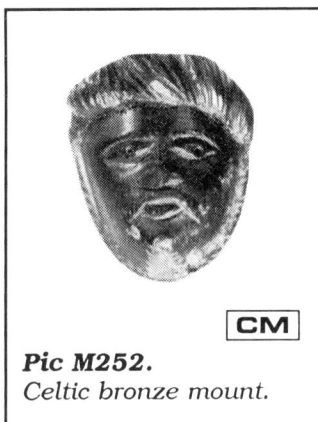

Pic M252.
Celtic bronze mount.

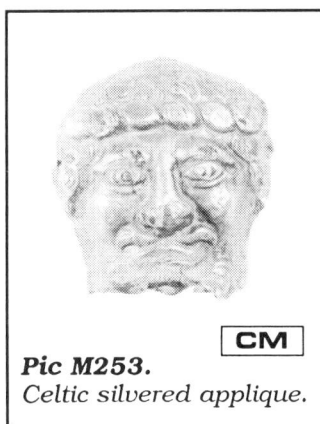

Pic M253.
Celtic silvered applique.

The small bronze mount or applique shown in **Pic M252** has a curved shape with a central iron rivet at the back for attachment, as decoration, to the outside of a vessel. The mount shows strong Celtic features with thick hair, a beard, and moustache. The eyes have indented pupils and there is a line of small dots around the forehead. It is thought to date 1st century AD.

Pic M253 shows another applique, this time made from a thin sheet of silver which has been stamped out from behind (repousse) and then filled with lead. The representation is mask-like, with staring eyes, curly moustache and a beard. There is a wreath around the forehead, and the figure's hair is composed of wavy curls. The

chin has broken away at the bottom.

The style again shows a strong Celtic influence, although the applique was found near Wroxeter, a Roman town. Possibly it is intended to be a representation of a Celtic god, although I have been unable to find any comparisons.

The most common Romano-British bronze mount is in the form of a lion's head as the example shown in **Pic M254**. These always take the form of circular bosses with hollowed-out backs and a central iron stud for attachment. The lion's head on the example illustrated is in high relief with an incised fringe or mane.

Mounts in this form vary both in size and quality; generally, they date from the 2nd century AD. It is believed that many would have been originally fixed to burial caskets. The smaller examples can range in price from £10 upwards, depending on condition.

Pic M255.
Female head applique.

The bronze applique shown in **Pic M255** is open backed and in the form of a mask-like female head. The hair is swept back in side tresses, and surmounted by a diadem.

The small mount illustrated in **Pic M256** is the head of a youth (probably Cupid) with long wavy hair, a rounded face and chin, and a short nose.

Pic M268

Pic M272

Pic M267

Pic M279

Pic M277

Pic M280

See text for details

Not to Scale

Pic M283

Pic M282

Pic M284

Pic M285

Pic M290

Pic M291

Pic M289

Pic M292

Pic M301

See text for details

Not to Scale

89

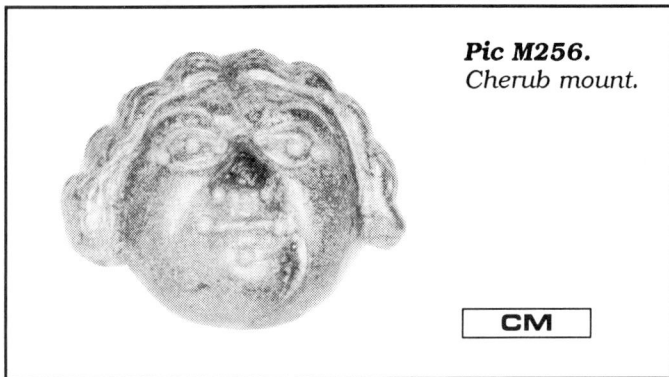

Pic M256.
Cherub mount.

CM

There are a series of bronze mounts which represent the foreparts (protome) of animals. They are solid cast with a projecting peg at the

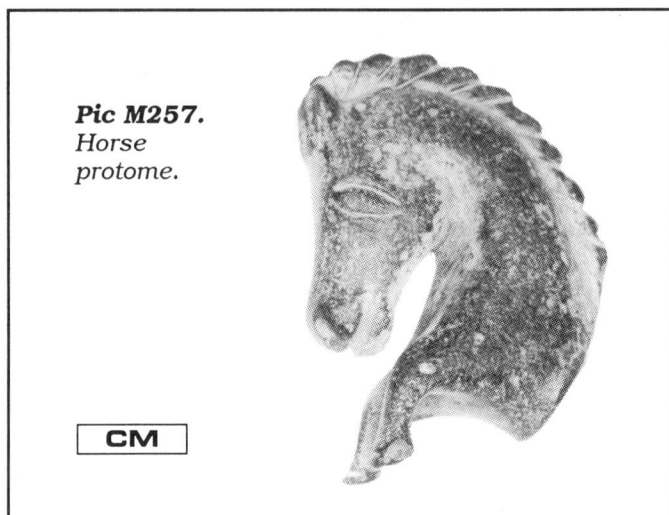

Pic M257.
Horse protome.

CM

rear. **Pic M257** shows the forepart of a horse, forelegs side by side, with a notched mane; its head is held down, and it has simple incised lines as eyes.

Rivetted to a base or stand, it would once have formed part of the tripod foot (combined with two other mounts) for a casket or lamp stand.

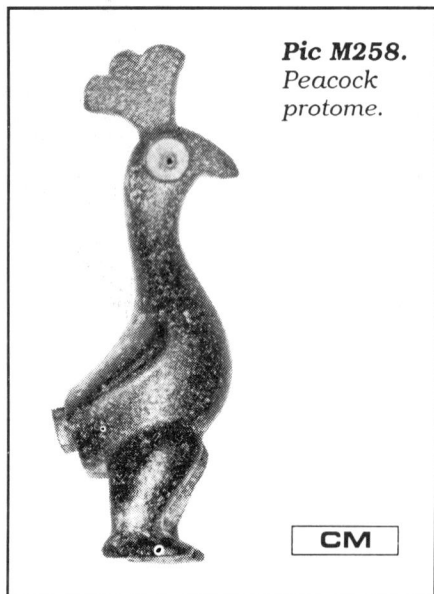

Pic M258.
Peacock protome.

CM

The peacock shown in **Pic M258** is similar but not as common. It has no tail, but does have a tall identifying crest on its head. The eyes would have been originally inset with enamel. The peacock was a cult emblem of Juno and consort of Jupiter.

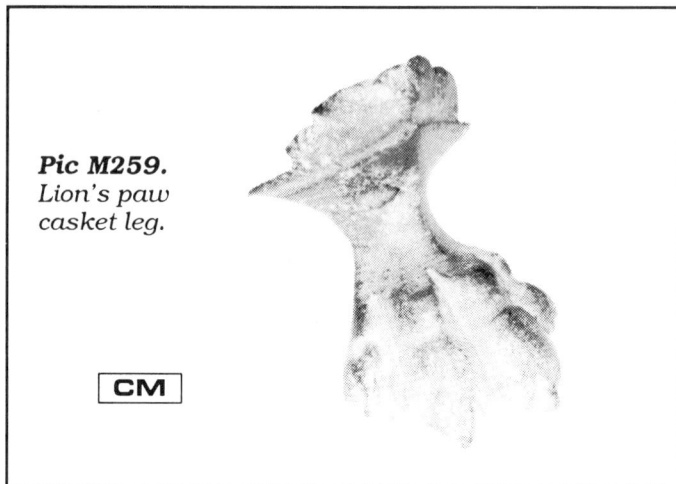

Pic M259.
Lion's paw casket leg.

CM

Many caskets and items of furniture in the Roman world stood on feet modelled as lions' paws, as the example shown in **Pic M259**. The shaft is curved with a flange at the top for attachment. This example was probably imported.

Pic M260.
Bust of Sol Invictus mount.

CM

Pic M260 shows a mount with a small circular peg at the rear. It is a crude representation of the bust of Sol Invictus, the sun god. He is shown wearing a radiate crown on his head (symbolising the rays of the sun). The Emperor Aurelian in the 3rd century

Pic M261.
*Head of Mars
mount.*

CM

The phallic mount shown in **Pic M262** has two rivets at the rear for attachment. Phalluses were a popular representation, and - unlike the situation today - were openly displayed on public buildings. This example may have been rivetted to a seal box lid or some other vessel. It has a recess on the shank and tip for enamel decoration, which is now missing.

Pic M263 shows a phallic pendant with a suspension loop. These were worn by the military as amulets or good luck charms to ward off the evil eye. This example is identical to one found at Corbridge, Northumberland. Such pendants were very popular in the 1st century AD.

Phalluses are sometimes represented with wings, while examples from Spain sometimes have a clenched fist at the opposing end. As a symbol of Priapus they also represent prosperity and fertility.

The Gorgon Medusa is well-known in mythology, her gaze being able to

established Sol Invictus as the supreme Roman deity, until the coming of Christianity. As a result, the sun became a common design on coins after this time.

The Celticised features of this mount (eg wedge-shaped nose and squared mouth) suggest local workmanship. It is probably late 3rd to 4th century in date.

The mount shown in **Pic M261** is Romano-Celtic in style and appears to represent Mars, the god of war. It has two rivets at the base which may have attached the mount to the rim of a vessel (or it might have been used as a terminal decoration).

Pic M262.
Phallic mount.

CM

Pic M263.
Phallic pendant.

CM

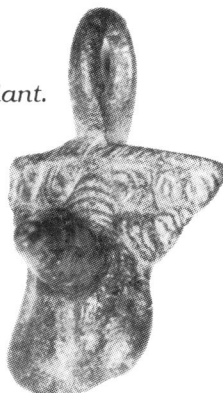

Pic M264.
*Medusa
mount.*

CM

turn an onlooker to stone. **Pic M264** shows a bronze mount representing the head of Medusa. The hair consists of coils of writhing serpents, and the Gorgon is shown with staring eyes and a grotesque face. The Medusa head was thought to be able to attract and destroy evil powers. The design was used on the military breast roundel known as an *aegis*.

The roundel shown in **Pic M265** may also have been a military decoration, in this instance for the belt. It shows the head of Mercury, with wings on each side sprouting from his hair. Around the diameter is a

Pic M265.
Roundel showing head of Mercury.

CM

Pic M266.
Rectangular plate showing figure of Diana.

CM

border of beading and pellets. This roundel was found on the Thames foreshore, hence its clean appearance. It is solid cast, with a flat back.

The rectangular flat bronze plate, shown in **Pic M266** was found in the Midlands. In the centre is a standing figure of Diana, her left hand raised and holding a bow. Her hair is tied back in a bun, and there is a cloak over her shoulder. At her feet is a hound. Diana is the huntress and moon goddess, and protector of women and children.

To the front of the figure can be seen hanging vine tendrils and the plate is bordered by a row of radiate lines. The plate is solid cast, but the design has been worked up by hand. This may have been an inset decorative panel.

Price Guide

		Fine	Very Fine
M239a:	lead steelyard weight	£1	£4
M239b:	bronze steelyard with hooks	£60	£150
M240:	component parts of steelyard	£5	£12
M241:	wrestler's head bronze steelyard weight	£450	£1,200
M242:	Romano-Celtic bronze weight	£35	£75
M243:	bronze steelyard weight of Victory	£400	£1,100
M244:	bronze steelyard weight, male head	£85	£200
M245:	Venus bronze steelyard weight	£180	£425
M246:	bronze hare steelyard weight	£500	£1,300
M247:	sleeping dog mount or weight	£35	£85
M248:	bronze male bust furniture mount	£325	£850
M249:	bronze bust of Mars	£65	£150

		Fine	Very Fine
M250:	bronze furniture mount showing youth	£275	£750
M251:	Silenus belt mount	£85	£200
M252:	Celtic bronze mount	£120	£275
M253:	Celtic silvered applique	£350	£1,000
M254:	lion's head casket boss	£25	£75
M255:	female head applique	£130	£300
M256:	cherub mount	£60	£140
M257:	horse protome	£30	£75
M258:	peacock protome	£40	£100
M259:	lion's paw casket leg	£20	£40
M260:	bust of Sol Invictus	£80	£175
M261:	head of Mars mount	£65	£150
M262:	phallic mount	£25	£45
M263:	phallic pendant	£35	£80
M264:	Medusa mount	£150	£350
M265:	head of Mercury roundel	£120	£275
M266:	rectangular plate depicting Diana	£160	£375

Figurines & Votive Objects

Many of the Roman artefacts presently being discovered, would originally have found their way into the ground as a result of accidental loss. For example, a brooch may have been lost when its pin snapped, or a decorative mount dropped after its fixing rivet had worked loose. It is equally true, however, that many objects were buried deliberately - often for safekeeping during troubled times and with the intention of recovering them at a later date.

Some objects were also buried as votive offerings. In such cases, the object was sacrificed as a present to a god in the hope of winning favour (or as a penance for a past transgression).

If you are lucky enough to find a Roman bronze figurine in the ground, it will almost certainly have been deliberately buried. Your find may have been mutilated before burial, but whatever its condition, it represents a bond between the Romans and their gods. As such it becomes one of the most inspiring and evocative objects of this period.

Representations of many different deities and animals occur as figurines and these would have been used as ornaments, votive offerings in a temple, or adornments to a household shrine (called a *Laraium*). Some small figurines were worn as amulets or talismans while life-size statues (especially of emperors) were displayed in the towns.

Pic M267 shows a Romano-British bronze figurine of Mercury, one of the most popular gods in the Roman Empire. Mercury was the inventor of the arts, and god of travellers and traders. He was adopted as one of the native Celtic deities which explains why so many figurines of Mercury were produced in Britain.

This example shows Mercury standing naked with the weight of his body resting on his left foot. The left leg is set slightly back. His right arm is extended forwards holding a purse with a pointed tip. The left arm is held sideways away from the body, and the hand is pierced for the insertion of the *caduceus* or wand which Mercury is usually shown holding.

Pic M268 shows a larger figurine of Mercury, and here part of the *caduceus* has survived. The purse

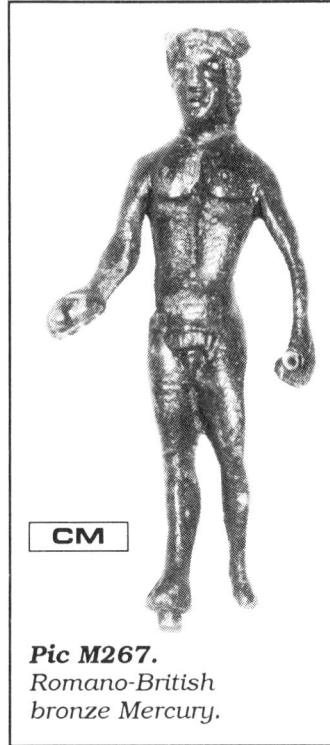

CM

Pic M267.
Romano-British bronze Mercury.

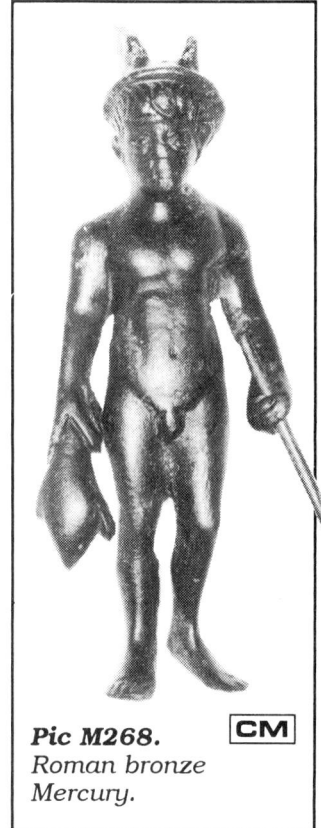

CM

Pic M268.
Roman bronze Mercury.

can be seen to be trilobate. Both figurines have the winged hat or *petasos*. Sometimes the ankles are also winged, and a cloak (*chlamys*) can be draped over his left arm.

The figurine in **Pic M268** is Romanised in style, being well-proportioned and naturalistic. Celtic depictions of gods are less stereotyped; often the body is out of proportion, and emphasis is put on the eyes and mask-like head.

A statue was normally fixed to a plinth or base, and in the case of Mercury the main statue would have been often flanked on either side by a cockerel (herald of the dawn), a ram (symbol of fertility), and a tortoise (in legend Mercury made the first lyre from a tortoise's shell). The usual height of such statues is from 7cms to 15cms, although they do range from 2cms to 52cms. Anything over 20cms, would be exceptional for Britain.

Cheaper versions of these figurines were produced in white pipe clay rather than bronze during the 1st-2nd century AD. This was because the poorer people wanted copies of the objects possessed by the

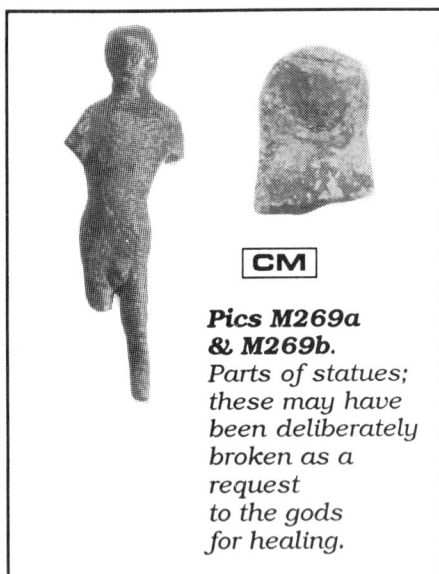

Pics M269a & M269b. *Parts of statues; these may have been deliberately broken as a request to the gods for healing.*

Pic M270. *Romano-Celtic bronze Apollo.*

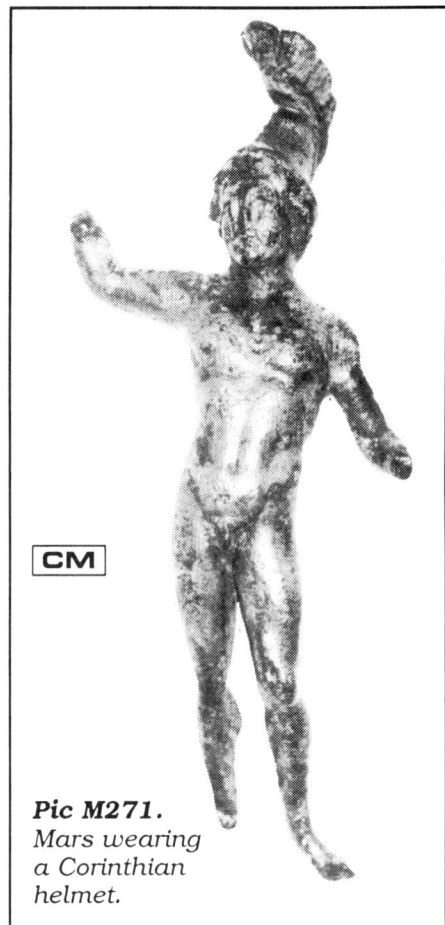

Pic M271. *Mars wearing a Corinthian helmet.*

rich. Figurines of Venus, the goddess of love, are quite common in pipe clay.

Pic M269a shows a smaller and quite crude bronze figurine which may have been produced locally; it shows a considerable amount of "wear and tear". The missing limbs on the figure may have been deliberately removed and then used by somebody as a votive offering to the gods. The idea behind this was that a person afflicted with a disease or injury would make an offering which was applicable to the part of the body which they wished healed. In the case of **Pic M269b** it appears to have been the thumb.

Some temples became depositories for a variety of wood, terracotta, and bronze representations of limbs and organs. Lead was more commonly used for curses which were hung from doors and walls, rather than for votive purposes.

Pic M270 depicts another male figure, in this case Apollo. Apollo was a sun god, and presided over healing sanctuaries and healing springs, warding off disease. He was also god of prophecy, music and hunting. Apollo figures are not common in Britain. This example has very crude facial features. Apollo is shown naked with his right arm extended forwards holding a plectrum. His left arm is bent at the elbow and holds a lyre (similar to a harp but having two curved horns and a yoke supporting the strings). The body is quite muscular. Both legs are broken: the right side at the ankle, the left just above the knee.

Mars the Roman god of war (see **Pic M271**) was popular in the north and west of England, where the military presence was stronger. In this example he is depicted standing nude

apart from a Corinthian helmet. The top of the helmet holds a crest of feathers, indicated by the scalloped edge.

The figurine stands on its right leg, the foot of which is now missing; the left leg is inclined backwards. The right arm is raised sideways, and would have originally held a spear. The left arm is extended forwards and would have held a sword. The slender, muscular body is curved at the hip with the right shoulder raised and the head turned to the right. This is a typical, classical representation of Mars. Generally he is shown as being young and clean shaven, but he can be depicted as being older and bearded, wearing a cuirass (armour).

Mars had several native names in Celtic Britain, and his sacred animals were the wolf and the woodpecker. The example illustrated was found in the Yorkshire Wolds.

The female counterpart to Mars was Minerva who is usually shown with a crested helmet and holding a spear. She also had a Celtic role, being associated with domestic prosperity and well-being.

Jupiter (see **Pic M272**) was the protector of the Empire and the Emperor. As a sky divinity, he was linked by the Celts to the sun and the thunder god Taranis. In this example

94

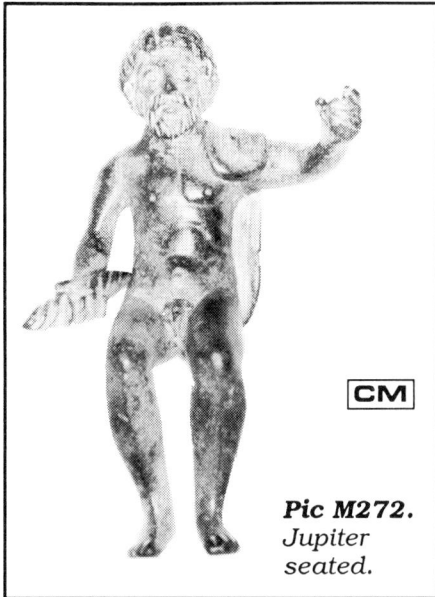

Pic M272. *Jupiter seated.*

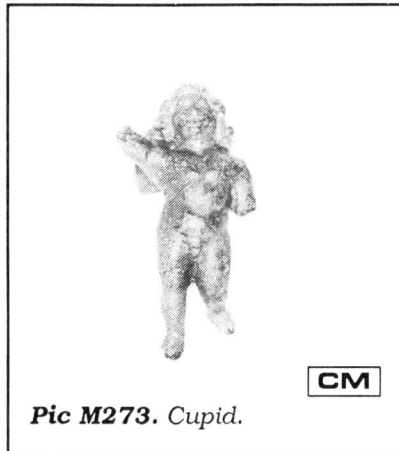

Pic M273. *Cupid.*

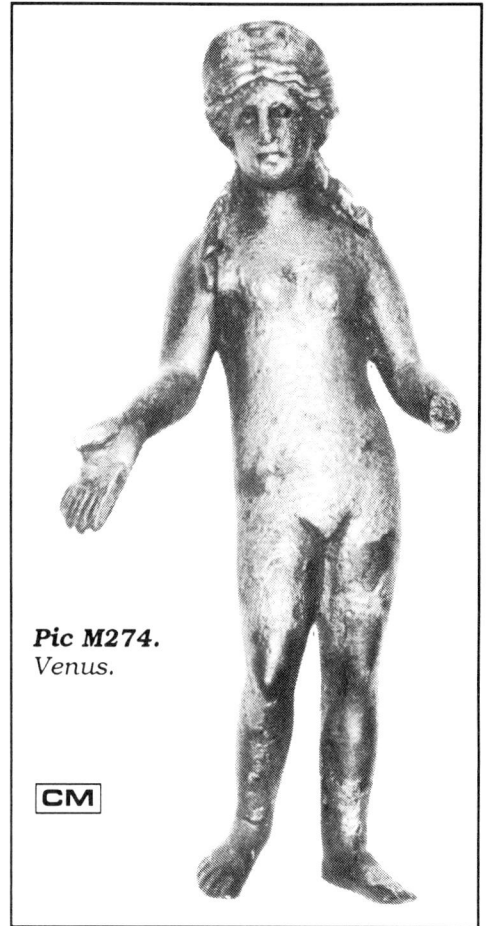

Pic M274. *Venus.*

he is depicted as a naked, bearded man in a seated position. He holds a thunderbolt with spiral grooves in his right hand, which is extended forwards. The left arm is raised, bent forwards at the elbow, and would have originally held a sceptre. There is a cloak (*chlamys*) over his left shoulder. The head is front-facing and has well-defined features; it is crowned with a laurel wreath intersected by straight grooves. This figure may be of Romano-British workmanship, and is thought to date 2nd century AD. The facial features are not unlike those of the Emperor Marcus Aurelius.

It is not easy to estimate the dating of Romano-British figurines so it is important to carefully note the find spot and any other related finds. Even when excavated from archaeological sites documentation is scarce, and dating is usually not much more than vague guesswork.

The small bronze figurine shown in **Pic M273** depicts Cupid or Amor (love) the son of Venus. He is a nude boy, with a pair of wings on his back. His right leg is placed forwards, his left leg backwards. The body is inclined backwards and the head is also thrown back. The right arm is stretched forwards while the left arm is held down (the forearm is missing). He has long, wavy hair which reaches the shoulders. In his hands he may have held a dove, a torch, a bunch of grapes, or a caduceus (wand). Cupids are closely linked to Venus (as goddess of love) and to Bacchus.

Another representation of a winged boy, but one that is rarely found in Britain, is Harpocrates. He was son of Isis (a moon and fertility goddess) and Sarapis (god of the sky and death). The figure is usually shown with his index finger touching his lips which the Romans interpreted as self-nourishment or symbolic of quiet.

Pic M274 shows Venus, goddess of love and beauty. She is depicted nude, but is wearing a diadem. Her hair is swept back and tied in a bun, with ringlets hanging down on either side onto her shoulders. The figure stands on its left foot which is straight. The right leg is bent backwards. The right arm is extended forwards with an open palm. The left arm is also extended forwards, but on this example is broken at the wrist. In her left hand, she may have been holding an apple or a mirror. Sometimes Venus is depicted with a hand touching her hair. The detailing of this figure is a little crude, and she has large hands in proportion to the rest of her body. There is a trace of silver remaining in the right eye. The clean appearance of this example is due to the fact that it was found in silt from the River Thames in London.

The female figure shown in **Pic M275** may be one of several deities; it is possible that this figurine was intended to represent Fortuna or Venus, but a mother goddess is another consideration. The figure is shown standing and wearing a *chiton* (long woollen garment) tied with a

Pic M275.
Venus walking.

Pic M276. Fortuna.

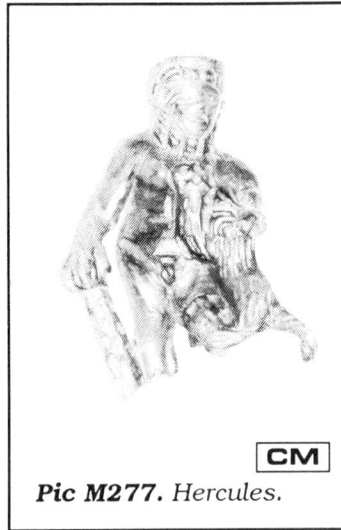
Pic M277. Hercules.

Pic M278.
Genius.

band around the waist. The right leg is straight and advanced forwards of the left leg. The right arm is extended forwards with the palm open but facing inwards. The left arm is missing. The figurine displays movement. The facial features are crude and the figure has been given a large wedge-shaped nose (now flattened). The hair is tied up in an intricate arrangement, crowned on top by a flat diadem.

Fortuna, shown in **Pic M276** was the goddess of good luck and fortune. The figure illustrated is standing upright on a plinth, and wearing a *chiton* which is draped down over her feet. Her right arm is extended downwards holding an upright rudder. The left arm is holding the horn of Amalthea (symbol of plentiful gifts of fortune) which rests against the shoulder. The head is turned to the right and is surmounted by a corn modius.

Fortuna was believed to have the power to change the direction of bad luck or evil forces by steering the rudder. She can also be shown with the rudder on a globe, and with a wheel besides her.

Hercules (see **Pic M277**) was a god admired for his strength and widely represented in statuette form, particularly in south-east England. He was adopted by the Celts as a god of healing and is usually depicted nude, holding a club in his raised right hand.

The example illustrated here shows a naked, well-muscled figure, with body inclined to the left. His right arm is extended downwards and is holding a club which rests of the ground (now broken away).

Hercules' left arm is grappling with a lion - paws and tail outstretched - against his left side. The head of the figure is bearded and he is shown with a cap.

In mythology, Hercules fought a lion with his bare hands and an olive wood club, eventually battering it to death. He wore a lion skin thereafter.

Pic M278 shows a statuette of the god Genius, a male youth who was a protector of places, and a spirit of prosperity and well-being. The figure stands on its right foot, while the left leg is bent backwards. The right arm is extended forwards and holds a *patera* (an offering plate which was held over an altar). The left arm extends downwards and holds a cornucopia which rests on the shoulder. The figure is clad in a *himation* which is draped over the left shoulder leaving the chest bare. The head has simple features, with a slit mouth and thick wavy hair.

Other examples of figurines from Britain include *Lars* (*Lares domestici*) or household gods. The figure shown in **Pic M279**, which comes from Salisbury, represents a dancing youth wearing a short tunic (tied at the waist) and boots. The right foot is raised forwards, while the left foot is straight. The right arm is raised up, holding a dolphin. The left arm is extended downwards and is holding a cornucopia which had three ears of corn protruding from the top. The Lar was considered to bring prosperity to the home.

Pic M280 shows a Romano-Celtic

Pic M279.
Lar or household god.

Pic M280. *River god.*

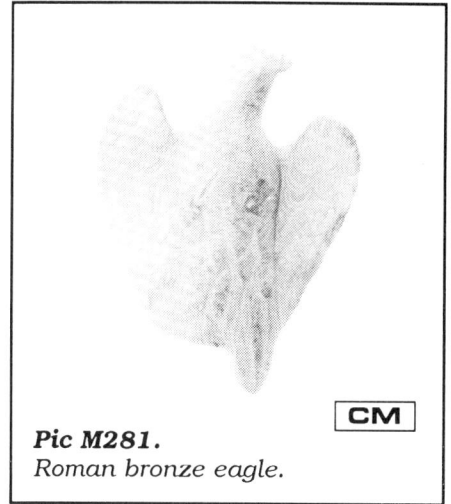

Pic M281.
Roman bronze eagle.

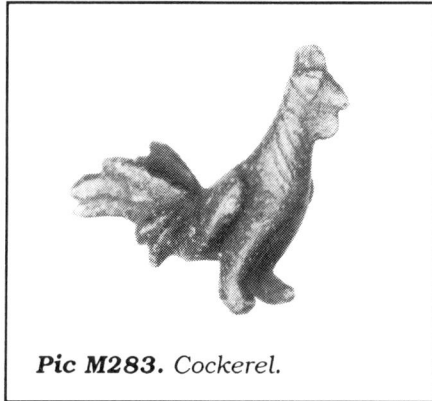

Pic M283. *Cockerel.*

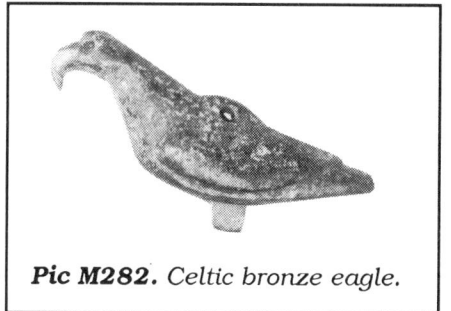

Pic M282. *Celtic bronze eagle.*

river god. The half-draped male figure has his head facing forwards and is reclining to the left on his elbow. There are simple, incised features, and the figure is of very thin, slightly-bowed construction. It would have been originally attached at the base to serve as a decorative mount. The gods of rivers and lakes received many offerings of metalwork from the Celtic tribes.

Most of the Roman gods were associated with animals or birds. The eagle, which was the emblem of the Legions, was also Jupiter's bird. The example shown in **Pic M281** is in typical classical style with its head turned and wings outstretched. It was found in Hertfordshire and may well have been a fitting for military equipment.

Pic M282 shows a Celticised eagle with its wings closed and sharply curved beak. Less detail appears than on the previous example. The eagle has a loop on its back and under its belly, so it may have been attached to a bull's head as part of a bucket decoration. This example is thought to date 1st century AD.

Birds were objects of worship because they could leave the earth and fly in the heavens. Carrion eaters represented death, while ducks were seen as a link between air and water, and had connections with healing.

The cockerel (**Pic M283**) is a fairly common figurine to turn up in Brit-

ain, probably because of its association with Mercury as the herald of the dawn. This example has crude detailing, suggesting it to be of Romano-British origin. It has large splayed tail feathers.

The ram (see **Pic M284**) and sometimes a tortoise were associated with Mercury. Both the ram and the goat represent fertility and sometimes the horns were exaggerated to depict aggression. This example has the ram, with a shaggy coat, standing on a flat base with its head turned to the right.

The mouse was rarely used as a representation in the Roman era. **Pic M285** shows an example of a mouse moulded in the round. It is squatting on its back feet and nibbling a cob of bread held between its extended front paws. It is thought that mice may

Pic M284.
Ram.

97

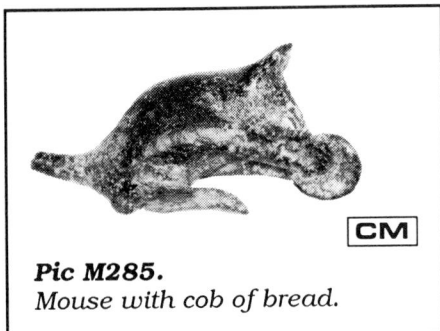

Pic M285.
Mouse with cob of bread.

Pic M286. *Owl.*

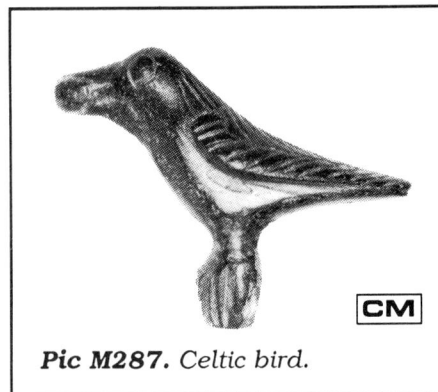

Pic M287. *Celtic bird.*

have been chthonic (used as a symbol of the underworld).

The owl (see **Pic M286**) is associated with wisdom and identified with the goddess Minerva. Examples of owls found in Britain are again rare. The owl is mounted on a solid, circular base, and has two cylindrical legs; its wings are folded. The rounded head is looking forwards. It has simple incised features with one side of its face and its beak damaged. This example was found in Suffolk.

The crow or raven (see **Pic 287**) is a Romano-Celtic representation. The raven is associated with Apollo, but is also a companion to several Celtic deities. The example shown here has deeply incised features and carries a piece of food in its beak. It was originally perhaps some form of terminal decoration.

One of the most interesting groups of figures to have come from Britain are the "horsemen". In eastern Britain there appears to have been a "Cult of the Horsemen" as a number of finds have testified. The horse represents speed and prestige and was linked in Celtic religion with the sun and warfare. The horseman held high status, and many of the Romano-

Celtic warrior gods are shown riding horses (especially by the Catuvellauni tribe).

An early representation of a rider is shown in **Pic M288**. It is very crude and almost "matchstick" in style. The figure is naked and stands with its legs apart. The right arm is extended sideways and bent at the elbow; originally, it would probably have held a spear. The left arm is also extended sideways and holds an oval shield. The face has protruding oval eyes and mouth (a Celtic feature) and is positioned above a thickened neck. This figure is thought to date from the 2nd century BC.

The horseman continues into the Roman period, reflected by the use of the design on Roman plate brooches (see **Pic M71**).

Pic M289 shows a rider dating from the 1st or 2nd century AD. He is wearing a short tunic with three bands running over the right shoulder. There is a fringe around the waist. The right arm is extended sideways and raised (it would originally have held a spear). The left arm is broken but would have held a shield. The head has incised circles for the eyes and a slit mouth. The figure is shown wearing a crested helmet.

The accompanying horse (see **Pic M290**) is depicted galloping and has its forelegs extended forwards. The underside of the body is hollowed out and there is a vertical hole to receive a lug to hold the rider in place. The head of the horse is looking forwards. The eyes are lozenge-shaped, and the ears large and pinned back. The long mane is raised and marked with incised lines.

The running dog or hound (see **Pic M291**) has very strong Celtic features, with two large cavities for eyes. These may well have been set with glass beads. The underside of the body is hollowed out, while vertical grooves on the side indicate the dog's rib cage. The tail is curved

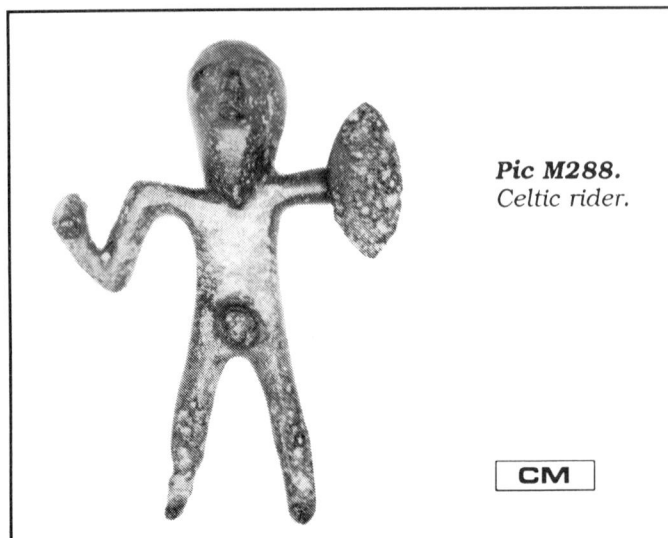

Pic M288.
Celtic rider.

98

Pic M289.
Romano-Celtic rider.

Pic M290. *Romano-Celtic horse.*

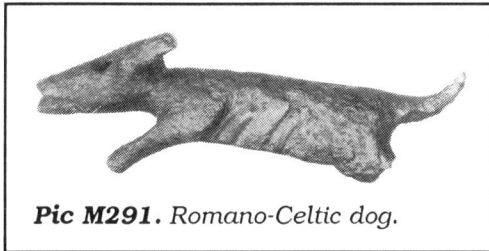

Pic M291. *Romano-Celtic dog.*

Pic M292.
Mother-goddess figure.

upwards. The dog sometimes accompanies the goddess Epona and, like her, is associated with both healing and death.

The female figure shown in **Pic M292** could be a Romano-Celtic representation of Epona, the horse goddess. She was worshipped in Britain throughout the Roman Occupation with a festival held on the 18th of December. She is always shown with horses, and sometimes with a dog and a raven. Epona is also linked with mother goddesses, the Celtic symbol of fertility and abundance.

The illustration shows the goddess standing, and wearing a long tunic (with heavy vertical ribbing) that touches the feet which are protruding from underneath. The head has a rounded face, with raised circular eyes. The hair is swept backwards in thick strands. The head is surmounted by a crested helmet.

Another type of Celtic rider from Yugoslavia and of Danubian Celtic origin is often confused with the British types, but is of inferior workman-

ship. So many items are traded as Romano-British, which are clearly not, that it is difficult for collectors and museums to establish the true provenance.

Another unusual figurine is the Romano-Celtic sphinx shown in **Pic M293**. This is quite a rare representation from Britain and appears to be some form of mount, perhaps from a ritual object. The sphinx first appears in Britain as a coin design during the reign of Cunobelin (10-40 AD). It has the face of a woman paired with the body of a lion, and is usually winged.

The captive figure shown in **Pic M294** is a nude male shown squatting. The ankles and wrists are tied and the rope continues around the figures neck linking everything together. There is a vertical hole through the body, and a horizontal hole through the chest. It has been suggested that these captive figures are amulets. However, they could have

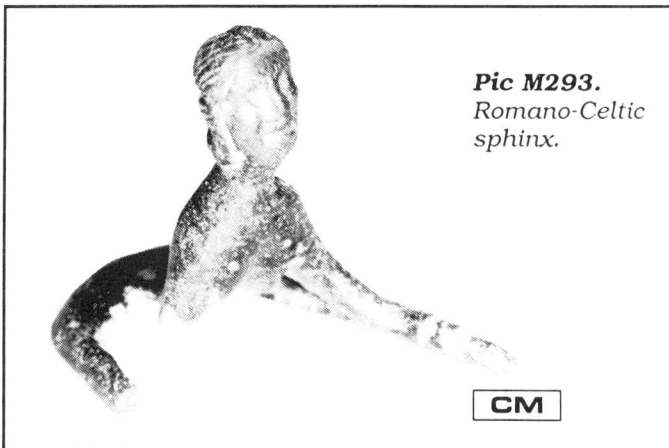

Pic M293.
Romano-Celtic sphinx.

CM

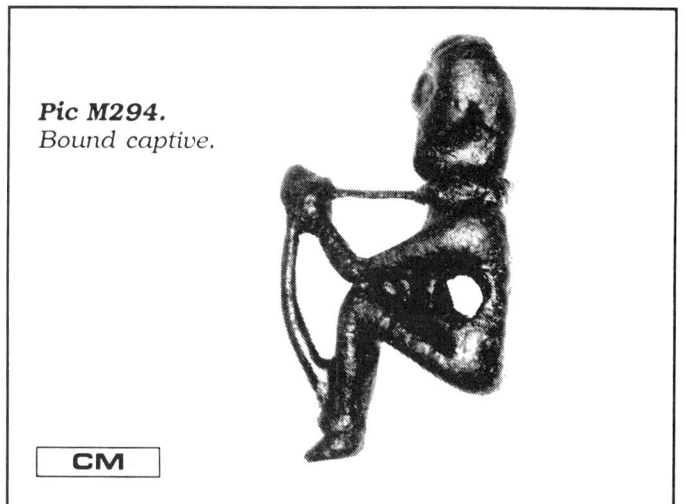

Pic M294.
Bound captive.

CM

99

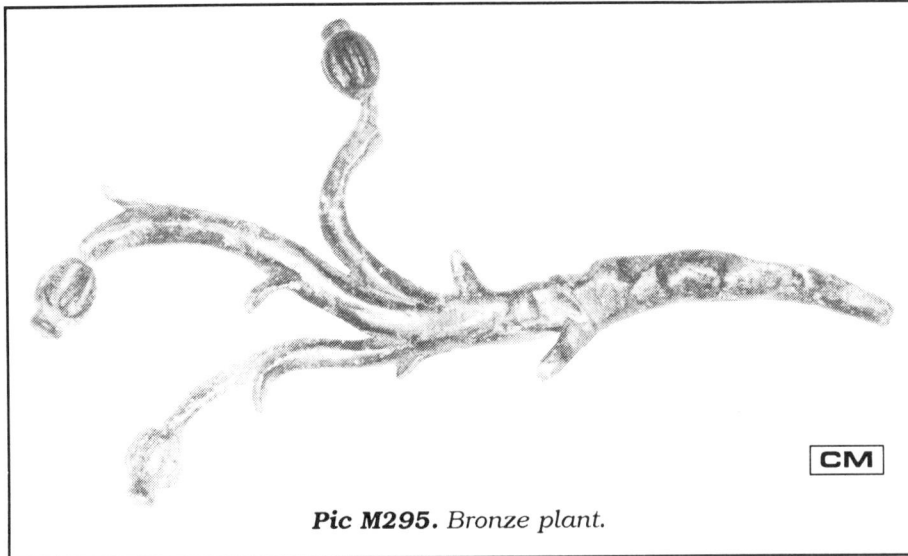

Pic M295. *Bronze plant.*

been mounted through the holes and perhaps even connected to another captive rather in the fashion of galley slaves.

The bronze branch shown in **Pic M295** is of Roman origin. Pine branches are a symbol of Atys who in legend castrated himself beneath a pine tree. The seed pods on this example, however, look like pomegranates.

Another interesting group of artefacts are the "model" objects. **Pic M296** shows a miniature replica of an axe in bronze. The axe is an ancient solar symbol and is also as-

sociated with Taranis, the wheel god. These little models may have been carried as good luck charms or have been used as votive offerings. It was a common practice for craftsmen to dedicate their tools to the gods, and also to have such objects buried in their graves with them. In making offerings it was obviously more practical to use small models, which may also have had ritual significance. Besides axes, miniature wheels, ploughs, anvils, daggers, bridles, saws and shears were also produced (see **Pics M297, M298, M299 and M300**).

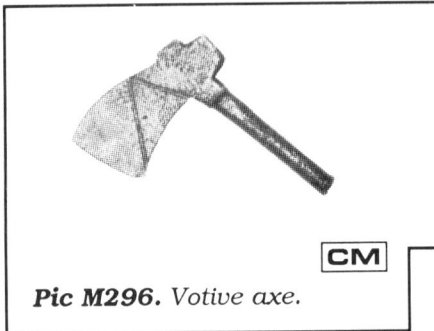

Pic M296. *Votive axe.*

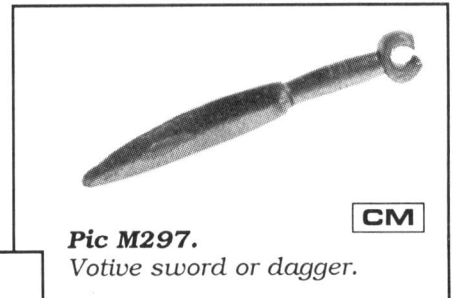

Pic M297. *Votive sword or dagger.*

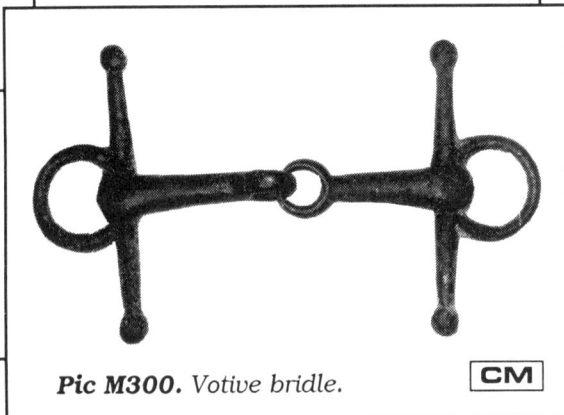

Pic M300. *Votive bridle.*

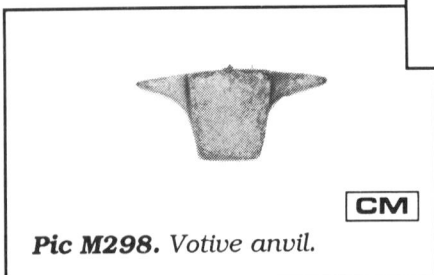

Pic M298. *Votive anvil.*

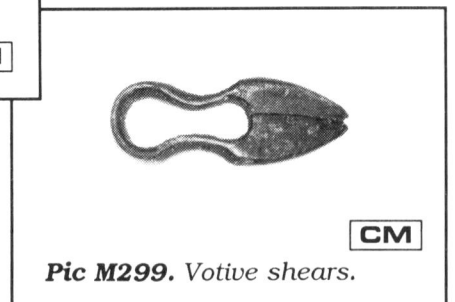

Pic M299. *Votive shears.*

The most interesting model objects are the pair of bronze enamelled altars (see **Pic M301**). The smaller of the two, fits on the top of the larger one. There is a circular hole through the middle and a projection at each corner. The side panels have three triangular enamelled recesses on each side. The larger example has a small circle inside each triangle. On the adjacent sides the design is lunular with involuted ends. Blue, green and red enamel has been used. The design of these altars suggests a 1st-2nd century date.

Most of these "model" altars have been found on fort sites, and all are of similar form. It has been suggested that they were used for burning perfume or incense.

At Roman forts, altars dedicated to the god Jupiter were replaced each year on the 3rd of January when the troops renewed their allegiance. The old altar was buried, and a new one put up in its place. Perhaps the stacking of the two miniature altars in this way, symbolises this.

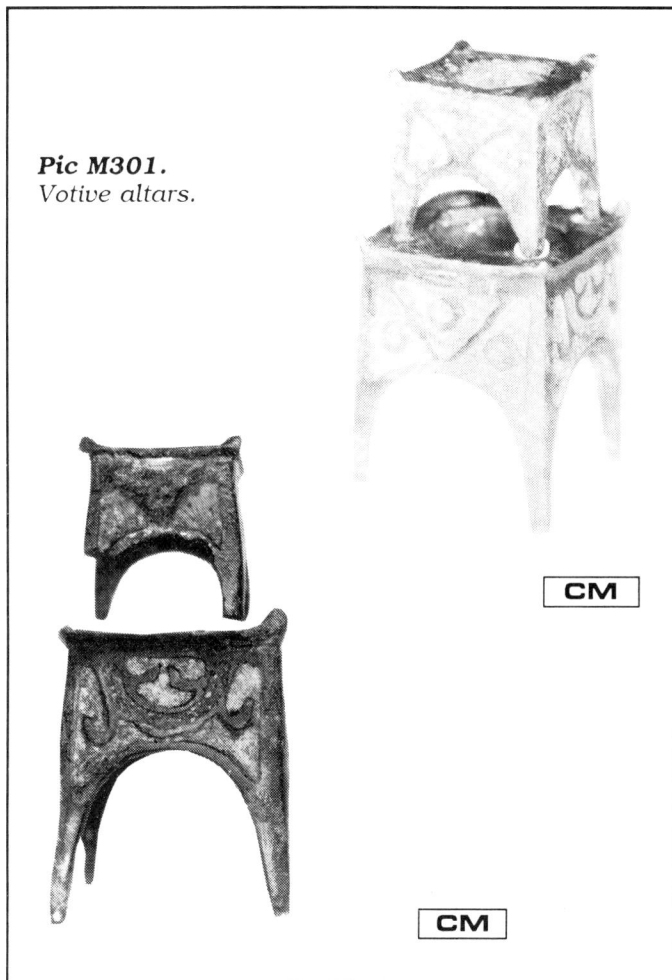

Pic M301.
Votive altars.

CM

CM

Price Guide

	Fine	Very Fine			Fine	Very Fine
M267: Romano-British bronze Mercury figurine	£150	£375	M283:	Cockerel	£80	£175
			M284:	Ram	£85	£185
			M285:	Mouse with bread	£120	£325
M268: Roman bronze Mercury	£650	£1,800	M286:	Owl	£140	£360
M269 a & b limbs or parts figurines	£15	£30	M287:	Celtic bird	£70	£150
			M288:	Celtic rider	£240	£650
M270: Romano-Celtic bronze Apollo	£500	£1,400	M289:	Romano-Celtic rider	£160	£400
M271: Mars wearing Corinthian helmet	£450	£1,300	M290:	Romano-Celtic horse	£130	£325
			M291:	Romano-Celtic dog	£175	£450
M272: Jupiter seated	£550	£1,500	M292:	Mother goddess	£400	£1,200
M273: Cupid	£120	£325	M293:	Romano-Celtic sphinx	£275	£800
M274: Venus	£650	£1,800	M294:	Captive	£180	£475
M275: Venus walking	£200	£550	M295:	Bronze plant	£120	£275
M276: Fortuna	£300	£850	M296:	Votive axe	£18	£30
M277: Hercules	£500	£1,400	M297:	Votive sword or dagger	£30	£55
M278: Genius	£550	£1,500				
M279: Lar	£500	£1,400	M298:	Votive anvil	£35	£75
M280: River god	£130	£325	M299:	Votive shears	£35	£75
M281: Roman bronze eagle	£70	£150	M300:	Votive bridle	£40	£90
			M301:	Votive altars	£220	£600
M282: Celtic bronze eagle	£75	£160				

Select Bibliography

R. Hattatt	**Ancient & Romano-British Brooches**	(1982)
R. Hattatt	**Iron Age & Roman Brooches**	(1985)
R. Hattatt	**Brooches of Antiquity**	(1987)
R. Hattatt	**Ancient Brooches & Other Artefacts**	(1989)
M. Green	**Dictionary of Celtic Myth & Legend**	(1992)
M. Green	**The Gods of Roman Britain**	(1983)
M. Green	**Religions of Roman Britain** BAR 24	(1976)
M. Green	**Roman Cult Objects** BAR 52	(1978)
Pitts	**Roman Bronze Figurines** BAR 60	(1979)
Bateson	**Enamel Working in Roman Britain** BAR 93	(1981)
British Museum Publication	**Wealth of the Roman World**	(1977)
British Museum Publication (Catherine Johns & T. Potter)	**The Thetford Treasure**	(1983)
British Museum Publication	**Jewellery Through 7000 Years**	(1976)
C. Marshall	**Buckles Through the Ages**	(1986)
L. Allison-Jones	**The Catalogue of Small Finds from South Shields Roman Fort**	(1984)
S. Frere & R. Tomlin	**The Roman Inscriptions of Britain** Vol II, F1	(1990) and F2 (1991)
Museum of London	**Treasure and Trinkets**	(1991)
John Ward-Perkins & Amanda Claridge	**Pompeii AD 79**	(1976)
Morna MacGregor	**Early Celtic Art in Northern Britain** 1 & 2	(1976)
B. Cunliffe	**Richborough, Fifth Report**	(1968)
John Wacher	**Roman Britain**	(1978)
Anthony Rich	**Dictionary of Roman & Greek Antiquities**	(1874)
J.S. Milne	**Surgical Instruments in Greek & Roman Times**	(1907)
British Museum	**Greek & Roman Life**	(1929)
British Museum	**Antiquities of the Early Iron Age**	(1905)
British Museum	**Antiquities of Roman Britain**	(1922)
British Museum	**Later Prehistoric Antiquities of the British Isles**	(1953)
London Museum	**London in Roman Times**	(1930)
Madrid	**Los Bronces Romanos en Espana**	(1990)
J.B. Wolters Groninlen	**Roman Bronze Statuettes From The Netherlands** I and II	(1967 & 1969)
M.C. Bishop and J.C.N. Coulston	**Roman Military Equipment**	(1993)
L'Erma and D. Bretschneider	**Rediscovering Pompeii**	(1992)
Michael Grant and John Hazel	**Who's Who Classical Mythology**	(1993)
Plantagenet Somerset Fry	**Roman Britain**	(1984).